FROM THE FARMERS' MARKET

Also by Richard Sax

COOKING GREAT MEALS EVERY DAY
(with David Ricketts)

OLD-FASHIONED DESSERTS

NEW YORK'S MASTER CHEFS

F·R·O·M FARMERS'

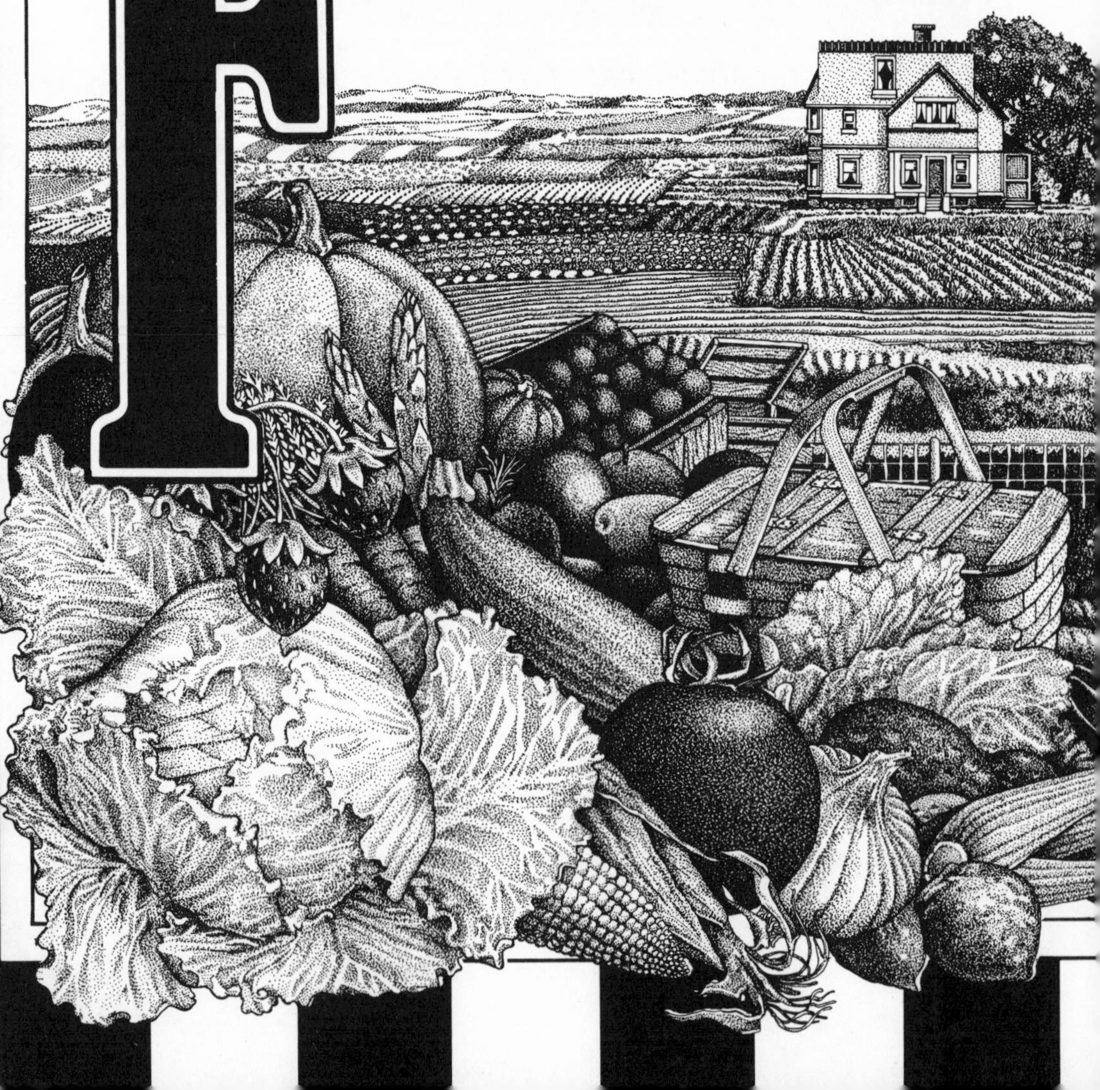

THE MARKET

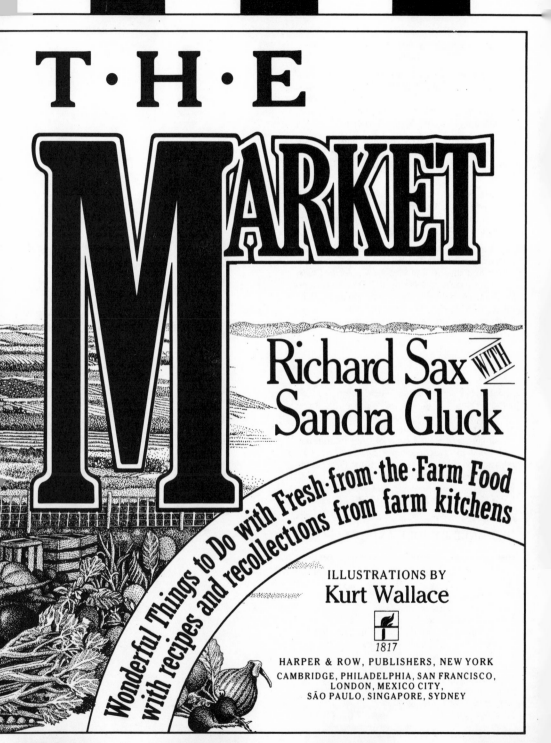

Richard Sax WITH Sandra Gluck

Wonderful Things to Do with Fresh-from-the-Farm Food with recipes and recollections from farm kitchens

ILLUSTRATIONS BY
Kurt Wallace

1817
HARPER & ROW, PUBLISHERS, NEW YORK
CAMBRIDGE, PHILADELPHIA, SAN FRANCISCO,
LONDON, MEXICO CITY,
SÃO PAULO, SINGAPORE, SYDNEY

Grateful acknowledgment is made for permission to reprint the following:

Excerpt from *Cross Creek,* by Marjorie Kinnan Rawlings. Copyright 1942 Marjorie Kinnan Rawlings; copyright renewed © 1970 Norton Baskin & Charles Scribner's Sons. Reprinted with the permission of Charles Scribner's Sons.

Excerpts from "Rice & Beans" and "Simple Cooking" by John Thorne. Copyright © 1981, 1984 by John Thorne; published by The Jackdaw Press.

Excerpt from *The Victory Garden Cookbook* by Marian Morash. Copyright © 1982 by Marian Morash and WGBH Educational Foundation; published by Alfred A. Knopf, Inc.

The Four Seasons recipes for Seppi Renggli's Gorgonzola Polenta and Hitch Albin's Cranberry Relish first appeared in *New York's Master Chefs* by Richard Sax, © 1985 by KQED/Golden Gate Productions; published by The Knapp Press. Permission to reprint these recipes was also graciously extended by Tom Margittai and Paul Kovi.

 For information address Harper & Row, Publishers, Inc., 10 East 53rd Street, New York, N.Y. 10022. Published simultaneously in Canada by Fitzhenry & Whiteside Limited, Toronto.

FIRST EDITION

DESIGNED BY JOEL AVIROM

Library of Congress Cataloging-in-Publication Data
Sax, Richard.
From the farmers' market.
Includes index.
1. Cookery, American. 2. Farm produce—United States—Marketing. I. Gluck, Sandra.
II. Wallace, Kurt. III. Title.
TX715.S2753 1986 641.5973 85-45658
ISBN 0-06-015555-8
86 87 88 89 90 10 9 8 7 6 5 4 3 2 1
ISBN 0-06-096072-8 (pbk.)
86 87 88 89 90 10 9 8 7 6 5 4 3 2 1

TO THE AMERICAN FARMER

CONTENTS

PART I

PART II

PART III

PREFACE

One morning nearly three years ago, I was having breakfast with Sandy Gluck when she told me she'd had an idea for a cookbook—"A farmers' market cookbook"—what to do with all the fresh ingredients found at farmers' markets.

In the past few years, in my capacity as a book reviewer, I've seen cookbooks come out in such profusion that I'm often skeptical when I hear of an idea for yet another one. But Sandy's seemed like a natural. The phenomenon of farmers' markets has found its way into just about every part of this country. And, with its emphasis on fresh, seasonal produce, it is one aspect of the current food revolution that brings together the so-called gourmet cooks and the healthy, "natural" ones. Because, when you really get down to it, it's all the same thing: the freshest possible ingredients, cooked in ways that bring out their flavors at their best.

I encouraged Sandy to pursue this project, and she wound up asking me if we might work on the book together. Collaborations aren't easy, but this one felt right. Sandy and I have known each other for over ten years. We met at cooking school, when we were both dissatisfied professionals in other fields, exploring what we could do with cooking, a field in which we were both enthusiastic amateurs. Since that time, Sandy has been working as a restaurant chef, presiding over first-rate kitchens, and, more recently, developing and testing recipes for food publications. She has evolved a distinctive style of cooking that, for all its simplicity, has remarkable finesse. Sandy has an ability to focus your attention on flavor above all else.

So, working together on a book did prove to be a harmonious experience for us both, a year of long and happy days in the kitchen and at the word processor. And the more we cooked, the simpler our preferences became.

Working with fresh-from-the-farm recipes appealed to us both for another reason, too. Cooking professionally and writing about food, we both get pretty impatient with the rarefied, trendy atmosphere that so often surrounds quality food. And it becomes increasingly absurd to watch the frantic race for cooks and food writers to "create" more and more "new" recipes—when good cooks everywhere, in both professional and home kitchens, are turning out such wonderful things.

This, then, is our salute to the farmers who work so hard to provide us all with the freshest possible produce. And to the people who still do good, simple, honest cooking, all over the country.

—Richard Sax
New York City, Fall 1985

WHAT THIS BOOK IS (AND IS NOT)

When people heard that we were working on a book about farmers' markets, they usually asked the same questions: "Are you including the one in Lancaster, Pennsylvania? Nashville, Tennessee? The Soulard Market in St. Louis?" The answer is yes and no —because this book is about the wonderful food available at farmers' markets, in a way, it's about all of them.

Today, farmers' markets are thriving. For most people, they are a reminder of an earlier time, when weekly market days were held in small towns, and before shopping malls let you know that you'd arrived somewhere. The markets range from permanent installations like Pike Place Market in Seattle and Philadelphia's Reading Terminal to small, once-a-week markets where farmers gather and sell just-picked produce from the back of a truck. Since the term is often abused, we will state for the record that we consider a farmers' market to be any place where the farmer sells produce he has grown himself, directly to the consumer.

While we do discuss the farmers' market phenomenon, this book is not a history of the movement in the country, nor a directory of market locations. Nor is it an encyclopedia of fruits and vegetables. (For that, we would direct you to, among others, The Victory Garden Cookbook *by Marian Morash [Knopf] and to Elizabeth Schneider's new guide to specialty fruits and vegetables,* Uncommon Fruits and Vegetables: A Commonsense Guide *[Harper & Row]. You'll also find helpful* Jean Anderson's Green Thumb Preserving Guide *[Quill paperback] and* Fancy Pantry *by Helen Witty [Workman].)*

Rather, From the Farmers' Market *is a collection of our favorite things to do with fresh-from-the-farm produce, once you've brought it home from the market. We've concentrated on produce grown in several parts of the country, so you won't find regional items like citrus fruits or avocados here. Some recipes are the simplest ways of dealing with a fruit or vegetable, which also happen to be the best: beets baked whole, ripe tomato salad, corn on the cob, vanilla and spice-stewed rhubarb, and strawberries in their own natural syrup.*

Others are recipes for soups, main dishes, vegetables, and desserts that put the produce to interesting use, without betraying the kind of good, honest cooking found on farms throughout the country. And we haven't restricted farm produce to fruits and vegetables; we've also included recipes for other items found at farmers' markets—fresh herbs, cheese, maple syrup, dried fruits, and nuts.

About half the recipes come from the farmers themselves, from all over the country. Contacting people we knew, and meeting others through County Agricultural Extension Services, we gathered recipes, whittling them down to our own favorites. Many farm wives told us, "Oh, I just cook simple—nothing you'd want to put in a cookbook." We had to convince them that that was exactly what we wanted to put in this cookbook. And when they shared their personal recollections along with the recipes, it all came to life.

So this food really is "fresh from the farm." This, more than any media-hyped trend practiced in professional kitchens, is the real American cooking.

INTRODUCTION

THE FARMERS' MARKET PHENOMENON

For the past few years, we've both looked forward to Wednesday and Saturday mornings, when we get up early and walk a few short blocks to our local Greenmarket, where farmers offer the freshest produce in season. Amid the New York morning craziness, it is a welcome oasis that seems almost like a visit to the country.

As we arrive at the market, it's hard to know where to start. We first see bushel baskets filled with tomatoes, vine-ripened and full of flavor. At the next table, loose, tender heads of butter lettuce share space with cucumbers, red and white radishes, bunches of spring onions with the moist earth still clinging to them, garlic and shallots, and bouquets of fresh herbs sitting in pails of water: flat and curly parsley, basil, chives, thyme, and tarragon. The effect is of a colorful seed catalog come to vibrant life. Farther along, there are plums, cherries, mushrooms, corn, cheeses, home-baked breads, and newly laid eggs (yes, there really is a difference).

New Yorkers, generally more at home among the subway throngs, or the skyscrapers uptown, are buying enthusiastically, while chatting about their favorite ways to bake apples or cook sugar snap peas. Everyone seems to smile, to enjoy being here. Walking back from Union Square, our bags bulging with fresh fruits and vegetables, the basis of several days' meals, we know that we not only have produce far fresher than anything available at even the best city shops, but also at a fraction of the price.

During the past ten or fifteen years, farmers' markets have sprouted up all around the United States, largely as a response to the awakened interest in fresh food. But while this might seem like a new phenomenon, farmers' markets actually have a long history in this country.

HISTORICAL BEGINNINGS

The farmers' market movement started when the nation was shifting its resources from agriculture to industry in the latter half of the nineteenth century, and the population shifted accordingly from rural areas to urban centers. At the same time, entire patterns of farming were changing. Fruits and vegetables were now being grown for year-round availability, visual appeal, and their ability to withstand the rigors of long-distance shipping—but often at the price of freshness and flavor. Which is why a ripe, juicy peach or tomato was becoming a fond memory.

The new city dwellers still wanted farm-fresh produce, though, and farmers' markets began to pop up around the nation, frequently sponsored by cities as public markets. Continuing a European tradition, farmers came to town in horse-drawn wagons to sell their goods in open lots along major city thoroughfares (many of which eventually became known as Market Street). Early examples include Philadelphia's Reading Terminal (whose site can be traced back to the city's origins), the Indianapolis City Market (for which space was included in the town plans of 1821), the French Market in New Orleans, Savannah's City Market, Boston's Haymarket, Cleveland's West Side Market, and the Pike Place Market in Seattle, which is listed on the National Register of Historic Places.

TYPES OF FARMERS' MARKETS

Today, as farmers' markets are flourishing more than ever, they range from indoor, year-round installations to weekly outdoor sites where farmers drive into cities and towns and sell directly from their trucks. Some are publicly funded and administrated: California certifies farmers' markets statewide, and insists that vendors sell only produce they have grown themselves.

Others are run by churches, by Chambers of Commerce and urban development groups, or by individuals. In many states, such as Minnesota and Iowa, Department of Agriculture Cooperative Extension Services direct market operations.

BENEFITS TO BOTH CONSUMER AND FARMER

What's behind the recent resurgence of farmer's markets? There are two major factors. The first, as we've already noted, is the renewed interest in fresh food of all sorts. The second, and even more critical, is that farmers' markets are one solution to agriculture's financial problems, in that they have allowed direct marketing of produce by the farmers themselves, without a middleman to skim profits. This has become a crucial outlet for the small, family-run farm, at a time when conglomerates and supermarket chains have forced many such farms to close down. In 1820, according to a recent report in *Newsweek,* nearly 75 percent of the United States population lived on farms. Today, only 3 percent does.

It's easy for those of us who live in cities to romanticize the idyllic side of farmers' markets, and by extension, farm life in general. We are prone to visions of farm kitchens where pitchers of thick cream stand ready to be poured over wedges of still-warm-from-the-oven pie. The reality, of course, is far different. Farming is hard work, and economically shaky at best (farmers and their wives must often seek outside sources of income), especially in today's political climate. Given the pro-big-business stance of the current conservative government, many small farmers find their very existence threatened.

In a small but critical way, farmers' markets have helped turn that tide.

STARTING A FARMERS' MARKET

Barry Benepe, the urban planner who is the guiding force behind New York City's Greenmarket program, recalls the factors that led him to start it, in 1976:

> *A lot of things sort of came together. The food at the supermarkets wasn't as fresh as it used to be. Also, I kept reading about farmers having problems selling their products.*
>
> *At the same time, I was doing some planning of a piece of land upstate which had beautiful apple orchards. One day, I was talking to the apple broker in the orchard, and I said that soon these orchards might not be here. The guy said, "It doesn't matter, in a few years all our apples will come from China anyway." And he said it with a perfectly straight face; he didn't care where his apples came from. Really, nobody seemed to care about the farmers at all.*
>
> *I was an urban consumer, and I wanted better produce. I'd go through a whole bin of peaches in August, and couldn't find a single ripe peach. The corn wasn't fresh, and you know what the tomatoes are like. And yet the farmers were out there with all that fresh food.*
>
> *All those things came together for the Greenmarket. Elinor Guggenheimer, the New York City Commissioner of Consumer Affairs at the time—her first idea was just one truck. There had also been a recent newspaper article by John Hess about a farmers' market in Syracuse. It was a real boon to the city—it had a good effect on downtown business. There was a 65 percent economic benefit from it. And we've found the same thing.*

Benepe's program is a huge success; today, there are nineteen Greenmarkets in New York City, some of them open all year.

IT'S NOT JUST AN EXCHANGE OF PRODUCE AND MONEY

Farmers' markets also encourage human exchange. One early summer morning we ran into fellow-cook Edna Lewis. "That's what I love about the farmers' market," she smiled in greeting. "You run into all kinds of people you know." Others tell how much elderly people appreciate having a congenial place to do their shopping. There are benches in some markets, and tables in the summer.

"It's wonderful," one customer enthused. "We don't have to go to the country . . . it makes the neighborhood more of a neighborhood . . . and it smells like the country! I feel like I'm in another time." "And look at this corn," said another, "it was just picked this morning!"

City people are not only interested in fresh food (often at 30 percent less than retail cost, in peak season), but in the farmers themselves. "The reaction of the city has been marvelous," says Barry Benepe. "The farmers were surprised at how warm the reception was."

For their part, the farmers enjoy the chance to meet city people. One said, "Before this year, I could care two cents about going to New York. Now I look forward to coming. Heck, there's a lot of nice people here."

"That's the part I like the best," Helen Kent, a farmer from Milton, New York, told us. "I enjoy it for the people—because I'm talking to the people as I sell. We've met some fascinating people, and I've learned a lot about cooking and about recipes." Mrs. Kent chats with her customers, while offering tastes of the several varieties of apples she grows, as well as expert advice on how to use them. And to encourage them to try quinces, she hands out a mimeographed sheet of her favorite recipes.

Selling at the farmers' market isn't easy. Helen Kent told us:

> *We pack till late at night. We get up at 4 in the morning, and we get to the market [in New York City] by 6 or 7. Then we sell until 5 or 6 o'clock. We get back late at night, and start all over again. We do this five days a week.*

But she goes on to say:

> *You know, people talk about city people. Well, I'm originally from Brooklyn, so I'm defensive. But city people are just like people anywhere else. And in New York City, they're from all over the world—different countries, everywhere. Some of the stuff you learn, talking to people. . . .*
>
> *Ninety percent of them are very nice. Sure, you get a few grouches—my husband talks to them. He must be telling them something right, because they wind up coming back again, to talk to him. But really, there are very few grouches.*

For those of us who live in bustling urban centers, disconnected from so much of nature and the year's changes, going to the farmers' market each week puts us back in touch with the passing of the seasons, and the kitchen rituals that attend them: as fall approaches, the apples, pears, and quinces arrive; and it's again time to make a big batch of pumpkin puree for the winter.

And the market offers the first signs of the spring thaw: first rhubarb, then spinach, asparagus, and strawberries. And then, the full-blown glory of summer, which means tomatoes, corn on the cob, basil, raspberries, plums, and peaches. And at the height of summer, when the best tomatoes can be had at bargain prices, both of us buy them by the bushel, to be hauled home, where we spend a whole day putting them up. Some will be canned whole, some made into a chunky tomato sauce (see page 138 for the recipe) to be canned or frozen, with a couple of whole fresh basil leaves tucked into each container. Soon, the fresh tomatoes will be flavorless and cottony, the basil will be gone, but we'll have the taste of summer on hand all year long, for quick pasta dishes, baked gratins, and home-baked pizza.

A TRANSFORMATION

Finally, it's not only people that benefit from farmers' markets—but the cities themselves. As Barry Benepe explains it:

> *The markets transform spaces in the city into pedestrian space. That's the biggest thing. City people were worried about the empty space, because the markets weren't going to be there every day. But the first thing I saw was a father coming out to teach his kid to ride a bike, and two kids with motorized cars, and roller skaters.*
>
> *That is a big plus. To get space back for people on foot. We have transformed spaces in the city in a profound way.*
>
> *There's no space equal to market space. You're in that space with the smells of fruit and vegetables. The odor is wonderful—like the first basil of the summer, and all the early morning smells. And the sounds are great—the people talking and walking. And just the sense of being in the sun. It's a nice place to be. To "cool out," and relax.*

In short, farmers' markets create a unique, mutually beneficial relationship between farmers and cities. Here again, we quote Barry Benepe:

> *It's the only urban project that depends on keeping the country green. So it's a perfect marriage of city and country. It's the only program geared to keep farmers farming, and making money, so that we can have good food.*

Perhaps Helen Kent, finally, explains best the secret of the farmers' markets' success:

> *"When you sell what you grow, you know what it is."*

A FEW NOTES ON INGREDIENTS

Ingredients used in these recipes are pretty straightforward; we rarely call for anything not readily available. You'll find that the recipes work best if you follow these few guidelines:

- Eggs—*All recipes were tested with eggs graded "large," unless otherwise noted.*
- Butter—*All recipes were tested with unsalted (sweet) butter.*
- Flour—*When we call for flour, use unbleached all-purpose flour, preferably measured by spooning lightly into a measuring cup, then leveling off.*
- Cake Flour—*If you don't have cake flour on hand, here's a satisfactory substitute: Spoon 2 tablespoons cornstarch into a measuring cup. Lightly spoon in unbleached all-purpose flour to measure 1 cup; this replaces 1 cup of cake flour.*
- Buttermilk—*If you don't have buttermilk on hand, you can substitute an equal volume of either:*
  - *plain yogurt, thinned with milk to the consistency of buttermilk,*
  - *or milk, soured by adding 1 tablespoon lemon juice or vinegar per cup of liquid, then letting the mixture stand for about 10 minutes.*
- Heavy Cream = *Whipping Cream, preferably not ultra pasteurized.*
- Parsley—*If it's available, we prefer flat-leaf parsley, sometimes called Italian parsley.*
- Nuts—*In just about all the recipes calling for them, you can use various nuts interchangeably. Substituting almonds for pecans, or walnuts for hazelnuts will give a different flavor, but equally good results.*

LIST OF RECIPES BY CATEGORY

(Consult the Index for page numbers)

APPETIZERS AND HORS D'OEUVRE

Eggplant Appetizer with Tomatoes and Herbs
Herbed Fromage Blanc
Onion Pie with Bacon
Pecan Cheese Crackers
Pierino's Baked Stuffed Pepper Wedges
Pumpkin-Filled Lasagne Rolls
Quesadillas
Red Pepper-and-Cheese-Stuffed Bread
Rice-and-Cheese-Stuffed Onions
Sautéed Wild Mushrooms with Garlic and Parsley

SOUPS

Arugula and Potato Soup
Bruna's Pasta e Fagioli with Mushrooms and Herbs
Cold-Weather Root Soup
Hearty Corn Chowder
Hungarian Hearty Bean Soup (Bableves)
Main-Dish Cabbage Soup
Mary's Escarole Soup with Tiny Meatballs

SALADS

Arlene's Summer Vegetable Salad
Cabbage and Pepper Slaw
Hungarian Marinated Cucumbers
Marinated Cauliflower
Marinated Green Beans with Red Onion
Nippy Potato Salad with Country Ham and Sour Cream
Raw Fennel with Lemon Dressing
Ripe Tomato Salad

EGGS AND OTHER LIGHT DISHES

ABC Sandwich
Apple Upside-Down Corn Bread
Asparagus Torte
Cheese Pancakes
Cherry Batter Pudding
Cornmeal Griddle Cakes
Herbed Spinach and Rice Bake
Red Pepper-and-Cheese-Stuffed Bread
Scalloped Tomatoes and Corn
Tomato and Cheese Strata
Zucchini and Potato Pancakes

MAIN DISHES

Baked Macaroni with Zucchini and Three Cheeses
Beer-Braised Beef with Onion Butter-Crumb Dumplings
Braised Veal Shanks with Wild Mushrooms
Bruna's Pasta e Fagioli with Mushrooms and Herbs
Chicken and Cheese Hash with Sweet Potato Corn Bread Squares
Chicken and Chips
Chicken in Succotash
Hungarian Hearty Bean Soup (Bableves)
Main-Dish Cabbage Soup
Mortimer's Chicken Fricassee with Shiitake Mushrooms
Onion Pie with Bacon
Pasta with Asparagus and Cheese
Pasta with Broccoli and Two Cheeses
Pasta with Sweet Onion Sauce
Pasta with Wild Mushrooms
Pork and Beans
Pumpkin-Filled Lasagne Rolls
Quick Bean and Sausage Bake
Red Beans and Rice
Red Flannel Hash
Red Pepper Boats Stuffed with Ricotta, Spinach, and Tomato Sauce
Red Peppers Stuffed with Sausage and Corn Kernels
Roast Loin of Pork with Apples and Cider
Sausage, Peppers, and Onions with Vinegar
Spicy Beef Pie with Corn Kernel Crust
Tomato and Cheese Strata

(Continued)

BREADS

Apple Upside-Down Corn Bread
Caramel Pecan Sticky Buns
Cheese Popovers with Fresh Herbs
Corn Kernel Muffins
Cornmeal Griddle Cakes
Edith's Virginia Spoon Bread with Corn Kernels
New Mexican Spoon Bread
Peanut Butter Bread
Pear Biscuits
Pecan Cheese Crackers
Potato Doughnuts or Biscuits
Pumpkin Cheese Bread
Red Pepper-and-Cheese-Stuffed Bread
Renita's Herb Bread
Rhubarb Nut Loaf
Sugarless Blueberry Muffins
Sweet Apple Muffins
Sweet Potato Biscuits
Sweet Potato Corn Bread

PRESERVES

Apple Cider Jelly
Cranberry Jelly (or Glaze for Roast Poultry or Ham)
Edna Lewis's Peach Chutney
Fresh Tomato and Vegetable Chutney
Hitch Albin's Cranberry Relish
Monique's Cranberry Sauce with Whiskey
Peg's Bread and Butter Pickles
Pickled Jerusalem Artichokes
Preserved Cherries
Preserved Spiced Seckel Pears
Pumpkin Butter
Quince Jam
Red Pepper Jam
Red Currant Jelly
Spiced Pear Butter

SAUCES & DRESSINGS

Basic Chunky Tomato Sauce
Basic Creamy Garlic Dressing
Black and Blue Compote
Currant Sauce for Poultry or Game
Double-Berry Sauce
Fresh Tomato-Pepper Salsa
Herb Butter Glaze for Fish or Chicken
Herbed Mayonnaise
Homemade Barbecue Sauce
Hitch Albin's Cranberry Relish
Maple-Walnut Sauce for Ice Cream
Monique's Cranberry Sauce with Whiskey
Sweet-and-Sour Rhubarb Sauce for Fish or Chicken
Vanilla Custard Sauce

MISCELLANEOUS

Basic Pie Pastry
Basic Sugar Syrup
Cranberry Coolers
Golden Chicken Broth
Herb Butters
Herbed Croutons
Homemade Fromage Blanc (Fresh White Cheese)
Homemade Nut Butters
Plum Cordial
Preserving Methods for Fresh Herbs
Pumpkin Puree
Rich Tart Pastry
Vegetable Broth

PART I
Vegetables

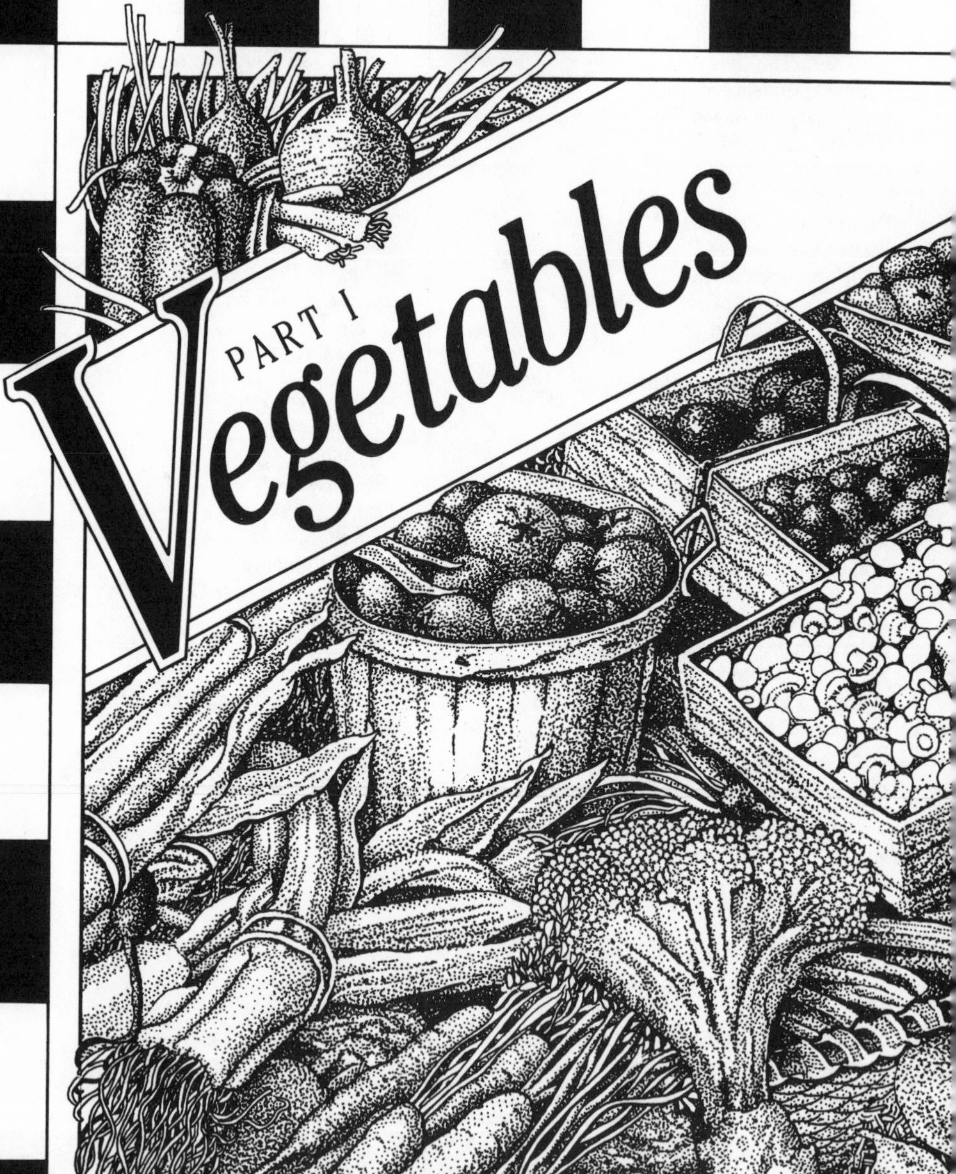

ASPARAGUS AND PEAS

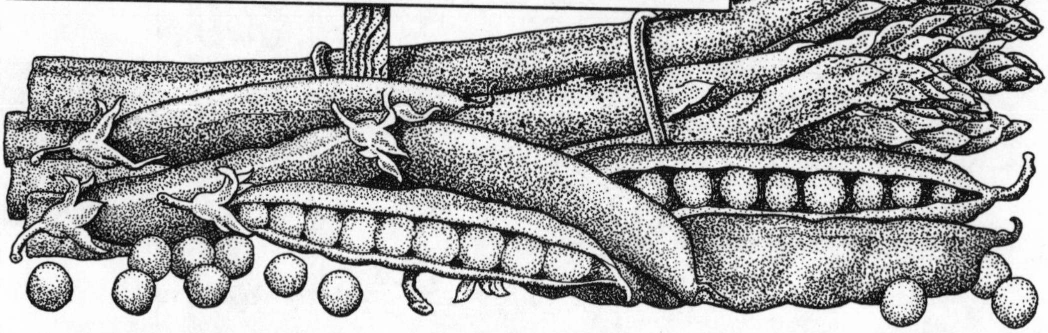

ASPARAGUS

The aristocrat of the vegetable world, asparagus has been prized since ancient times (the Roman expression *velocius quam asparagi coquantur*—"quicker than you can cook asparagus"—is the equivalent of our "as quick as a wink"). Did you know that asparagus is a member of the lily family, which also includes onions, leeks, garlic, and tulips?

BEST OF THE BEST: CRISP, BRIGHT GREEN ASPARAGUS

***F**orget all those complicated directions for using asparagus steamers. The best way to cook crisp, bright green stalks is also the easiest. Here's how:*

- ***Trim off the woody bottoms of the asparagus stalks.***
- ***With a sharp vegetable peeler, carefully peel the bottom halves of the stalks. Don't take off too much.***
- ***Bring a wide skillet of water to a rolling boil. Salt the water, then drop in the asparagus. (If they vary in size, add thickest stalks first; cook about a minute, then add the rest.) Boil, uncovered, just until crisp-tender, 3 to 4 minutes.***
- ***With tongs, transfer asparagus to a plate lined with paper towels to drain.***

That's it. Serve either:

- ***Hot, as is, with freshly ground pepper and a squeeze of lemon juice or balsamic vinegar, or***
- ***Hot, drizzled with olive oil or butter, with a squeeze of lemon, or***
- ***Lukewarm or cool, dressed with a vinaigrette, Basic Creamy Garlic Dressing (page 46), or an herbed mayonnaise (page 148).***

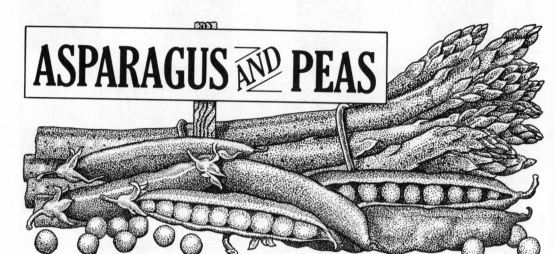

AN INTERESTING ALTERNATIVE: ROAST ASPARAGUS

This easy, unusual method comes from old friends Johanne Killeen and George Germon, wonderful cooks. Pay them a visit at Al Forno Restaurant in Providence, Rhode Island.

- *Trim and peel asparagus stalks as directed in the box on the opposite page.*
- *Place in a shallow baking dish and drizzle with fruity olive oil.*
- *Roast in a preheated 500° F. oven just until crisp-tender, 8 to 10 minutes. Serve immediately.*

Asparagus Torte

This tasty dish, similar to a baked omelet or frittata, is from Clara Bartlett of Hoodsport, Washington. Try this for brunch, or as a main dish for a light supper.

Serves 4 to 6

2 pounds asparagus, bottoms trimmed, bottom halves of stalks peeled, sliced diagonally in 1- to 2-inch lengths
4 tablespoons (½ stick) unsalted butter
1 large onion, coarsely chopped
2 garlic cloves, minced
Salt and freshly ground black pepper
10 eggs, lightly beaten
½ cup milk
¼ cup chopped parsley
1 tablespoon chopped fresh basil, or pinch each of dried basil and marjoram
Pinch of cayenne pepper
½ cup cracker meal, or finely crushed bland crackers
1½ cups grated Parmesan or Cheddar cheese, or a combination

1. Preheat the oven to 350° F. Blanch the asparagus in a large pot of boiling salted water until crisp-tender, 3 to 4 minutes. Drain in a colander, refresh under cold running water, and drain again thoroughly.

2. Heat the butter in a large skillet over medium heat. Add the onion and garlic and sauté, tossing occasionally, until wilted, about 8 minutes. Add the drained asparagus, tossing to coat, and sprinkle the mixture with salt and pepper. Sauté 2 minutes longer to bring out the flavor of the asparagus. Set aside.

3. In a large mixing bowl, whisk together the eggs, milk, parsley, basil, cayenne, cracker meal, and all but ¼ cup of the cheese. Add salt to taste; then stir in the asparagus mixture. Transfer the mixture to a buttered shallow 6-cup casserole, such as a 7 x 11-inch rectangular, 9-inch square, or 11-inch oval baking dish. Top with the reserved ¼ cup grated cheese.

4. Bake until lightly golden and set in the center, 25 to 30 minutes. Serve hot or at room temperature.

A WINNING VARIATION:
PASTA WITH ASPARAGUS AND CHEESE

For a quick but special dinner, try serving pasta with asparagus and cheese. Here's how: Cook 1½ pounds asparagus as explained in the box on page 28; cut the cooked spears diagonally into 1-inch lengths. Then, just follow the recipe for Pasta with Broccoli and Two Cheeses on page 44, substituting the asparagus for the broccoli. Get ready for something good. . . .

PEAS

There's nothing as sweet as freshly shelled peas. You should, however, avoid pods with overlarge peas; they tend to be starchy rather than sweet. In the past few years, snow peas have also become widely available, and even better, to our taste, are sugar snap peas. Introduced in 1979, the sugar snap is a hybrid whose tender pod is edible, as are the sweet, fully formed peas within. Remove their strings, then blanch them just until crisp-tender, usually not much more than 45 seconds. Then serve hot or cold. Our favorite pea variety name: Dwarf Telephone (or Daisy) peas.

Fresh Peas Stewed with Lettuce

You can also cook frozen peas this way, partially thawing them first.

Serves 4

- **2** ***teaspoons unsalted butter***
- **2** ***scallions, thinly sliced***
- **1½** ***cups shredded greenleaf or iceberg lettuce***
- **2** ***cups shelled fresh peas (about 2 pounds unshelled) or 10 ounces partially thawed frozen peas***
- **½** ***teaspoon fresh summer savory or marjoram, or pinch of dried***
- **⅛** ***teaspoon salt***
- ***Large pinch of sugar***

1. Heat the butter in a saucepan. Add the scallions and shredded lettuce, tossing to coat. Cook, uncovered, until wilted, about 4 minutes.

2. Add the peas, savory or marjoram, salt, and sugar, stirring gently to combine the ingredients. Cover the pan tightly and cook until the peas are just tender, stirring once or twice, 5 to 8 minutes for fresh peas. Serve hot.

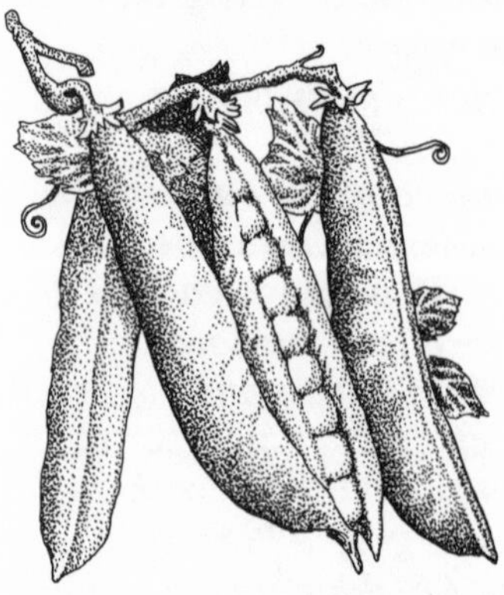

Arlene's Summer Vegetable Salad

From Arlene Sarappo, an old friend who frequently conducts farm tours for the New Jersey Department of Agriculture. Arlene and her husband, Lou, recently built a glorious kitchen that opens onto a lush backyard. They are both excellent cooks, and make their own pasta, sausages, and home-baked bread.

Serves 4

***2** red bell peppers*
***½** pound sugar snap peas, strings removed*
***1** tablespoon sesame seeds*
***½** pound mushrooms*
***6** ounces fresh spinach leaves, stems removed, washed carefully, and patted dry*

SESAME-HONEY DRESSING

***5** tablespoons olive oil*
***1** tablespoon Oriental sesame oil (or use another tablespoon olive oil)*
***1** tablespoon apple cider vinegar, plus more as needed*
***1** tablespoon lemon juice*
***1** garlic clove, smashed and peeled*
***1½** teaspoons honey*
***¼** teaspoon salt*
Freshly ground black pepper

1. *Sesame-Honey Dressing:* Place the olive oil, sesame oil, vinegar, lemon juice, garlic, honey, salt, and pepper in a blender or food processor. Blend until smooth; then add a little more vinegar, if needed, to give the dressing a pleasant tang.

2. Roast the peppers (page 102). Peel, trim away seeds and ribs, and cut the peppers into strips ½ inch wide. Set aside.

3. Blanch the sugar snap peas in a large pot of boiling salted water, uncovered, until just crisp-tender, about 1 minute. Drain, refresh under cold running water, and drain again. Set aside on paper towels to dry.

4. Toast the sesame seeds in a small dry skillet over medium heat until very lightly golden, 1 to 2 minutes (Watch carefully to prevent burning.) Transfer to a plate; set aside.

5. *Assembly:* Wipe the mushroom caps with a damp paper towel. Trim stems flush with caps; slice the mushrooms thin. In a mixing bowl, combine the mushrooms, reserved pepper strips, sugar snap peas, sesame seeds, and the dressing, tossing gently. Line four chilled salad plates with spinach leaves and mound the vegetable salad on top. Serve immediately.

BEANS

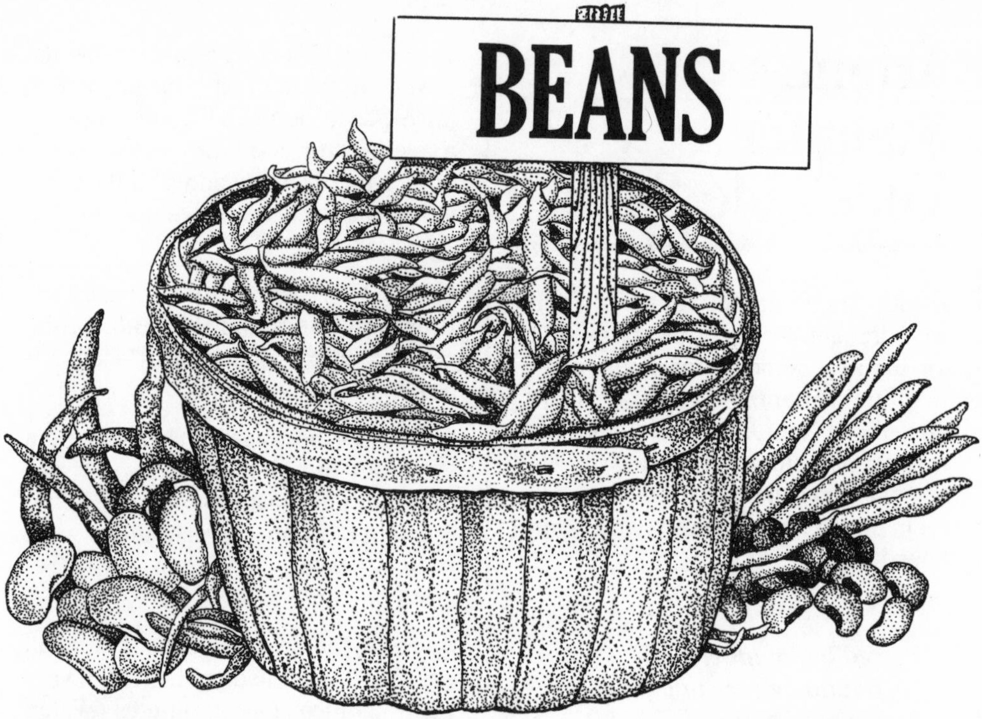

We've included here recipes for fresh green (snap) beans, shell beans (such as fresh limas and black-eyed peas), and protein-rich dried beans. To quote Marian Morash in *The Victory Garden Cookbook* (Knopf), "Snap, shell, and dried beans represent different phases in the bean's development. . . . Any bean allowed to grow long enough will give you all three stages (but not necessarily the same good flavor at each stage)."

A RESTAURANT SHORTCUT FOR BRIGHT GREEN BEANS

You can save time, and last-minute worry at dinner parties about whether they are done, by using this restaurant shortcut for precooking green beans so they stay bright green:

- ***Blanch the green beans in advance (see recipe for Marinated Green Beans, page 33).***
- ***Drain and cool completely under cold running water.***
- ***Chill the green beans in a dish lined with paper towels to absorb excess moisture.***
- ***At serving time, simply toss the green beans in butter in a large skillet, just until heated through. Season with salt, pepper, and a squeeze of lemon juice.***

Use this method for any firm vegetable—carrots, asparagus, broccoli, cauliflower, snow peas, sugar snap peas, etc.

Marinated Green Beans with Red Onion

Adding the lemon juice to this refreshing salad just before serving ensures that the color stays bright.

Serves 4 to 6

***1** pound green beans, ends trimmed*
***½** small red onion, cut in thin slivers (about ½ cup)*
***2** or 3 garlic cloves, smashed and peeled*
***½** cup olive oil*
***¼** teaspoon salt*
Freshly ground black pepper
***3** tablespoons chopped fresh dill*
***3** to 4 tablespoons lemon juice*

1. Bring a large pot of water to a full rolling boil; salt lightly. Add the green beans a handful at a time, so that the water remains at a boil. Boil, uncovered, just until crisp-tender, 3 to 4 minutes (the timing can vary, depending on the size and age of the beans). Drain in a colander under cold running water until cool; drain well. Transfer the beans to a large mixing bowl. (Do not chill.)

2. Add the onion, garlic, olive oil, salt, pepper, and dill to the beans; toss gently to combine ingredients and coat the beans.

3. Just before serving, remove the garlic cloves and add the lemon juice, tossing to coat; correct seasonings. Serve at cool room temperature.

Fresh Butter-Stewed Lima Beans

Lima bean haters will be surprised at how good these are.

Serves 4 to 6

***2** pounds fresh lima beans, in the shell*
***1** cup cold water*
***6** tablespoons (¾ stick) unsalted butter, cut into pieces*
***½** teaspoon fresh marjoram leaves, or pinch of dried*
***1** bay leaf*
Zest of ¼ orange in strips
***½** teaspoon coarse (kosher) salt*
***2** tablespoons chopped parsley*

1. Shell the beans. Place them in a saucepan with the water, butter, marjoram, bay leaf, and orange zest. Cook over low heat, uncovered, for 25 minutes, or until the beans are tender but not mushy.

2. Season with salt. Garnish with parsley and serve hot.

"UNINTERRUPTED JOY"—BLACK-EYED PEAS, CORN BREAD, TOMATOES, AND ONIONS

Marion Travis, who now lives in Houston, recalls:

When I was growing up on our Little Rock Stock Farm in central Texas in the 1930s, a smart-alecky cousin told me, "Northerners don't eat black-eyed peas. They call them cow feed."

I was incredulous. Fresh black-eyed peas with hot corn bread, fresh garden tomatoes, and fresh onions were among my favorite foods—in the same class with my Grandmother Brewer's crisply fried chicken and Blue Bird vanilla ice cream from the Palace of Sweets in Cameron.

Properly selected, prepared and served, they are uninterrupted joy—the kind that clings in memory from Texan childhood throughout adulthood.

Fresh black-eyed peas. They will poppedy-pop-pop from their long, greenish purple pods into the pan in your lap as you shell them. Each pea is plump and a delicate green with a purplish black eye. Snap a few young pods into the shelled peas. If you pick them yourself, a full-packed gallon bucket (in the hull) will serve four.

Now for the eating:

While the peas are cooking, make your best recipe of corn bread. (See the Sweet Potato Corn Bread, page 132, or use your own favorite recipe.) Perfect this in advance. Good corn bread is essential to the quality of the meal. . . .

The layered feast should be arranged as follows: Serve your plate with several spoonfuls of hot black-eyed peas. Mound them into the center of your plate. Take a large piece of warm corn bread and crumble it quickly over the peas. It should have its stove heat when you begin eating. Do not butter your corn bread. Place cool tomato slices to taste on top of the corn bread and slices of crisp, cool onion to taste on top of tomatoes. Immediately ladle out several spoonfuls of warm pot liquor onto the plate. Not too many. You are not making soup, just a good eating consistency. Take knife in one hand, fork in the other and cut—over and over. This cuts up the tomatoes and onions, completes the corn bread crumbling, and mixes the whole culinary marvel together. Dissimilarity in food textures, vegetable and bread temperatures, and flavors makes this combination surpassingly delicious.

Ralph's Fresh Black-Eyed Peas

Serves 4

1 pound black-eyed peas (in the shell)
1 ripe plum tomato, peeled, seeded, and chopped
2 garlic cloves, cut in slivers
2 sprigs fresh thyme
3 tablespoons olive oil
Salt and freshly ground black pepper
3 tablespoons chopped parsley (optional)

1. Shell the peas; place them in a skillet with cold water to cover. Add the tomato, garlic, thyme, and 2 tablespoons of the olive oil. Cover the skillet and bring the mixture just to a boil.

2. Simmer, covered, for 30 minutes. Uncover and continue cooking for 15 minutes longer, or until the peas are tender. Season with salt, pepper, and the final tablespoon of olive oil. If you like, stir in 3 tablespoons chopped parsley. Serve hot.

QUICK METHOD FOR SOAKING DRIED BEANS

Recipes usually call for soaking dried beans overnight. If you don't have time, use this quick-soaking method instead:

- *Place the dried beans (picking out any bad ones or stones) in a large pot with cold water to cover by about two inches.*
- *Bring to a boil, covered. Boil 2 minutes.*
- *Remove from heat and let stand 1 hour. Drain off the liquid. The beans are now ready to cook.*

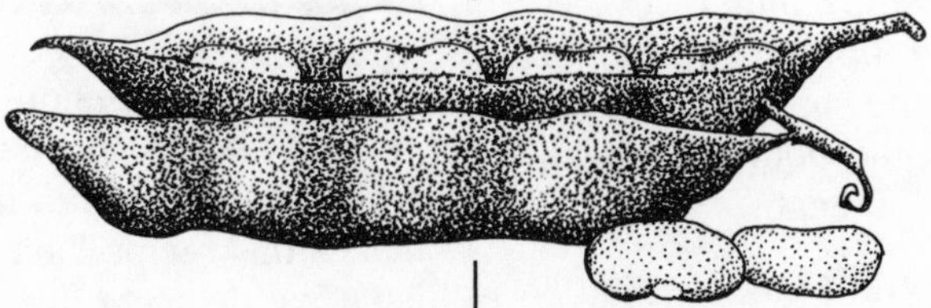

Pork and Beans

A far cry from the canned version.

Serves 6

1½ cups dried cranberry, kidney, or pinto beans, picked over (9 to 10 ounces)
4 tablespoons olive oil
⅓ cup diced bacon (about 1½ ounces)
2 cups coarsely chopped onions
4 garlic cloves, smashed and peeled
1½ pounds boneless pork shoulder or butt, cut in 1-inch cubes
Reserved bean liquid
½ cup tomato paste
½ cup molasses
1 tablespoon red wine vinegar
1 tablespoon prepared strong mustard, such as Dijon
1 quarter-size slice peeled fresh ginger
Salt and freshly ground black pepper

1. Soak the beans overnight or use the quick-soaking method (page 35). Drain and place in a large saucepan. Add cold water to cover by several inches. Bring to a boil; skim. Simmer, covered, until tender but not mushy (timing varies). Drain the beans, reserving about 2 cups of the liquid. Set beans and liquid aside, off heat.

2. In a Dutch oven or large casserole, heat 2 tablespoons of the olive oil. Add the bacon and cook over medium-low heat, stirring occasionally, for 5 minutes. Stir in the onions and garlic and cook 6 to 7 minutes longer.

3. Preheat the oven to 350° F. While the onions are cooking, heat the remaining 2 tablespoons of olive oil in a skillet over medium-high heat. Brown the pork on all sides, about 8 minutes total. With a slotted spoon, transfer the pork to the bacon-onion mixture. Discard fat from the skillet. Deglaze the pan: Add ½ cup of the reserved bean-cooking liquid to the skillet, scraping up all the browned bits in the pan. Stir in the tomato paste, molasses, vinegar, mustard, and ginger. Bring to a boil; pour over the pork. Cover the Dutch oven with a sheet of foil, then with the lid. Place it in the lower third of the oven.

4. Bake 1 hour. Stir in the beans; if the mixture seems dry, moisten with a little of the bean liquid. Bake until pork is tender, 45 to 60 minutes longer. Season with salt and pepper; serve hot.

Bruna's Pasta e Fagioli with Mushrooms and Herbs

A personal version of the Italian peasant classic, this has become a favorite supper. The ingredients list makes this recipe look complicated; it isn't. We dedicate this, with gratitude, to Everett Quinton, whose performance as Bruna in *Galas* gave us more pleasure than he'll ever know.

Serves 6

- ***2*** ***tablespoons fruity olive oil, plus more for serving***
- ***2*** ***onions, thickly sliced***
- ***2*** ***small carrots, peeled, trimmed, and thickly sliced***
- ***½*** ***red bell pepper, seeds and ribs removed, cut in thin strips about 1 inch long***
- ***4*** ***garlic cloves, finely chopped***
- ***½*** ***cup shredded fresh basil leaves, or ½ teaspoon dried***
- ***Pinch of dried oregano***
- ***8*** ***ounces smoked ham, cut in ¼-inch dice (about 1⅓ cups)***
- ***1*** ***cup drained canned tomatoes***
- ***6*** ***cups Chicken Broth (page 239) or Vegetable Broth (page 240)***
- ***1*** ***pound dried beans, such as cranberry beans, Great Northern beans, or red kidney beans, picked over, soaked, and cooked (see Pork and Beans, step #1, opposite page, or 2 cans (19 ounces each) red kidney beans, drained and rinsed***
- ***2½*** ***cups (5 ounces) dried rotelle pasta (wheels; or substitute rigatoni, penne, shells, or other short pasta)***
- ***Salt and freshly ground black pepper***
- ***¾*** ***cup sliced fresh mushrooms***
- ***⅓*** ***cup sliced scallion greens***
- ***Freshly grated Parmesan cheese***

1. In a deep heavy saucepan, heat the olive oil over medium-high heat. Add the onions, carrots, and pepper and cook, tossing occasionally, until softened slightly, about 8 minutes. Add the garlic, 3 tablespoons of the fresh basil (or ½ teaspoon dried), the oregano, and the ham and cook, tossing, for 2 minutes longer.

2. Add the tomatoes and cook, crushing the tomatoes, until they have reduced to the consistency of a thick tomato sauce, about 6 minutes. Add the broth and the beans and bring to a boil. As the mixture comes to a boil, mash about one quarter of the beans against the side of the pot to thicken the soup slightly (the broth should be quite thin at this point; it will thicken later). Skim off froth from the surface as necessary. Lower the heat and simmer, covered, about 20 minutes. (Soup can be prepared in advance to this point.)

3. Shortly before serving, return the soup to a boil, degrease thoroughly, and stir in the pasta. Boil gently, uncovered, until the pasta is nearly, but not quite *al dente,* 6 to 7 minutes. Remove from heat, degrease again, and season to taste with salt and pepper. Scatter the mushroom slices on the surface of the soup. Cover and set aside 5 minutes.

4. Return the soup to a boil, stirring. Correct seasoning, adding a generous amount of freshly ground pepper and the remaining fresh basil. Serve immediately, sprinkling each serving with scallion greens and drizzling with a little more olive oil. Pass freshly grated Parmesan cheese and a pepper mill at the table.

Hungarian Hearty Bean Soup (Bableves)

A meal in itself, with a robust red wine and a salad. The combination of dried beans and smoked pork is found in many traditional American farm recipes. Bean soup is also a Hungarian favorite, and this version, from Chef György Szente of the Vámosi Betyár Csarda in Nemesvámos, in the resort region of Lake Balaton, is especially tasty. If you can't get smoked pig's feet, you can substitute an equal weight of smoked spareribs, or bacon with bones, if available. Home-cured pork products, by the way, can be found at many farmers' markets.

Hungarian paprika is available by mail order from Paprikas Weiss, 1546 Second Avenue, New York, N.Y. 10028; telephone (212) 288-6117.

Serves 8 to 10

1½ pounds dried red kidney beans, picked over
2 tablespoons lard, bacon fat, or vegetable oil
2 medium onions, chopped
2 small ribs celery with leaves, trimmed and chopped
1 small celery root (6 to 8 ounces), pared and diced
1 tablespoon medium-hot or sweet Hungarian paprika
2 smoked pig's feet, or 2 pounds smoked pork ribs, cut up; or 2 pounds slab bacon with rind, cut up
2½ quarts cold water
¼ teaspoon dried marjoram

ROUX

5 tablespoons lard, bacon fat, or vegetable oil
½ cup flour
4 to 6 large garlic cloves, finely grated or minced
½ teaspoon Hungarian paprika
1 cup warm water

¼ cup red wine vinegar, or more to taste
2 to 3 tablespoons sugar
Salt and freshly ground black pepper
Chopped parsley
Thin slivers of red and/or green pepper, for garnish
Thin slivers of tomato, for garnish (optional)

1. Place beans in a large bowl with enough cold water to cover by several inches. Soak overnight (or use quick-soaking method, page 35).

2. In a large kettle or casserole, heat lard or other fat over medium heat. Sauté the onions, celery, and celery root until softened but not browned, 5 to 7 minutes. Add the paprika; remove the pan from the heat, and stir for a few moments.

3. Drain the beans and add to the kettle with the pork, water, and marjoram. Bring to a boil, covered, then lower heat and simmer, partially covered, until beans and meat are tender, 1½ hours or longer. Skim and stir occasionally. Remove the meat and let stand until cool enough to handle. Pick meat from the bones, discarding fat and bones. Cut meat into bite-size chunks and return it to the soup.

4. *Roux:* In a small heavy saucepan, heat the fat over medium heat, then stir in the flour with a wooden spoon and continue stirring until the mixture is opaque, 3 to 4 minutes. Add the garlic; then cook, stirring constantly, until the roux is a medium tan color, 10 to 15 minutes (watch carefully; timing can vary). Stir in the paprika; then whisk in the water gradually until smooth.

5. Return the soup to a simmer; skim off all fat. Add about half the roux mixture, whisking. Stir together the vinegar and 2 tablespoons sugar in a small bowl; add to soup. Now add enough of the remaining roux to bring soup to desired consistency; the soup should be full-bodied, but not too thick. Add salt, pepper, and more vinegar and/or sugar to taste (the soup should have a nice sweet-sour tang). Serve hot, sprinkled with chopped parsley, slivers of pepper, and tomato slivers.

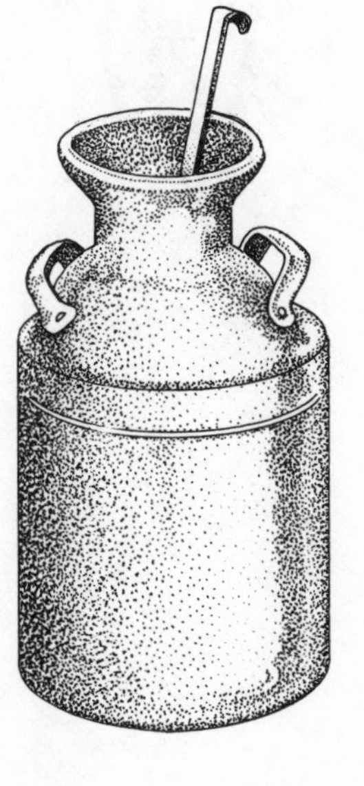

Red Beans and Rice

Adapted from a recipe by John Thorne, which appears in his booklet *Rice & Beans.** Mr. Thorne explains his basic formula: "...rather than reproducing a dozen or so very similar recipes, I have composed a master recipe, explaining the options so the individual cook can fine-tune the dish to his or her particular tastes." Instructions for his onion salad, served as a condiment with the beans and rice, are found at the end of the recipe.

Serves 8

1 ***pound dried red beans or red kidney beans, picked over, washed, soaked overnight or by quick-soaking method (page 35), and drained***
1 ***ham bone with plenty of meat, sawed in half or cracked by a butcher (or, if unavailable, 1 pound lean salt pork, cubed and boiled in ample water for 15 minutes to reduce saltiness)***
1 ***pound smoked Creole sausages, or chorizo, or smoked kielbasa (optional but recommended)***
2 ***medium onions, finely chopped***
1/4 ***cup chopped parsley***
1 ***bunch scallions, (first reserve 1/2 cup sliced green portions for garnish), finely chopped***
1 ***large carrot, peeled, trimmed, and finely diced***
1 ***medium green or red bell pepper, seeds and ribs removed, chopped (optional)***
2 ***ribs celery, trimmed and finely diced (optional)***
6 ***garlic cloves, minced (amount optional)***
Generous pinch of fresh thyme leaves, or small pinch of dried
2 ***bay leaves***
1 ***small hot red pepper (fresh or dried), seeds and ribs removed, finely chopped, or a generous hand with the Tabasco bottle***
Salt and freshly ground pepper to taste
2 ***cups raw long-grain rice***

1. Put the soaked beans, ham bone, sausages, onions, parsley, scallions, carrot, green pepper, celery, 4 cloves of garlic, thyme, bay leaves, and hot pepper into a very large iron pot with a cover. Add a generous 2 quarts of water. Heat over low heat (so as not to annoy the beans), and bring to a simmer, never a boil. The cooking process will take up to 3 hours. Add liquid if needed; never let the pot go dry. Add salt and pepper to taste as the beans cook.

2. When the beans begin to soften, mash some of them against the side of the pot to make a thick, creamy sauce. When the beans are soft and the sauce thick and richly flavored, bring 4½ cups water to a boil in a separate pot. Boil the rice gently with the remaining 2 cloves of garlic and a little salt until the liquid has evaporated and the rice is tender, about 20 minutes. Turn off the flame and let both the rice and the beans sit on the stove for about 15 minutes. If you like, cut the meat from the ham bone into bite-size pieces, discard the bone, and stir the meat into the beans.

3. Fluff the rice and top with the beans. Top with the reserved scallion tops. Serve, if you like, with additional hot sauce and vinegar. Another popular topping is:

Onion Salad

Thinly slice 1 large red onion and divide into rings in a large bowl. Cover with ¼ cup olive oil, 1 tablespoon wine vinegar, and salt and black pepper. Let marinate while the beans are cooking, and serve as a condiment.

* Mr. Thorne publishes a series of booklets and a quarterly newsletter, both called *Simple Cooking.* Anyone interested in food should become familiar with his highly individual writing, which combines fine recipes, solid research, and a wild sense of humor. Send for information to *Simple Cooking Series,* Box 371, Essex Station, Boston, MA 02112.

Quick Bean and Sausage Bake

Here's a hearty supper for a blustery winter night.

Serves 6

- ½ ***pound bacon, cut in squares or cubes***
- 1 ***large onion, coarsely chopped***
- 2 ***ribs celery, trimmed and sliced***
- 2 ***carrots, peeled, trimmed, and sliced***
- 1 ***red pepper, seeds and ribs removed, diced***
- 4 ***garlic cloves, sliced***
- 1 ***tablespoon red wine vinegar***
- ½ ***teaspoon dried herbs (thyme, marjoram, or a combination)***
- 2 ***ripe tomatoes, cored, seeded, and chopped, or ¾ cup canned crushed tomatoes***
- 2 ***cans (19 ounces each) cannellini beans, drained and rinsed, or 4 cups cooked dried beans***
- ¾ ***pound kielbasa or other cooked garlic sausage, simmered briefly, peeled and sliced***
- ⅔ ***cup Chicken Broth (page 239) or Vegetable Broth (page 240), or as needed***
- ¼ ***cup bread crumbs***
- ¼ ***teaspoon paprika, preferably Hungarian***
- 2 ***tablespoons chopped parsley***
- ***Freshly ground black pepper***

1. Sauté the bacon slowly in a wide skillet until golden, about 10 minutes. Transfer to a plate lined with paper towels to drain, leaving the fat in the skillet. Set aside 2 tablespoons of the bacon fat, leaving about 3 tablespoons in the skillet.

2. Preheat the oven to 400° F. Raise heat under the skillet. Add the onion, celery, carrots, and pepper and sauté until the vegetables begin to wilt, about 6 minutes. Add the garlic and sauté 2 minutes longer. Add the vinegar; boil until nearly dry. Add the herbs and tomatoes; cook, stirring, until lightly thickened, about 3 minutes. Remove from heat.

3. Add the reserved bacon and the beans to the mixture in the skillet, stirring gently to combine. Use 1 tablespoon of the reserved bacon fat to grease a 1½-quart casserole. Layer the bean mixture and slices of sausage alternately, ending with a layer of sausage. Pour on enough broth to come to the top layer of beans without covering them.

4. Sprinkle the casserole with bread crumbs, then with paprika and the reserved tablespoon of bacon fat. (You can add a few bits of butter if dry.) Bake until golden, about 35 minutes. Sprinkle with parsley and pepper and serve hot.

BROCCOLI AND CAULIFLOWER

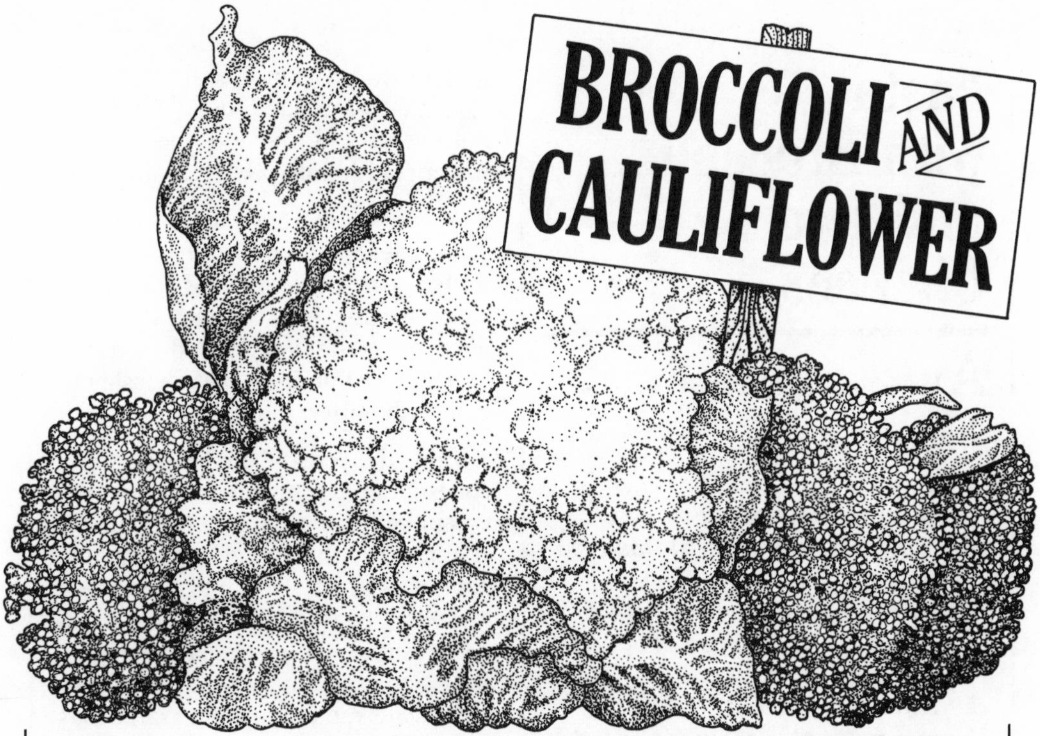

There is now purple cauliflower available, called Violet Queen, which, though a pretty novelty, turns the familiar green once cooked. (It's actually a cross between cauliflower and broccoli.) One interesting thought: though most people prize the broccoli tops (flowerets), others, us included, prefer the taste and texture of the stalks. The stalks, by the way, are best peeled, if you want to take the trouble.

BASIC STEAMING METHOD FOR BROCCOLI

1 bunch broccoli, 1¼ to 1½ pounds

1. Separate the broccoli flowerets from the stems. Trim off and discard the bottom inch or so from the stems; then peel the stems with a paring knife. Slice diagonally into ¼-inch-thick pieces.

2. Set up a steamer, or improvise by placing a metal colander in a large pot. Bring about an inch of water to a boil in the bottom of the steamer; salt lightly. Place the broccoli stem pieces in the top of the steamer, then top with the flowerets. Cover the steamer tightly and steam the broccoli just until crisp-tender, 2 to 4 minutes. The broccoli can be served immediately, drizzled with a little lemon juice and/or butter, and a sprinkling of salt and pepper. If not to be served right away, drain the broccoli under cold running water. Transfer to a dish lined with paper towels and chill, covered, until needed.

Note: *Try broccoli served cold, marinated as in the cauliflower recipe (page 45). Or try a mixture of broccoli and cauliflower, marinated together.*

Pasta with Broccoli and Two Cheeses

A luscious dish, quickly assembled.

Serves 4 to 6

- ***1** pound penne, ziti, or other short tubular pasta*
- ***4** tablespoons (1/2 stick) unsalted butter*
- ***2** garlic cloves, finely chopped*
- ***1** recipe basic steamed broccoli (page 43)*
- ***1** cup heavy cream*
- ***1/2** cup milk, plus more if needed*
- ***1/3** cup crumbled goat cheese (cream cheese or another soft cheese can be substituted)*
- ***3/4** cup freshly grated Parmesan cheese, plus more for serving*
- ***1/2** cup slivered cooked ham or prosciutto (optional)*
- *Salt and freshly ground black pepper*

1. Cook the pasta in a large pot of boiling salted water until just *al dente;* do not overcook. Drain and rinse quickly under cold running water; drain again.

2. Return the pasta cooking pot to the stove over medium-low heat. Add the butter. When melted, add the garlic. Sauté, tossing, for 2 minutes. Raise the heat to medium-high and add the broccoli and drained pasta, tossing to coat with butter.

3. Add the cream, milk, and goat cheese. Cook, tossing gently, until the cream begins to boil and the sauce is smooth. Add the grated Parmesan and ham; toss gently just until the cheese is melted. Season lightly with salt and pepper; thin the sauce, if necessary, with a splash of milk or cream. Serve immediately, passing more grated Parmesan and a pepper mill separately.

BASIC METHOD FOR COOKING CAULIFLOWER

1 head cauliflower (about 12 ounces), leaves trimmed
2 tablespoons white wine or apple cider vinegar

1. Place the whole head of cauliflower in a saucepan; cover with cold water and add the vinegar. Place a small heavy pot lid or plate on the cauliflower to keep it submerged. Bring to a boil, lower the heat, and simmer just until crisp-tender, about 30 minutes (timing can vary).

2. Drain the cauliflower and rinse under cold water. The cauliflower is now ready to serve any way you like; on the opposite page we offer two simple, tasty treatments.

Butter-Crumbed Cauliflower for Cauliflower Haters

Serves 4

- **1** ***head cooked cauliflower (page 44)***
- **4** ***tablespoons (½ stick) unsalted butter***
- **¼** ***teaspoon salt***
- **1½** ***tablespoons coarse bread crumbs, preferably homemade***

1. Break the cauliflower into flowerets; shake dry.

2. Heat the butter over medium heat in a large skillet. Add the cauliflower, sprinkle with salt, and toss until very lightly golden, about 7 minutes.

3. Add the bread crumbs, tossing to coat. Continue to cook, tossing frequently, until the bread crumbs are crisped and golden, about 3 minutes longer. Serve immediately.

Marinated Cauliflower

Serves 6

- **1** ***head cooked cauliflower (page 44)***
- **1** ***recipe Basic Creamy Garlic Dressing (page 46)***
- **½** ***red bell pepper, seeds and ribs removed, cut in thin julienne strips 1 inch long***

1. Separate the cauliflower into flowerets; shake dry.

2. In a large bowl, toss together the garlic dressing and red pepper strips. Add the cauliflower pieces, tossing to coat. Cover and refrigerate at least 1 hour. Remove from the refrigerator about 20 minutes before serving. Toss gently and correct seasonings.

BASIC CREAMY GARLIC DRESSING

This dressing is good for all sorts of salads and marinated vegetables, since the egg yolk makes it coat well. It's also tasty when made with balsamic vinegar. You can keep this refrigerated for about three days in a tightly covered jar.

Makes about 1 cup

- Half an egg yolk
- Juice of 1 lemon
- 2 tablespoons red wine vinegar, plus more as needed
- 1 tablespoon Dijon mustard
- 3 garlic cloves, peeled and thinly sliced
- ½ teaspoon salt
- Freshly ground black pepper
- ½ cup olive oil
- ¼ cup light vegetable oil
- ¼ cup chopped parsley

1. Whisk together the egg yolk, lemon juice, vinegar, mustard, garlic, salt, and pepper until blended and smooth.

2. Add the olive oil a drop at a time, whisking. When the dressing begins to thicken, continue to add the oil in a thin stream. Whisk in the vegetable oil and chopped parsley. Correct all seasonings; be sure the dressing is nicely pungent with vinegar and mustard.

CABBAGE

One of the humbler products of the garden, cabbage is enjoyed all over the world, and has been since ancient times. In the middle of winter, when there's little else around, cabbage saves the day. It can be used in a variety of ways, especially if you take advantage of the different types available: green, red, crinkly Savoy, and the elongated Chinese cabbage. With bok choy, the thick stems need longer cooking than the leaves.

A member of the mustard family, genus *Brassica,* cabbage has a long line of relatives which include Brussels sprouts (called *rosenkohl*—"rose cabbage"—in German), kohlrabi, kale, turnips, broccoli, cauliflower, and rutabaga. In *De Re Culinaria,* the first century A.D. cookbook that gives a fairly clear picture of dining in ancient Rome, Apicius includes seven cabbage recipes, including one flavored with caraway, with which it is still frequently prepared.

Braised Cabbage with Wine and Caraway

Adapted from a recipe of Andy Kisler, the young chef at New York's Vienna '79. A tasty side dish.

Serves 4

3 ***tablespoons unsalted butter***
1 ***medium onion, sliced***
1 ***tablespoon sugar***
1/2 ***head green cabbage, outer leaves removed, quartered, cored, and shredded (about 4 cups)***
1 ***apple (McIntosh or Granny Smith), peeled, cored, and shredded***
1 ***cup dry white wine***
3/4 ***cup Chicken Broth (page 239) or Vegetable Broth (page 240)***
1/4 ***cup heavy cream***
1 ***tablespoon white wine vinegar***
1 ***teaspoon caraway seeds***
1/2 ***teaspoon salt***
Freshly ground black pepper

1. Melt the butter in a large skillet over medium-high heat. Add the onion and sugar and cook, stirring constantly, until lightly golden, about 5 minutes. Add the cabbage and toss for 3 minutes. Add the apple, wine, broth, cream, vinegar, caraway, and salt and pepper, and lower the heat to medium.

2. Cook, uncovered, until the cabbage is just tender and the liquid is nearly absorbed, 20 to 25 minutes. Correct seasonings. Serve hot. (This dish can be prepared in advance and reheated.)

Main-Dish Cabbage Soup

Like many Hungarian soups, this soul-satisfying winter soup combines fresh cabbage with sauerkraut. With dark bread and marinated cucumbers (page 76), it's a meal in itself. We prepare this with sauerkraut that's home-cured by a local Polish butcher; if that's not available, look for vacuum-packed sauerkraut in a plastic pouch.

Serves 8

***8** ounces bacon, cut in strips or squares*
***2** tablespoons vegetable oil*
***2** medium onions, coarsely chopped (about 2 cups)*
***3** garlic cloves, gently crushed and peeled*
***2** medium carrots, peeled, trimmed, and sliced (about 1 cup)*
***2** pounds boneless beef shin or chuck, cut in 3 or 4 pieces*
***3** cups canned tomatoes, with their liquid or puree*
***9** cups beef broth, homemade or canned*
***¼** teaspoon caraway seeds*
***1** dried hot chili pepper*
***1** head green cabbage (about 2½ pounds), quartered, cored, and cut in ½-inch strips*
***12** to 16 ounces sauerkraut, drained and rinsed in cold water*
Salt and freshly ground black pepper
***¼** cup snipped fresh dill, plus more for garnish*
Sour cream

1. In a large casserole, cook the bacon in the oil over low heat, stirring frequently, until the bacon is golden and the fat is rendered, about 15 minutes. Pour off all but about 3 tablespoons bacon fat; reserve fat.

2. Add the onions and garlic to the casserole, tossing to coat. Raise heat to medium and sauté for 10 minutes, tossing occasionally. Add the carrots and cook 4 minutes longer. Add the meat, pushing vegetables aside, and brown lightly, turning once or twice.

3. Add the tomatoes, broth, caraway seeds, and chili pepper. Bring to a boil, skimming. Lower the heat, partially cover the casserole, and simmer 1½ hours.

4. Meanwhile, heat reserved bacon fat in a large skillet. Add the cabbage and cook over medium heat, tossing, until wilted, about 10 minutes. Add the sautéed cabbage and the sauerkraut to the soup after it has simmered for 1½ hours. Simmer, partially covered, 2 hours longer, skimming occasionally.

5. Skim all possible fat from the surface. Remove the meat and cut in bite-size pieces. Add salt and pepper to taste. Just before serving, stir in fresh dill. Serve hot, topping each bowlful with sour cream and a small sprig of fresh dill.

Cabbage and Pepper Slaw

Serves 8 to 10

- ***1** medium head green or Savoy cabbage (about 1¼ pounds)*
- ***2** red bell peppers, seeds and ribs removed*
- ***3** carrots, peeled, trimmed, and coarsely grated (about 2 cups)*
- ***½** cup sliced scallions (green and white portions)*

DRESSING

- ***1** cup mayonnaise*
- ***½** cup lemon juice*
- ***½** cup buttermilk (or plain yogurt thinned with milk)*
- ***2** tablespoons Dijon mustard*
- ***2** tablespoons coarse-grain mustard (or substitute 1 additional tablespoon Dijon mustard)*
- ***4** teaspoons sugar*
- ***2** teaspoons vinegar*
- ***¾** teaspoon salt*
- *Freshly ground black pepper*
- ***⅛** teaspoon cayenne pepper*

1. Remove outer cabbage leaves; discard. Quarter the cabbage, cut out the core, and shred the cabbage ¼ to ½ inch thick (you should have about 8 cups shredded cabbage). Transfer to a large mixing bowl. Cut the peppers crosswise in strips 1 inch wide; cut the strips in thin julienne. Add the pepper strips, grated carrots, and scallions to the cabbage, tossing to combine.

2. *Dressing:* In a separate mixing bowl, whisk together the mayonnaise, lemon juice, buttermilk, mustards, sugar, vinegar, salt, black pepper, and cayenne pepper. Pour the dressing over the vegetable mixture and toss with your hands to combine. Correct seasonings. Chill at least 1 hour.

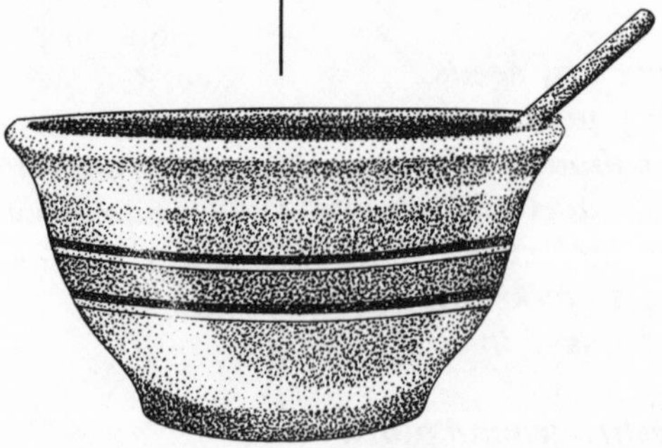

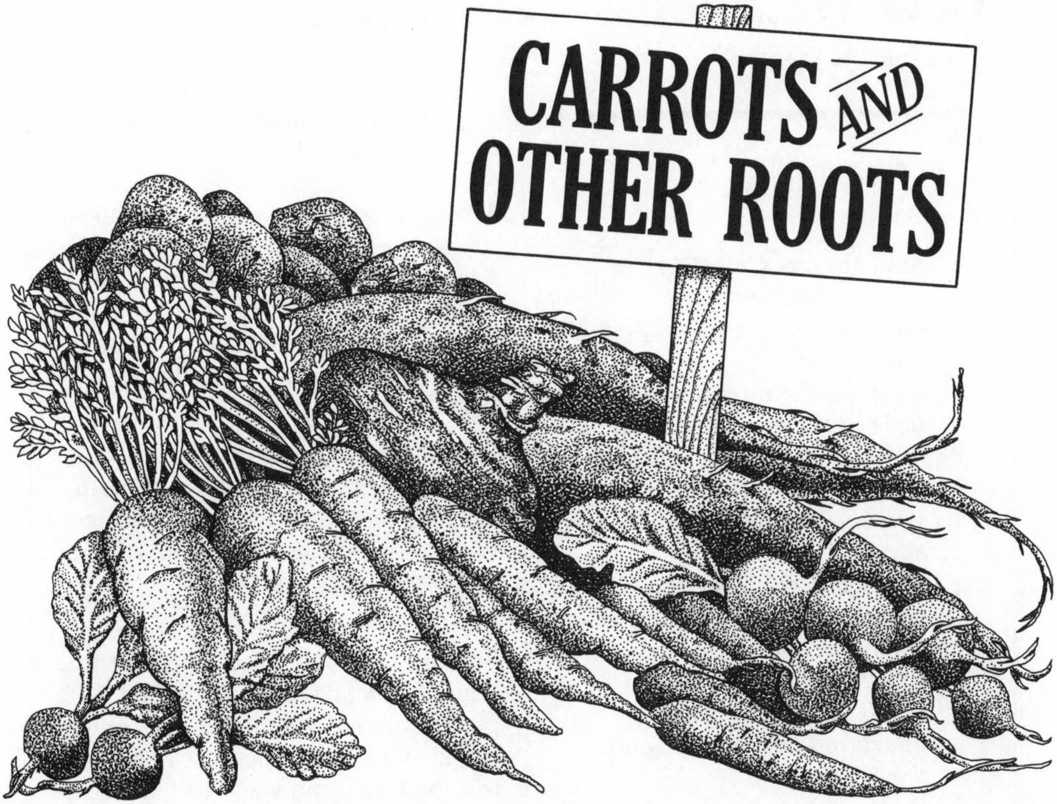

Though kids sometimes find them dull, carrots and the other root vegetables—celery root, turnips, and parsnips—are among the most adaptable vegetables in the kitchen. We think of them as a foundation for preparing many dishes.

In making all sorts of soups and stews, we usually begin with a mixture of onions and such root vegetables as carrots and a small amount of turnips and/or parsnips. They contribute a subtle earthy flavor, and in the case of carrots, a pleasant rounded sweetness, too.

But the uses of these vegetables go beyond just flavor. Rather than using flour to thicken soups or the juices of a stew, try pureeing some of the cooked root vegetables, then adding them back to the liquid. You'll have a smooth, lightly thickened finished product, with lots more flavor (and fewer calories).

Maybe the reason we grew up finding root vegetables dull is that they were cooked in dull ways. Dealt with imaginatively, they can add a special touch to any main dish. And have you ever tried carrots baked in a tart?

Cold-Weather Root Soup

One of our favorites.

Serves 8

- **4** ***tablespoons (1/2 stick) unsalted butter***
- **3** ***medium-large onions, peeled and sliced***
- **2** ***leeks (white portions and a little of the green), trimmed, halved lengthwise, washed well, and sliced***
- **5** ***carrots, peeled, trimmed, and sliced***
- **3** ***garlic cloves, smashed and peeled***
- **1** ***teaspoon salt***
- **1** ***small bay leaf***
- **2** ***small turnips, peeled, quartered lengthwise, and thinly sliced***
- **3** ***thin parsnips, peeled, halved lengthwise, and thinly sliced***
- **2** ***medium potatoes, peeled, quartered lengthwise, and thinly sliced***
- **6 1/2** ***cups Chicken Broth (page 239) or Vegetable Broth (page 240)***
- **1/4** ***teaspoon freshly grated nutmeg***
- **1/3** ***cup heavy cream***
- ***Freshly ground white or black pepper***
- ***Pinch of cayenne pepper***
- ***Freshly grated Parmesan or Cheddar cheese***

1. Heat 3 tablespoons of the butter in a large casserole. Add the onions, leeks, carrots, garlic, salt, and bay leaf, tossing to coat. Cover the pan and cook over medium heat, stirring occasionally, until the vegetables are wilted, about 15 minutes.

2. Add the turnips, parsnips, potatoes, broth, and nutmeg. Bring to a boil, stirring. Simmer, covered, until the vegetables are very tender, about 1 hour. Remove the bay leaf.

3. With a slotted spoon, transfer about half the vegetables and a little of the liquid to a food processor or food mill; puree until smooth. Return the puree to the soup, add the cream, and bring to a boil. Add the white or black and cayenne pepper, plus salt, if needed. Just before serving, remove from heat and swirl in the remaining tablespoon of butter. Serve hot, sprinkling each portion with freshly grated Parmesan or Cheddar Cheese.

Note: This soup may need to be thinned slightly with additional broth or milk when reheated.

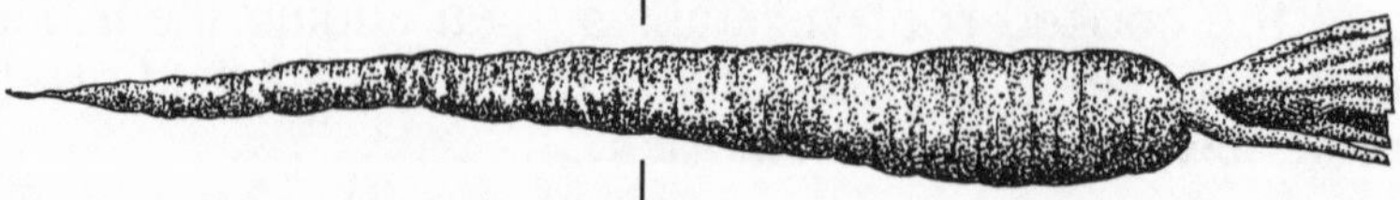

Sautéed Turnips with Butter and Sugar

Serves 4

- **3** ***tablespoons unsalted butter***
- **2** ***tablespoons sugar***
- **1** ***pound white turnips, peeled, halved, and cut into wedges about 1/2 inch wide at their widest***
- ***Salt***
- **1/4** ***cup water***
- ***Freshly ground black pepper***

1. Melt the butter and sugar in a medium skillet over medium heat. Cook 3 to 4 minutes, or until the sugar begins to color slightly. Add the turnips, salt lightly, and toss to coat. Cook over medium heat, tossing occasionally, for 10 minutes or until lightly browned.

2. Add the water, raise the heat to medium-high, and cook, tossing, until the turnips are tender and the water has evaporated, coating the turnips with a light glaze, about 3 minutes. Sprinkle with pepper and serve hot.

Turnips and Parsnips au Gratin

From the Minnesota Department of Agriculture, which administers the state's roadside stands, a creamy gratin of grated root vegetables, topped with oven-crisped bread crumbs. This is guaranteed to convince even determined non-root eaters. Grated carrots and/or celery root can be added, too.

Serves 6 to 8

- **6** ***tablespoons (3/4 stick) unsalted butter***
- **1** ***pound turnips, peeled and grated***
- **1** ***pound parsnips, peeled and grated (or use all of either vegetable)***
- **1** ***teaspoon salt, or to taste***
- **1/2** ***teaspoon sugar***
- **1/4** ***teaspoon freshly ground white pepper***
- **1** ***cup heavy cream, or as needed***
- **1/3** ***cup coarse fresh bread crumbs***

1. Preheat the oven to 375° F. Heat 4 tablespoons of the butter in a wide skillet or casserole over medium heat. Add the turnips and parsnips and sprinkle with the salt, sugar, and pepper. Sauté, uncovered, tossing often, until nearly tender, about 10 minutes.

2. Transfer the mixture to a buttered shallow casserole, such as an 11 x 7-inch rectangular or 9-inch-square baking dish. Add enough heavy cream to nearly cover, then sprinkle with an even layer of bread crumbs. Dot with the remaining 2 tablespoons of butter.

3. Bake until the crumbs are crisp and golden, 45 to 50 minutes. Serve hot.

Baked Celery Root

Celery root (also called celeriac) has a warm, earthy flavor. It makes a delicious soup, can be grated and baked *au gratin* as in the preceding recipe, and is terrific mixed half and half with mashed potatoes (see the box on page 108). Here is an unusual cooking method that brings out celery root's natural sweetness.

Serves 6 to 8

- ***4 small whole celery roots, washed and trimmed of roots but unpared***
- ***4 tablespoons (1/2 stick) unsalted butter***
- ***Salt and freshly ground pepper***

1. Preheat the oven to 375° F. Wrap each celery root in foil and place on a baking sheet. Bake until tender when poked with a small knife, about 1 hour. Remove from the oven, unwrap the foil, and cool until celery root can be handled easily.

2. Peel each celery root with a stainless paring knife and cut in ½-inch dice. Heat the butter in a large skillet over medium heat. Add the diced celery root, sprinkle with salt and pepper, and toss until heated through, about 5 minutes. Serve immediately.

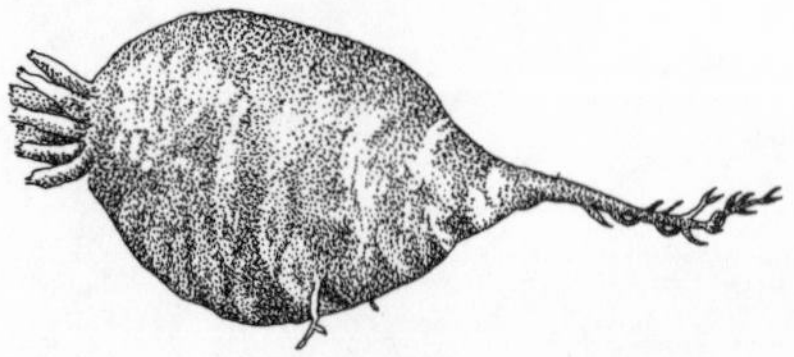

Puree of Root Vegetables and Apples

Serves 4

- ***5 tablespoons unsalted butter***
- ***1 medium onion, coarsely chopped***
- ***1 rib celery, trimmed and sliced***
- ***2 garlic cloves, smashed and peeled***
- ***Salt***
- ***1 medium apple, peeled, cored, and sliced***
- ***2 medium white turnips, peeled and thinly sliced***
- ***2 medium celery roots, pared and thinly sliced***
- ***1 quarter-size slice peeled fresh ginger***
- ***1/2 cup heavy cream, or as needed***
- ***Freshly ground pepper***
- ***Pinch of freshly grated nutmeg***

1. Melt 3 tablespoons of the butter in a skillet over medium-low heat. Add the onion, celery, and garlic; sprinkle lightly with salt, and toss to coat. Cover the skillet and sweat the vegetables, tossing occasionally, until wilted, about 10 minutes.

2. Stir in the apple, tossing to coat. Cover and sweat 5 minutes. Stir in the turnips, celery root, ginger, and cream. Cover and simmer until everything is tender, about 30 minutes. If the mixture becomes dry, add a little more cream or milk.

3. Puree the mixture in a food processor or blender. (Recipe can be pre-

pared in advance to this point.) Return to the skillet and heat gently. Stir in the remaining 2 tablespoons of butter and cook until the mixture is hot and quite thick. Season to taste with salt, pepper, and nutmeg; serve hot.

Gingered Carrot Tart

Several early American cookbooks include recipes for carrot puddings and pies. This recipe is based on one from Lydia Maria Child's *American Frugal Housewife,* published in Boston in 1833. "Carrot pies are made like squash pies," Mrs. Child advised. "The more eggs, the better the pie.... [Ground] Ginger will answer very well alone for spice if you use enough of it. The outside of a lemon grated in is nice."

Serves 8 to 10

1 pound carrots, peeled, trimmed, and thinly sliced
Basic Pastry Dough for a One-Crust Pie (page 241), or Rich Tart Pastry dough (page 240)
2 eggs
1/4 cup light brown sugar
2 tablespoons granulated sugar
1 1/2 teaspoons flour
3/4 cup heavy cream
1/2 cup milk
2 1/2 tablespoons finely chopped crystallized ginger
Pinch each of freshly grated nutmeg and freshly ground black pepper
Grated zest of 1 lemon
1 tablespoon bourbon or rum

1. *Carrot Puree:* In a large saucepan, boil or steam the carrots until they are very tender. Drain thoroughly and return to the empty pan over moderate heat. Toss constantly until all excess moisture evaporates. Puree the carrots in a food processor or through a sieve into a mixing bowl; there should be about 1 1/4 cups. Set aside.

2. On a lightly floured surface, roll out the dough to a thickness of 1/8 inch. Fit it loosely into a 10-inch tart pan with removable bottom; trim excess dough. Form a high border and flute the edge. Chill briefly.

3. *Partially Baking the Pastry Shell:* Preheat the oven to 400° F. Prick the dough lightly with a fork and line it with foil. Weight the foil with rice and bake the shell, on a heavy baking sheet, until the sides have set, about 8 minutes. Carefully remove the foil and rice and continue to bake until the pastry is very pale golden but has not baked through, about 6 minutes longer. Prick any air bubbles with a fork as the pastry bakes. Remove the tart shell from the oven to cool on a wire rack, and lower the oven heat to 350°.

4. Add the eggs, brown and white sugars, and flour to the carrot puree, whisking until smooth. Whisk in the cream, milk, crystallized ginger, nutmeg, pepper, lemon zest, and bourbon. Pour the mixture into the pastry shell and return the tart to the oven.

5. Bake until set in the center, about 30 minutes. Cool on a rack to cool room temperature. Remove the tart from the rim of the pan before serving.

BEETS

If root vegetables are underrated, beets are probably considered the worst of the lot. So much so, in fact, that many people have never cooked fresh ones (since boiled beets make such a mess in the kitchen, that's probably not such a bad idea).

Our answer: try baking beets whole, wrapped in foil (see box below). Not only will you discover a whole new flavor, but cleanup is a snap. And when you try them, make a few extra. Beets are a delicious and colorful addition to many dishes: You can dice or slice them and add to a salad; cut in julienne, toss in butter, and serve as a side dish or garnish; or marinate them and serve as part of an antipasto plate (with a slice of salami, some good olives, a bit of cheese, etc.). Or puree the baked beets smooth or coarse, season with a touch of nutmeg and work in a piece of sweet butter, and discover a whole new vegetable dish. And of course, beets are a time-honored basis for soups, including ruby-hued borschts both hot and cold.

One nice part of buying beets at farmers' markets is that you can often find them with their green tops attached. To prepare the greens, cut them from the roots, wash well, trim off thick stems, and steam or sauté in butter. And a new development, found at some farmers' markets, is golden beets, which taste like red beets but lack their pigment, betanin.

CAN'T BEET 'EM—BAKING BEETS WHOLE

For sweetest flavor, try baking beets whole. Here's how:

- ***Trim the tops from the beets (try cooking the beet greens separately; see page 121); leave them unpeeled. Wrap each one in aluminum foil (wrap 3 to 4 per package if small). Place on a baking sheet.***
- ***Bake in a preheated 400° F. oven until the beets are tender, about 1 hour (time can vary according to size). Remove from the oven.***
- ***When cool enough to handle, unwrap the packages and slip off the skins—using a paper towel will prevent staining your hands.***

The beets are now ready to be served, either:

- ***Hot, tossed in butter, or***
- ***Dressed with oil and balsamic vinegar with fresh dill, or***
- ***With Basic Creamy Garlic Dressing (page 46).***

Or use to make Red Flannel Hash (opposite page), or in any other recipe calling for cooked beets.

Red Flannel Hash

The great New England favorite. *The Yankee Cookbook* (Stephen Greene Press) notes that "a sauce made by blending 2 tablespoons freshly grated horseradish with ½ cup whipped cream is excellent with hash. Sliced green tomato pickles are a perennial favorite."

Follow these instructions carefully and you'll be famous for your hash at brunch or late supper.

Serves 2

- **6** ***small beets, baked (see page 56), peeled and cut in ¼-inch dice***
- **¾** ***pound corned beef, trimmed and cut in ¼-inch dice (about 2 cups)***
- **1½** ***cups diced (¼ inch) cooked all-purpose potatoes***
- **1** ***medium onion, chopped***
- ***Salt and freshly ground black pepper***
- **2** ***egg yolks***
- **2** ***tablespoons heavy cream, or more if needed***
- **4** ***tablespoons (½ stick) unsalted butter, or more if needed***
- **2** ***teaspoons chopped parsley***
- **2** ***fried or poached eggs (optional)***

1. In a large mixing bowl, gently toss together the beets, corned beef, ½ cup of the diced potatoes, the onion, and salt and pepper to taste (go easy on salt; corned beef can be quite salty).

2. In a food processor, process the remaining potatoes, the egg yolks, and 1 tablespoon of the cream until smooth. Gently fold into the hash mixture.

3. Heat 2 tablespoons of the butter in an 8-inch nonstick skillet over medium heat. When the foam subsides, gently add the hash mixture. Let it sizzle in the pan for 2 or 3 minutes; then carefully turn the mixture over and over for a minute or so, to impregnate with the butter. Let sizzle about 1 minute. Now tuck 1 tablespoon of butter under the hash in the center of the bottom of the skillet and flatten the hash mixture into an even pancake, pressing with a spatula.

4. Brown the hash, shaking the skillet often, 8 to 10 minutes. Lay a plate over the skillet; invert the hash onto the plate. Add another 1 to 1½ tablespoons butter to the skillet; when hot, very carefully slide the hash back into the pan, browned side up. Cook over medium heat, shaking the skillet often, for 4 minutes.

5. Dribble the remaining tablespoon of cream down the sides of the skillet, letting it run under the hash, forming a browned crust. Continue to shake the pan for another 4 to 6 minutes, until the bottom is nicely browned. Add another spoonful of cream if necessary to keep the bottom coated evenly. Invert the hash carefully onto a serving plate; top with parsley and the eggs.

JERUSALEM ARTICHOKES

They're not from Jerusalem, and they're not true artichokes. They are delicious, however, with a nutty flavor all their own. In some markets, you might find them under the name sunchokes—look for gnarled (but not shriveled) little nubby tan roots. As with beets and celery root, the flavor seems to come out sweetest when Jerusalem artichokes are baked whole. (There are some people who find that Jerusalem artichokes cause flatulence.)

An interesting note: Jerusalem artichokes are dried and milled into flour, used to prepare pasta for low-gluten diets.

Baked Whole Jerusalem Artichokes

This method of cooking Jerusalem artichokes—a favorite of Marian Morash—results in tender flesh with a sweet, nutty flavor. And try cooking them in duck fat instead of olive oil.

Serves 6

2 tablespoons olive oil
2 garlic cloves, skin on
3 juniper berries
1 pound Jerusalem artichokes, scrubbed (unpeeled), quartered if large
Salt

1. Preheat the oven to 400° F. Place the oil, garlic, and juniper berries in a shallow baking dish, such as a cake, pie, or gratin dish. Place the dish in the oven and heat until the fat is sizzling, about 5 minutes.

2. Add the Jerusalem artichokes, sprinkle with salt, and toss gently to coat. Roast, tossing occasionally, until the artichokes are golden and fork-tender, 35 to 45 minutes.

Pickled Jerusalem Artichokes

A quick, easy pickle from Bob and Mary Van Nostrand, who grow cauliflower, broccoli, potatoes, Jerusalem artichokes, and cranberry beans, as well as herbs and flowers, at their farm in Orient Point, New York, on Long Island's north shore.

Makes about 3 pints

1 pound Jerusalem artichokes, scrubbed (unpeeled) and cut in 1½-inch chunks if large
2 cups apple cider vinegar
3 slices onion
4 cloves
1 bay leaf
6 peppercorns, or 1 dried hot chili pepper

1. Soak the artichokes in cold water for 2 hours. Drain and place them in Mason or stoneware jars, or heavy plastic refrigerator containers.

2. Place the vinegar, onion slices, cloves, bay leaf, and peppercorns or chili pepper in a saucepan and bring slowly to a boil. Pour the mixture over the artichokes. Cool, then refrigerate. The artichokes will be ready to eat in 24 hours, and will keep, refrigerated, for two weeks.

Many favorite foods, such as tomatoes, chocolate, vanilla, and corn, are native to the Americas. Corn originated in southern Mexico or Central America, and has been around for nearly ten thousand years. New hybrids continue to be developed, and some of the most exciting have been introduced in just the past decade. With names like StaySweet, Summer Sweet, and Crisp n' Sweet, these varieties of corn will stay sweet for five or six days past harvest without refrigeration, twelve to fourteen days refrigerated.

Such dramatic breakthroughs have not been easily won, because corn experts often disagree violently about everything from its origins to methods of cross-breeding. Corn seems to bring out passion in the people who spend their lives working with it. Dr. Stephen Marshall, who is at the vanguard of corn research at the Crookham Company in Idaho (over 93 percent of the world's sweet corn seed is produced in Idaho's Treasure Valley), immediately referred to corn as his "second love." (We didn't ask the obvious question.)

The one thing experts do agree on is how corn should be eaten. When we asked Tom Lunkley, who oversees the farmers' markets in Johnson County, Iowa, for some of his favorite corn recipes, he laughed, "Just cooked on the cob, with plenty of butter. If you're into sweet corn, that's the best—it can't be beat!" At Iowa County fairs at the height of summer, large pots are layered with just-picked ears and lots of butter, and for once, instead of serving as a supper side dish, corn *is* supper, with everyone putting away five or six large, juicy ears.

Other natives of the "Tall Corn State" admit to enjoying creamed corn (made with the corn's own milky pulp, with no added cream), or old-fashioned corn relish. And in What Cheer, Iowa, there is even a highly regarded corncob jelly.

Many of our parents' generation recall being offered several varieties of sweet corn at a single farm stand. Some of the most popular over the years have been Iochief, Golden Cross Bantam, Illini Xtra Sweet, Silver Queen (a white variety found throughout the United States), and Kandy Korn (with both white and yellow kernels). Many of these can still be found, alongside the new hybrids.

Although the recipes that follow do go beyond corn on the cob, we've developed them to preserve corn's fresh, sweet flavor.

BEST OF THE BEST: CORN ON THE COB

Until the new hybrids of sweet corn were developed, the only way to enjoy truly sweet corn was to put a pot of water on to boil, run out to the field and pick the corn, and rush it to the waiting pot. While such extreme measures are no longer necessary, this advice from* The Yankee Cook Book *(The Stephen Greene Press, originally published in 1939) still holds true:

> **"One of the commonest faults of cooking corn on the cob in water is overcooking it. Drop corn into boiling, salted water. When water returns to boil, turn off heat and let stand in water exactly 5 minutes."**

We agree, but prefer to boil the corn without salt, adding a splash of milk to the water. Salt at the table, and offer plenty of sweet butter.

ROASTING ON THE COB

If you've got the barbecue going, try roasting corn on the cob. For the traditional version: Pull back the husks without detaching; remove silk. Wrap the leaves back around the corn and soak in cold water for about 10 minutes to prevent burning.

Alternatively, try this easy method for foil-wrapped cobs:

- ***Husk the corn. Place each ear on a sheet of aluminum foil.***
- ***Brush the corn generously with melted butter. Wrap tight.***
- ***Grill until tender, turning occasionally, 15 to 20 minutes (or roast in a moderately hot oven for 20 to 25 minutes).***

Hearty Corn Chowder

Good stuff.

Serves 6

- ***3*** ***tablespoons bacon fat or vegetable oil***
- ***1/2*** ***pound smoked ham, cut in 3/8-inch dice***
- ***3*** ***medium onions, coarsely chopped***
- ***2*** ***ribs celery, trimmed and coarsely chopped***
- ***3*** ***carrots, peeled, trimmed, and thickly sliced***
- ***2*** ***sprigs fresh thyme, or 1/4 teaspoon dried***
- ***1*** ***small bay leaf***
- ***1*** ***pound boiling potatoes, peeled and cut in 1/2-inch dice***
- ***2*** ***cups Chicken Broth (page 239), Vegetable Broth (page 240), or water, plus more as needed***
- ***3/4*** ***teaspoon salt***
- ***1 1/2*** ***cups milk, plus more as needed***
- ***2/3*** ***cup heavy cream***
- ***5 1/2*** ***cups corn kernels with pulp, cut from 8 to 11 ears***
- ***Freshly ground black pepper***
- ***Unsalted butter (optional)***
- ***Fresh thyme leaves, for garnish***
- ***Diced red bell pepper, raw or roasted, for garnish***
- ***Pilot crackers***

1. Heat the bacon fat in a large heavy casserole. Add the ham and toss over medium heat until lightly golden and fragrant, about 5 minutes. With a slotted spoon, transfer the ham to a plate, draining the fat back into the pot. Add the onions, celery, carrots, thyme, and bay leaf to the fat and toss over medium heat until the vegetables are wilted but not brown, about 10 minutes.

2. Add the potatoes, broth or water, and salt to the casserole. Add more liquid, if necessary, just to cover the solids. Bring to a boil, cover, lower the heat slightly, and boil gently until the potatoes are just tender but not mushy, 20 to 25 minutes.

3. Skim any foam from the surface of the soup; remove and discard the thyme sprigs and bay leaf. Add the milk and cream to the soup; bring to a boil. Stir in the corn kernels and simmer gently, partially covered, for 5 minutes.

4. With a slotted spoon, transfer about half the solids to a food processor. Puree until smooth. (If you wish a fuller-bodied chowder, puree a bit more of the solids.) Return the puree to the soup, stirring. Add the reserved ham and a generous sprinkling of pepper; simmer 5 minutes longer, adding milk, if necessary, to bring the chowder to a medium-thick consistency. Correct seasonings.

5. Serve hot, topping each bowl of chowder with a thin pat of unsalted butter, then sprinkling with a few fresh thyme leaves and a few pieces of diced red pepper. Pass pilot crackers alongside.

WHEN CORN'S NOT IN SEASON....

If fresh corn on the cob is not available, we prefer canned corn kernels (crisp-pack) to frozen. Just substitute cup for cup:
1 can (12 ounces) = 1¾ cups drained corn kernels, which equals kernels cut from about 3 medium ears.

Edith's Virginia Spoon Bread with Corn Kernels

From Edith Peroff of Richmond. Starting this spoon bread with a cooked cornmeal "mush" results in a more delicate texture; stirring the cornmeal with a little cold milk prevents lumps. The result—the tenderest, creamiest spoon bread you'll ever try.

Serves 6 to 8

3 cups milk
1 cup cornmeal, preferably stone-ground
1 tablespoon sugar
1 teaspoon salt
3 tablespoons unsalted butter, cut into pieces, plus more for serving
1 cup corn kernels, cut from 2 small ears
7 eggs, very well beaten

1. Preheat the oven to 400° F. Scald 2½ cups of the milk in a heavy saucepan.

2. In a mixing bowl, stir together the cornmeal, sugar, and salt; then stir in the remaining ½ cup cold milk until smooth. When the milk is almost boiling, gradually add the cornmeal mixture to the saucepan, stirring constantly to prevent lumps. Cook, stirring, over medium heat until the mixture is thick and smooth, about 3 minutes. Stir in the butter and corn kernels; remove the pan from the heat.

3. Very slowly add a little of the hot cornmeal mixture to the bowl of beaten eggs, stirring vigorously. Repeat. Add all the cornmeal mixture to the eggs, stirring well to combine. Scrape the mixture into a buttered 12-inch oval gratin dish or a 9-inch square pan.

4. Bake until the spoon bread is golden and a knife inserted in the center just comes out clean, 25 to 30 minutes. Serve immediately, giving each person some of the browned top and soft interior, and topping with a pat of sweet butter.

New Mexican Spoon Bread

From the New Mexico Cooperative Extension Service, a creamy southern spoon bread with Southwest touches of jalapeño peppers and cheese. Serve as a side dish.

Serves 8

***2** cups milk*
***3/4** cup cornmeal*
***5** tablespoons unsalted butter, cut into small pieces*
***4** eggs, lightly beaten*
***1** teaspoon baking powder*
***1/2** teaspoon baking soda*
***1** teaspoon salt*
***1** teaspoon sugar*
***1** cup corn kernels, cut from 2 small ears*
***4** ounces fresh jalapeño peppers, seeds and ribs removed (or one 4-ounce can), chopped*
***1/3** cup diced, trimmed red bell peppers*
***2** cups grated sharp Cheddar cheese, loosely packed (5 to 6 ounces)*

1. Preheat the oven to 375° F. In a small mixing bowl, stir together ½ cup of the cold milk with the cornmeal until smooth. Meanwhile, bring remaining 1½ cups milk nearly to a boil. Stir the cornmeal mixture into the hot milk until smooth. Bring to a boil; boil 2 minutes, stirring constantly. Remove from heat.

2. Stir the butter into the hot cornmeal mixture until melted. Add the beaten eggs gradually, stirring. Then stir in the baking powder, baking soda, salt, sugar, corn kernels, and jalapeño and bell peppers.

3. Place half the batter in a well-buttered 1½-quart soufflé dish or casserole. Top with half the grated cheese. Repeat, adding another layer of batter and topping with remaining cheese. Bake until puffed and golden, 40 to 45 minutes. Serve immediately.

Corn Oysters

"Corn oysters," according to the nineteenth-century American cookbooks in which they frequently appear, were thought to capture the briny flavor of real oysters. True, they do *look* like fried oysters, and feel like them as you break through their crisp coating, but we're not sure we'd confuse them with oysters. They are delicious, though.

In her 1848 *Directions for Cookery,* Eliza Leslie offers "Mock Oysters of Corn," noting that "this is an excellent relish at breakfast, and may be introduced as a side dish at dinner."

Makes about 20 corn oysters

***2** cups corn kernels with pulp, cut from 4 ears*
Milk, if needed
***1/4** cup sifted flour*
Salt and freshly ground black pepper
***2** eggs, separated*
***2** tablespoons bacon fat or vegetable shortening*
***1** tablespoon unsalted butter, plus more as needed*

1. Place the corn kernels, with their pulp, in a mixing bowl. If the corn is not milky, add about a tablespoon of milk. Gently stir in the flour, salt and pepper to taste, and the egg yolks.

2. Beat the egg whites until stiff and fold into the corn mixture.

3. Heat the bacon fat and butter in a large heavy skillet over medium-high heat. When sizzling, add generous tablespoons of the corn mixture, which will spread into oyster shapes. Cook until lightly golden, about 3 minutes; then turn and brown the second sides lightly. Keep the oysters warm on a plate lined with paper towels while you cook the remaining mixture, adding fat as needed. Serve immediately.

Corn and Cheese Pudding

Serve as a side dish with meats, poultry, or fish.

Serves 6

2 cups corn kernels with pulp, cut from about 4 ears
3 tablespoons cornstarch
½ cup thinly sliced scallions (green and white portions)
1 teaspoon unsalted butter
3 eggs
1 cup milk
½ cup Chicken Broth (page 239) or Vegetable Broth (page 240)
1 teaspoon salt
1 teaspoon sugar
Freshly ground black pepper
Pinch each of nutmeg and cayenne pepper
½ cup mozzarella cheese, cut in ¼-inch dice
½ cup Italian Fontina or Swiss cheese, cut in ¼-inch dice, plus 2 tablespoons grated Fontina

1. Preheat the oven to 375° F. Bring a kettle of water to the boil and set aside. Puree 1¼ cups of the corn kernels with the cornstarch in a food processor or blender. Set aside.

2. In a small skillet, stew the scallions in the butter slowly over low heat until softened slightly, about 5 minutes. Set aside briefly to cool.

3. In a large mixing bowl, whisk together the eggs, milk, broth, salt, sugar, a generous sprinkling of pepper, the nutmeg, and cayenne. Stir in the pureed corn mixture, the reserved ¾ cup corn kernels, the scallions, and the diced mozzarella and Fontina cheeses. Pour the mixture into a well-buttered 8-inch-square baking pan and top with the grated Fontina.

4. Place the baking pan in a larger roasting pan; set on the center rack of the oven. Pour hot water into the larger pan to come halfway up the sides of the pudding. Bake until lightly golden and just set, 40 to 45 minutes. Serve hot.

Chicken in Succotash

Succotash is a direct legacy from the Indians, who taught the white settlers how to prepare it. There are versions in early American cookbooks from all over the country, including summer versions made with green beans instead of limas, and winter versions that use dried limas.

Although the majority of recipes for succotash use only vegetables, the tradition of including meat in succotash is an old one. In the "Original Plymouth Succotash," which is traditionally served on Forefathers' Day (December 21), a large cut of corned beef and whole fowl were boiled first. Their cooking liquor was then used to simmer pea beans and corn, which were served alongside.

Here, the flavor combination has been used to sauce a light summer chicken sauté in a home-style chicken cream gravy flecked with fresh herbs.

Serves 4

***1** 3½-pound chicken, cut in small serving pieces*
Salt and freshly ground black pepper
***2** tablespoons bacon fat, or 1 tablespoon each unsalted butter and vegetable oil*
***1** medium onion, chopped*
***¾** cup Chicken Broth (page 239), preferably homemade*
***2** cups shelled fresh lima beans, or 1 package (10 ounces) frozen baby lima beans, partially thawed*
***1** sprig fresh thyme leaves, or ¼ teaspoon dried*
***1** sprig fresh chervil leaves, or ¼ teaspoon dried*
***1½** cups heavy cream, or as needed*
***1½** to 2 cups corn kernels, cut from 3 ears*
Few drops of fresh lemon juice
***2** tablespoons chopped parsley*
***2** tablespoons chopped fresh chervil leaves or chives*

1. Pat the chicken pieces dry, including the neck, back, and giblets (reserve the liver for another use). Season the chicken with salt and pepper. In a wide heavy skillet, heat the bacon fat or butter and oil until foaming. Add half the chicken pieces in a single, well-spaced layer and sauté over medium-high heat until lightly golden, shaking the pan occasionally to prevent sticking, about 8 minutes. Turn and brown the other side. Remove the chicken to a plate lined with paper towels and sauté the remaining chicken pieces.

2. Discard all but 1 tablespoon of the fat from the skillet. Add the onion and cook, stirring, for 2 minutes. Add the chicken broth, scraping the pan well to dislodge all the browned bits. Bring the broth to a boil. Arrange the chicken pieces in the pan, with the breast pieces on top. Cover the pan tightly, lower the heat, and simmer gently 15 minutes.

3. Scatter the lima beans, thyme, and sprig of chervil around the chicken, cover the pan again, and continue to simmer just until the chicken is tender, 10 to 15 minutes longer. Use tongs to remove the chicken pieces to a plate. Discard the neck, back, and giblets.

4. Add the cream to the pan and boil, stirring occasionally, until very lightly thickened, 6 to 8 minutes. Skim the fat from the surface as the cream reduces. Add the corn kernels and simmer 1 minute. Return the chicken pieces to the pan, spooning the cream and vegetables over. Cover and simmer 3 to 5 minutes to heat through, spooning the gravy over the chicken once or twice. Correct seasonings. Remove the pan from the heat and stir in the parsley and chopped chervil or chives. Serve hot, with freshly baked biscuits.

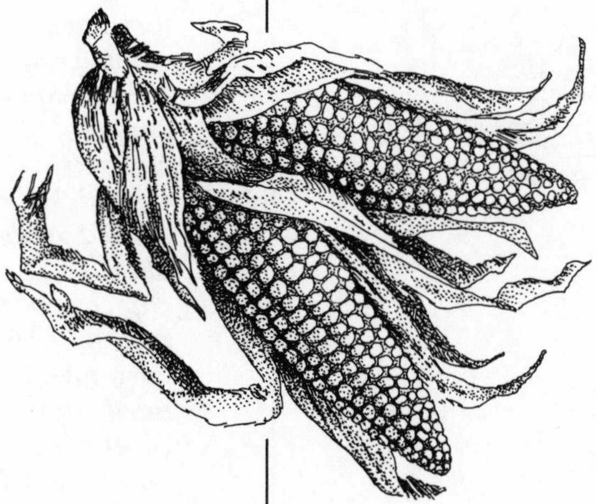

Spicy Beef Pie with Corn Kernel Crust

The English food writer Elisabeth Lambert Ortiz makes a delicious *pastel de choclo con relleno de pollo,* a Bolivian chicken pie with a tender topping made with pureed corn kernels. Here, a similar corn mixture is layered with a spicy ground beef filling; serve this with cold beer.

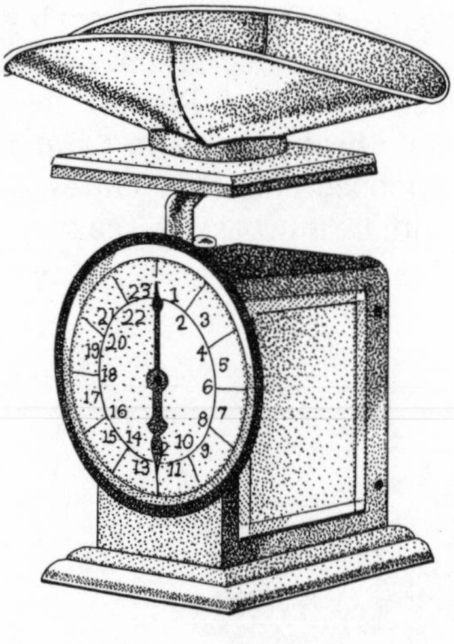

Serves 6 to 8

CORN CRUST

1/2 ***cup (1 stick) unsalted butter***
4 ***cups corn kernels, cut from 6 to 8 ears***
2 ***teaspoons sugar***
1 ***teaspoon salt***
4 ***eggs, lightly beaten***

FILLING

2 ***tablespoons bacon fat or vegetable oil***
1 1/2 ***pounds lean ground beef, such as round***
2 ***medium onions, chopped***
1 ***small red bell pepper, seeds and ribs removed, diced***
3 ***garlic cloves, minced***
1 1/2 ***teaspoons salt***
1 ***teaspoon ground cumin***
1 ***teaspoon ground cinnamon***
1/2 ***teaspoon crumbled oregano***
2 ***tablespoons red wine vinegar***
1 ***to 1 1/4 pounds ripe tomatoes, peeled, seeded, and chopped (or a 1-pound can of crushed tomatoes)***
1/3 ***cup beer, or as needed***
1/4 ***to 1/2 teaspoon cayenne pepper***
1/4 ***cup raisins***
1/4 ***cup thickly sliced pimiento-stuffed green olives (10 to 12 olives)***
1/4 ***cup chopped parsley (or a mixture of fresh parsley and coriander)***
2 ***hard-cooked eggs, sliced (optional)***
Sweet paprika

1. *Corn Crust:* Melt the butter in a heavy saucepan. Meanwhile, puree 3 cups of the corn kernels in a food processor or blender until nearly smooth; add the puree, sugar, and salt to the butter, stirring over low heat to combine. Stir in the reserved cup of corn kernels. Stir in the beaten eggs very gradually. Cook, stirring constantly, over low heat, until thickened slightly, about 3 minutes. Remove from heat and cool.

2. *Filling:* Preheat the oven to 375° F. Heat the bacon fat or oil in a large, heavy skillet over low heat. Add the ground beef and cook, stirring to break up the meat, until about half of it has lost its raw look, 3 or 4 minutes. Add the onions and red pepper and cook the mixture, stirring often, until the vegetables wilt, about 8 minutes.

3. Add the garlic, salt, cumin, cinnamon, and oregano and cook for 2 minutes, stirring to combine the ingredients. Add the vinegar and cook until nearly dry. Add the diced tomatoes and simmer about 3 minutes. Add the beer and bring to a boil. Partially cover the pan and simmer 10 minutes. The mixture should now be quite moist but not soupy; if too wet, boil for a few minutes uncovered, stirring. If dry, add a little more beer. Remove the pan from the heat and stir in the cayenne, raisins, olives, and parsley. Correct all seasonings (salt, spices, vinegar); the mixture should be well seasoned.

4. Spread a little more than one quarter of the corn mixture in a buttered deep baking dish, such as a 2-quart casserole. Gently spoon half the meat filling over; then top with half of the hard-cooked egg slices, if you are using them. Top with a second quarter of the corn mixture, then with remaining meat, then remaining eggs. Very gently spoon the remaining corn mixture over the filling, smoothing it. Sprinkle with sweet paprika.

5. Bake until the crust has set and is lightly golden, about 45 minutes. Remove from the oven and let settle for 5 or 10 minutes before spooning out deep, thick wedges of the pie.

Stewed Corn and Tomatoes

Corn and tomatoes, which reach their seasonal peak together, have been combined in several regions of the United States. One Midwest recipe daintily instructs the housewife to "thrust a small wooden skewer (toothpick) through a small clove of garlic, drop it into the mixture and stir lightly until a delicate flavor is imparted to mixture. Remove garlic (the skewer will help to locate garlic)."

This version, loosely based on Creole recipes, is tasty with broiled or fried chicken, or with charcoal-grilled steaks.

Serves 6

***2** tablespoons unsalted butter*
***1** tablespoon olive oil*
***1/2** cup thinly sliced scallions (green and white portions)*
***1** small garlic clove, minced*
***3** medium-large ripe tomatoes, peeled, seeded, and cut in large dice (about 2 1/2 cups)*
***1** teaspoon salt*
***1/4** cup chopped parsley*
***2** sprigs fresh thyme leaves, or 1/4 teaspoon dried*
***1** sprig fresh tarragon leaves, chopped, or 1/4 teaspoon dried*
***1** small bay leaf*
***2 1/2** to 3 cups corn kernels, cut from about 4 ears*
Tomato juice or water, as needed
Freshly ground black pepper

1. Heat 1 tablespoon of the butter with the olive oil in a wide, noncorrosive skillet. Add the scallions and garlic and stew gently over low heat, stirring occasionally, until softened but not brown, about 5 minutes.

2. Add the diced tomatoes, salt, half the parsley, the thyme, tarragon, and the bay leaf, and bring the mixture to a boil over medium heat. Simmer, stirring, until the tomatoes give off their liquid and the mixture begins to thicken lightly, about 6 minutes.

3. Stir in the corn kernels. Partially cover the pan, lower the heat, and simmer the mixture gently until the corn is tender, the flavors have blended, and the mixture is lightly thickened, about 15 minutes. Stir occasionally as the vegetables cook; if the mixture becomes too thick, add a little tomato juice or water and cover the pan.

4. Remove the skillet from the heat. Stir in the remaining tablespoon of butter, 2 tablespoons parsley, and plenty of black pepper. Correct the seasonings and serve hot.

Seppi Renggli's Gorgonzola Polenta

A favorite dish from New York's legendary restaurant, The Four Seasons. Try this as a side dish with roast poultry; it can be prepared in advance except for the last step.

Serves 6

3 ***cups milk***
3 ***tablespoons unsalted butter***
3/4 ***cup cornmeal (not stone-ground)***
3 ***tablespoons sour cream***
2 1/2 ***tablespoons grated Gruyère or Swiss cheese***
2 1/2 ***tablespoons freshly grated Parmesan cheese***
1/3 ***cup crumbled Gorgonzola cheese, plus six 1 x 1-inch thin slices***
1/3 ***cup (generous) golden raisins***
Freshly grated nutmeg
Salt and freshly ground black pepper
Fine bread crumbs

1. In a heavy-bottomed saucepan, bring the milk and butter to a boil. Pour in the cornmeal in a thin stream, whisking constantly. When the mixture becomes very thick, change to a wooden spoon. Boil, stirring constantly, until smooth, about 5 minutes.

2. Stir in the sour cream, grated Gruyère and Parmesan cheeses, crumbled Gorgonzola, raisins, and a little nutmeg, beating until smooth. Remove from heat and add salt and pepper to taste.

3. Spoon the cornmeal mixture into six 1/2-cup ramekins or custard cups, banging the molds gently on a work surface to settle the mixture, and smoothing the tops with a spatula. Cool at least 15 minutes. (Recipe can be prepared in advance through this step.)

4. Preheat the oven to 450° F. Carefully run a knife around the polenta molds and unmold them onto a generously buttered baking dish. Place a slice of Gorgonzola on top of each one; sprinkle with a fine layer of bread crumbs. Bake for 10 to 12 minutes; then run the baking dish briefly under the broiler, just until lightly golden. Serve immediately.

Corn Kernel Muffins

Makes 12 to 14 muffins

- ***2** ears corn, or 1 cup corn kernels*
- ***1** cup flour*
- ***1** tablespoon baking powder*
- ***1** teaspoon salt*
- ***½** teaspoon baking soda*
- ***½** teaspoon sugar*
- *Pinch of cayenne pepper*
- ***1** cup cornmeal, preferably stone-ground*
- ***2** eggs, lightly beaten*
- ***1¼** cups buttermilk*
- ***4** tablespoons (½ stick) unsalted butter, melted*
- ***⅓** cup grated sharp Cheddar cheese*

1. Preheat the oven to 425° F. With a sharp knife, cut the corn kernels from the cobs, cutting off only the outer half of each kernel. Use a teaspoon to scrape the milky pulp from the cobs. Combine the kernels and pulp and measure 1 cup.

2. Sift onto a sheet of wax paper the flour, baking powder, salt, baking soda, sugar, and cayenne. Stir in the cornmeal. In a mixing bowl, beat the eggs with the buttermilk until blended; then add the melted butter and corn and stir until blended. Add the dry ingredients and stir very briefly, just until moistened. The batter will be lumpy; do not overmix.

3. Spoon the batter into deep, well-buttered muffin tins, filling them a little over three-quarters full. (A nonstick muffin pan works well; if your pan is shallow, use 2 buttered custard cups or ramekins to use up the remaining batter). Sprinkle the batter with cheese and bake until lightly golden and a toothpick inserted in the center of a muffin emerges clean, about 25 minutes. Serve hot, with plenty of butter.

Cornmeal Griddle Cakes

From Oakgrove Mills in Pittstown, New Jersey. People from Oakgrove can be found at several of the area's farmers' markets, selling plastic bags of freshly ground cornmeal, buckwheat flour, and other grains. They also offer helpful recipe cards for breads and other baked goods that use their grains.

Makes about 2 dozen 3½-inch pancakes

1½ cups yellow cornmeal
¼ cup flour
2 tablespoons sugar
1 teaspoon baking soda
½ teaspoon salt
2 cups buttermilk
2 tablespoons unsalted butter, melted
1 egg, separated
Vegetable oil for frying
Butter and maple syrup, for serving

1. In a mixing bowl, combine the cornmeal, flour, sugar, baking soda, and salt. Make a well in the center of the dry ingredients; pour in the buttermilk, melted butter, and egg yolk. Stir gently to combine the ingredients.

2. In a separate bowl, beat the egg white until stiff but not dry. Gently fold the egg white into the cornmeal batter.

3. Heat a griddle or wide heavy skillet over medium heat. Add enough vegetable oil to film the bottom. Pour about 2½ tablespoons of the batter for each pancake; the batter should spread to about 3½ inches wide. Cook until the bottom surface is golden and the top is bubbly, 2 to 3 minutes. Flip the pancakes and cook until the second side is golden, about 2 minutes longer. Transfer to a platter and keep warm while you fry the remaining pancakes. Serve immediately, with butter and warm maple syrup.

Red Peppers Stuffed with Sausage and Corn Kernels, page 102
Sweet Potato Corn Bread, page 132
Scalloped Tomatoes and Corn, page 141
Apple Upside-Down Corn Bread, page 153

CUCUMBERS, SUMMER SQUASH AND ZUCCHINI

"A cucumber should be well sliced, and dressed with pepper and vinegar, and then thrown out, as good for nothing."

Dr. Samuel Johnson, quoted by Waverley Root

CUCUMBERS

We don't agree. In fact, few things are more refreshing than cucumbers on a warm day (why else the expression, "cool as a . . ."?). They can be grated into coleslaw, add crunch and cool flavor to Chinese sesame noodles, and are used to garnish cocktails, from Pimm's cup in England to sake in Japan. And if you've only tried cucumbers cold or in a salad, try them as a hot vegetable, tossed in butter with fresh herbs (see box on opposite page)—a perfect accompaniment to fish.

Cucumbers have long been reputed to be the secret of clear skin—remember Cybill Shepard's face plastered with cucumber slices in *At Long Last Love*? And when pickled, cucumbers really come into their own; an easy Hungarian version is on page 76. At many farmers' markets, you can find small Kirby and seedless cucumbers, perfect for this purpose. About the more involved brine-pickled version, John Thorne has this to say:

> *. . . Cucumbers are okay—so is dill. Put together, they make a friendly flavor combination, no doubt about it. But my mouth only starts to moisten when they go plunge together into the salty brine—that tug on the taste buds is the cure's rationale. Not to preserve but to enhance.*

EVER HAD CUCUMBERS AS A HOT VEGETABLE?

They couldn't be easier. Just peel cucumbers, preferably Kirby or seedless (also called burpless). Halve lengthwise, scrape out seeds with a spoon, and slice 1/4-inch thick. Sauté gently in butter just until crisp-tender, 3 to 5 minutes. Top with snipped chives, fresh dill, or chopped parsley.

Peg's Bread and Butter Pickles

From Margaret Stieber of Sheboygan, Wisconsin. Mrs. Stieber told us that the thin slicing disk of a food processor makes quick work for slicing the cucumbers, onions, and peppers.

Makes about 8 pints

1 gallon Kirby cucumbers (about 5 pounds), washed (unpeeled) and thinly sliced
4 medium white or yellow onions, thinly sliced
1 green pepper, seeds and ribs removed, thinly sliced
1 red bell pepper, seeds and ribs removed, thinly sliced
1/2 cup coarse (kosher) salt
4 cups ice cubes

PICKLING SYRUP
5 cups sugar
2 tablespoons mustard seeds
1 teaspoon celery seeds
1 1/2 teaspoons turmeric
5 cups apple cider vinegar
1/3 cup cold water

1. Place the sliced cucumbers, onions, and peppers in a large mixing bowl. Toss with the salt and ice cubes. Cover with a plate, weight down with a heavy pan, and let stand for 3 hours.

2. Drain the vegetables completely; set aside.

3. *Pickling Syrup:* In a large heavy saucepan, combine the sugar, mustard and celery seeds, and turmeric. Add the vinegar and water, stirring to combine. Add the drained vegetables and place the pan over low heat. Cook, stirring, until the sugar has dissolved and the syrup begins to simmer. Do not boil.

4. Pack the pickles and syrup in sterilized jars, leaving 1/4-inch headspace. Remove air bubbles; set canning lids and screw bands in place. Process in a boiling water bath for 10 minutes.

Hungarian Marinated Cucumbers

Crunchy and slightly sweet; a refreshing side dish with meat stews or broiled fish. Salting the cucumber slices removes excess liquid, making them nice and crisp.

Serves 4

- ***2** large cucumbers, preferably seedless, peeled and thinly sliced*
- ***1½** teaspoons coarse (kosher) salt*
- ***¼** cup (or more) fresh lemon juice or mild vinegar*
- ***1** tablespoon cold water*
- ***2** teaspoons superfine sugar*
- ***1** small garlic clove, minced*
- ***2** tablespoons chopped fresh dill (optional)*

1. Layer the cucumbers and salt in a colander set over a bowl. Let the mixture stand for 1 hour.

2. In a glass serving bowl, whisk together the lemon juice, water, sugar, garlic, and dill. Squeeze the cucumbers gently to extract as much liquid as possible. Add them to the bowl, tossing to coat with the dressing. Cover and refrigerate until ready to serve. Add a little more lemon juice, if needed.

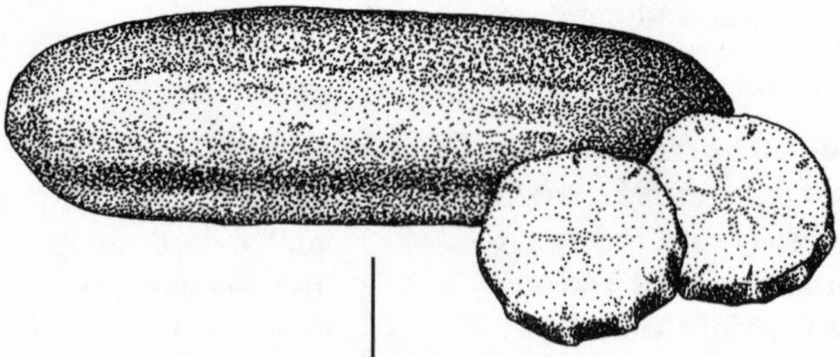

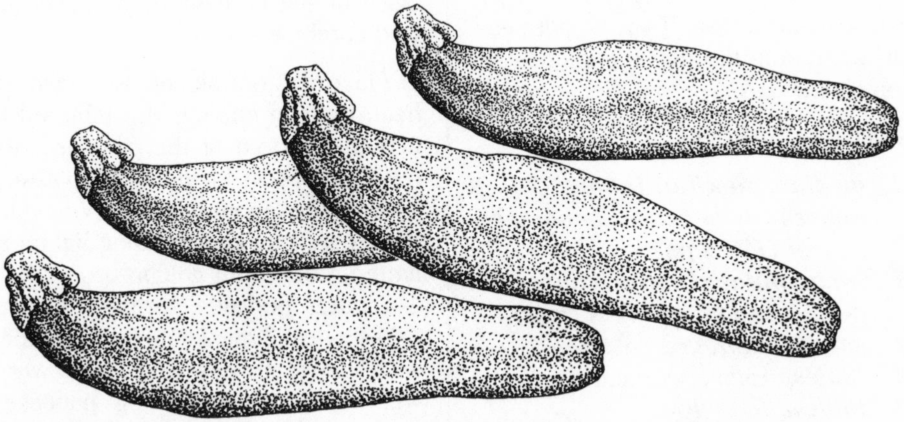

ZUCCHINI AND SUMMER SQUASH

Sorry, we don't share the enthusiasm of those gardeners who proudly hold up their baseball-bat-size zucchini. In fact, we both have to admit that neither zucchini nor squash are our favorite vegetables. (M. F. K. Fisher once referred to "... anyone honest enough to confess to a basic loathing of zucchini.")

But cooked right, zucchini and summer squash can be sweet and tender. Look for small specimens, with firm, bright flesh. Summer squash varieties you're likely to encounter at farmers' markets include yellow squash, both crookneck and straight neck. You may also be able to find small pattypan (or cymling) squash. And whatever variety you choose, take care not to overcook.

WHAT ARE THOSE ORANGE THINGS, ANYWAY?

Lately, some markets have been offering zucchini with their blossoms still attached, or selling the bright orange blossoms separately. If you can find them, try stuffing the blossoms with mozzarella or a soft cheese such as ricotta or **fromage blanc** ***(page 157) and herbs, then dipping them in a light batter and deep frying until crisp and golden. Serve with a wedge of lemon.***

Zucchini and Potato Pancakes

Don't count on saving these crispy pancakes for a meal if you've got people wandering through the kitchen as you fry them.

Makes about 1 dozen

- ***2 medium zucchini (about 12 ounces), trimmed and coarsely grated (1½ cups)***
- ***1 Idaho potato (about 8 ounces), peeled and grated (1¼ cups)***
- ***1 small onion, grated***
- ***2 tablespoons cornmeal***
- ***2 tablespoons flour***
- ***¾ teaspoon salt***
- ***1 egg, lightly beaten***
- ***Vegetable oil, as needed***
- ***Sour cream***

1. Place the grated zucchini in a colander and press firmly to remove all possible liquid. Transfer to a mixing bowl and combine with the grated potato and onion. Stir in the cornmeal, flour, and salt; then add the beaten egg, stirring until the ingredients are well combined.

2. Place a large skillet over medium heat. Pour in enough vegetable oil to film the bottom of the pan. Heat the oil; then spoon in the vegetable mixture, using about 2 tablespoons for each pancake, and pressing lightly to flatten. Cook until golden brown, 3 or 4 minutes per side, turning the pancakes once. Transfer to a plate lined with paper towels and keep warm while you fry remaining pancakes. Serve immediately, with sour cream.

AND NOW, A FEW WORDS FROM THE BIBLE....

Sally Piland and her husband grow a beautiful vegetable garden in Allwyn, Washington. When she heard that we were seeking recipes using fresh vegetables, she sent us this advice: "Read Daniel I on vegetables."

Curious, we did. Chapter I of the Book of Daniel, it seems, is referred to as "The Food Test." It tells the story of Nebuchadnezzar, the Babylonian king who had taken siege of Jerusalem. The king ordered several noble young Israelites to be brought to his palace. After three years' training, they were to enter the king's service. We read:

> **. . . The King allotted them a daily portion of food and wine from the royal table.**
>
> **But Daniel was resolved not to defile himself with the King's food or wine; so he begged the chief chamberlain to spare him this defilement. Though God had given Daniel the favor and sympathy of the chief chamberlain, he nevertheless said to Daniel, "I am afraid of my lord the King; it is he who allotted your food and drink. If he sees that you look wretched by comparison with the other young men of your age, you will endanger my life with the King." Then Daniel said to the steward whom the chief chamberlain had put in charge of Daniel [and the others], "Please test your servants for ten days. Give us vegetables to eat and water to drink. Then see how we look in comparison with the other young men who eat from the royal table, and treat your servants according to what you see." He acceded to this request, and tested them for ten days; after ten days they looked healthier and better fed than any of the young men who ate from the royal table. So the steward continued to take away the food and wine they were to receive, and gave them vegetables.**

Summer Squash Casserole

Based on a recipe from Edris Sitzer, who sells her produce at the Heart of the City Farmers' Market in San Francisco.

Serves 4 to 6

3 ***tablespoons unsalted butter***
1 ***pound summer (yellow) squash, thinly sliced (about 4 cups)***
Salt and freshly ground black pepper
½ ***cup sour cream***
1 ***tablespoon fresh chives and/or parsley***
¼ ***teaspoon paprika***
2 ***tablespoons plus ¼ cup grated Swiss cheese***
3 ***tablespoons fresh bread crumbs***

1. Preheat the oven to 375° F. Heat the butter in a large skillet over medium-high heat. Add the sliced squash, sprinkle with salt and pepper, and sauté, tossing frequently, until tender and very lightly golden, about 5 minutes.

2. In a mixing bowl, stir together the sour cream, chives and/or parsley, paprika, and 2 tablespoons of the cheese. Add the cooked squash, stirring to combine the ingredients, and transfer the mixture to a buttered, shallow baking dish, such as a 9 x 6-inch rectangular or 8-inch round pan. Sprinkle the bread crumbs over the surface.

3. Bake 10 minutes; then scatter the remaining ¼ cup grated cheese on top and bake 5 minutes longer. Run briefly under the broiler until golden brown, about 1 minute. Serve immediately.

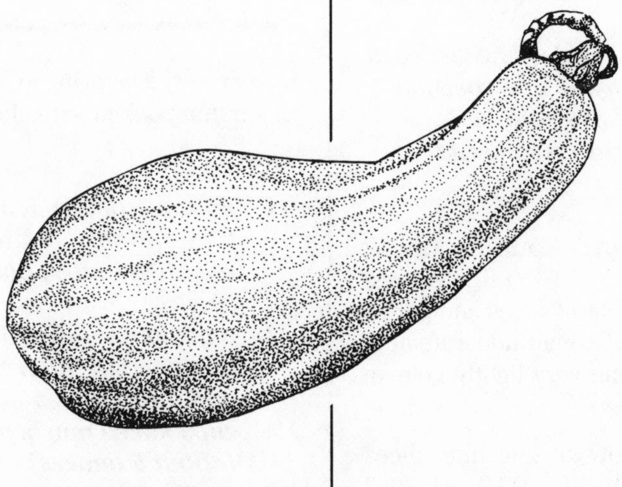

Baked Zucchini, Pepper, and Tomato Gratin

Beautiful to look at, with neat rows of colorful vegetable slices. Terrific with chicken, fish, or steak. Prepare this in advance; it's especially good at room temperature.

Serves 4 to 6

5 ***tablespoons olive oil***
2 ***cups sliced onions***
2 ***garlic cloves, smashed and roughly chopped***
1 ***pound zucchini, trimmed and sliced***
1 ***large red bell pepper, seeds and ribs removed, cut in ½-inch dice***
1¼ ***pounds ripe tomatoes, cored, halved, seeded, and sliced***
Salt and freshly ground black pepper
1 ***tablespoon mixed herbs, such as fresh thyme and rosemary, and dried oregano***
2 ***tablespoons fresh bread crumbs***

1. Preheat the oven to 375°F. Heat 2 tablespoons of the olive oil in a large skillet. Add the onion slices and garlic; toss to coat. Sauté over moderate heat until softened and very lightly golden, about 12 minutes.

2. Arrange a row of zucchini slices across the width of an 11-inch oval gratin dish or other comparable shallow baking dish, standing them upright. Add a row of the onion mixture, then a row of diced pepper, and then sliced tomatoes; repeat until you have used them all.

3. Sprinkle the salt, pepper, and herbs over the vegetables, then scatter the bread crumbs on top in an even layer. Drizzle the remaining 3 tablespoons olive oil over all. Bake until the vegetables are tender, about 1 hour. If you'd like a little more color on top, run the dish under the broiler until the crumbs and vegetables are lightly golden, 1 minute or less (watch carefully). Serve hot or at room temperature.

Baked Macaroni with Zucchini and Three Cheeses

Everybody's favorite, in a new, colorful version packed with cheese.

Serves 6

1 ***pound elbow macaroni***
6 ***tablespoons (¾ stick) unsalted butter, plus more if needed***
1 ***tablespoon olive oil***
2 ***medium zucchini, trimmed and thinly sliced***
1½ ***cups sliced mushrooms (about 5 ounces)***
1 ***medium-large onion, coarsely chopped***

1 ***medium red bell pepper, seeds and ribs removed, cut in ½-inch dice***
2 ***garlic cloves, minced***
¼ ***cup flour***
1 ***quart cold milk***
1 ***teaspoon salt, plus more to taste***
¼ ***teaspoon freshly grated nutmeg, plus more to taste***
½ ***cup sour cream***
1 ***teaspoon Worcestershire sauce, plus more to taste***
Few drops Tabasco sauce
1½ ***cups grated sharp Cheddar cheese (about 4 ounces)***
1¼ ***cups grated Swiss cheese (about 3 ounces)***
½ ***cup freshly grated Parmesan cheese, packed (about 1½ ounces)***

1. Preheat the oven to 400°F. Cook the macaroni in a large pot of boiling salted water until just *al dente,* about 8 minutes. Drain, rinse under cold water, and drain again. Set aside.

2. Meanwhile, heat 2 tablespoons of the butter with the olive oil in a large skillet over medium-high heat. Add the zucchini and the mushrooms and sauté, tossing occasionally, for 5 minutes. Transfer to a plate; set aside.

3. Add 3 tablespoons of the butter to the skillet and lower the heat to medium. Add the onion, red pepper, and garlic and sauté, tossing occasionally, until the vegetables are softened but not brown, about 8 minutes.

4. Sprinkle the vegetables in the skillet with the flour and stir with a wooden spoon. If the mixture is too dry to stir, add a bit more butter. Cook until the flour is opaque, about 4 minutes. Add the milk to the skillet and bring to a boil, stirring occasionally. Add the salt and nutmeg and simmer the sauce 5 minutes. Remove the sauce from the heat and stir in the sour cream, Worcestershire, and Tabasco. Correct all seasonings.

5. In a large mixing bowl (or the pot used to cook the macaroni), toss together the drained macaroni, reserved zucchini mixture, and the sauce. Combine the grated Cheddar and Swiss cheeses; set aside ¼ cup of this mixture. Add the grated cheese mixture to the macaroni, stirring gently to combine thoroughly, and transfer to a buttered 9 x 13-inch baking dish. Combine the reserved ¼ cup cheese with the grated Parmesan; scatter this mixture over the macaroni and dot with the remaining tablespoon of butter.

6. Bake until crusty, about 45 minutes. Run under the broiler just until nicely golden, about 45 seconds (watch carefully). Serve immediately.

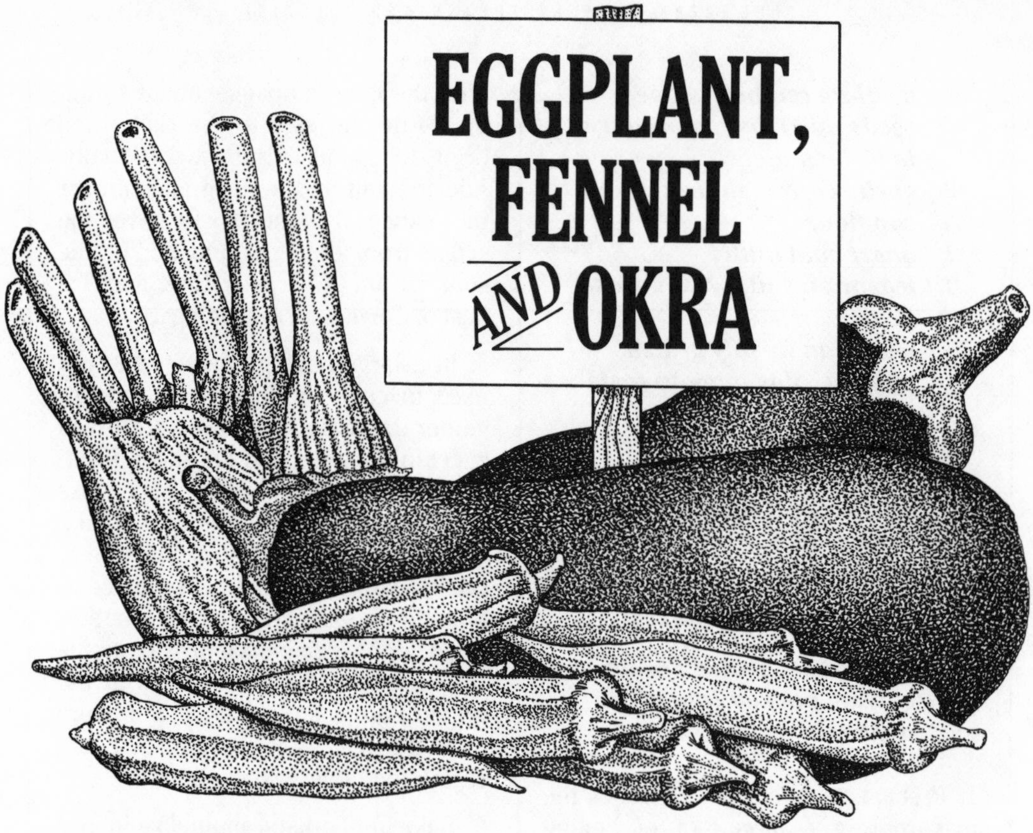

EGGPLANT

Because of eggplant's substantial texture, it is often compared to other foods: many people find it "meaty" when cooked *alla parmigiana;* when pureed, Middle Eastern style, it's called eggplant caviar.

Eggplant is a member of the nightshade family, which also includes peppers, potatoes, and tomatoes. All of these, which are now so taken for granted in our diets, were once suspected and feared. Curiously, some people with arthritis are advised to avoid all members of the nightshade family.

At the farmers' market, you may be able to find several eggplant varieties. Have you ever tried white eggplant, sometimes called Easter egg eggplant? They have fewer seeds than the more common purple variety, and are usually less acidic in flavor. Or the slender Japanese ichiban, which can grow up to ten inches long, but is only about two inches in diameter? One of the most beautiful of all vegetables is the Chinese eggplant, with pale lavender skin and white flesh.

With all eggplant varieties, look for firm, tight skin that is not shriveled.

BASIC METHOD FOR BAKED EGGPLANT

Lots of people avoid cooking eggplant, because it can easily turn out bitter, greasy, or both. This quick, no-effort method is our favorite; it results in a meaty texture and sweet flavor.

2 **eggplants (about 2½ pounds total weight), halved lengthwise**
½ **cup water, plus more as needed**

1. Preheat the oven to 350° F. Lay the eggplants, cut sides down, on a foil-lined jelly roll pan. Pour ½ cup water into the pan. Bake until the eggplant is tender when poked with a small knife, about 45 minutes. As the eggplant bakes, add more water, if necessary, so there is always a small amount in the pan.

2. Remove from the oven and cool. Remove the skin with a small knife. You can sauté the chunks of eggplant in butter, adding salt, pepper, or a sprinkling of chopped herbs, or serve it mashed and seasoned. Or use it as the basis for Eggplant Appetizer with Tomatoes and Herbs.

Eggplant Appetizer with Tomatoes and Herbs

Because this is served at room temperature, you can prepare it in advance. Serve as a summer first course or salad, or on a buffet table, lining the platter with lettuce leaves.

Serves 6

2 ***baked eggplants (see above)***
3 ***tablespoons olive oil, plus more for drizzling***
1¾ ***cups coarsely chopped onions***
2 ***or 3 garlic cloves, chopped***
Salt and freshly ground black pepper
5 ***tablespoons balsamic or red wine vinegar, plus more to taste***
1¼ ***cups peeled ripe fresh tomatoes (about 2 medium), or drained canned tomatoes, seeded and cut in large dice***
3 ***tablespoons chopped parsley and/or basil***

1. Prepare the eggplant as directed; peel, then cut the flesh in ¾-inch cubes and place in a mixing bowl.

2. In a large skillet, heat the olive oil over low heat. Add the onions and garlic; sprinkle with salt and pepper. Sauté slowly, stirring occasionally, until lightly golden, about 30 minutes. Add 4 tablespoons of the vinegar and simmer for 3 minutes. Raise the heat to medium, add the tomatoes, and cook, stirring, until lightly thickened, 8 to 10 minutes. Add this mixture to the eggplant, stirring to combine.

3. Add the parsley, another tablespoon of vinegar, and additional salt and pepper to taste. Cool to room temperature, correct seasonings, and add a little more vinegar, if necessary, to give the mixture a pleasant tang. Serve at room temperature, drizzled with good olive oil.

MORE EGGPLANT

To sauté or grill eggplant, rather than baking, we suggest salting beforehand to remove bitterness.

- **To Sauté:** ***Peel (optional), cut in chunks, and sprinkle with coarse salt. After about ½ hour, rinse, squeeze dry, and sauté gently in sweet butter or olive oil.***
- **To Grill:** ***Slice, leaving peel on. Salt and rinse as above; then pat dry. Drizzle with olive oil and grill until golden.***
- **Grilled Eggplant Wedges:** ***For a special treat, mix together chopped fresh basil, chopped garlic, salt, freshly ground pepper, and enough olive oil to moisten. With a paring knife, poke small incisions in thick wedges of unpeeled eggplant. Insert the basic mixture into the slits with your fingers; then drizzle with olive oil and grill.***

FENNEL

Just about every part of fennel can be used in cooking. In this chapter, we deal mainly with the bulb, which looks like a plump cousin of celery, with feathery green tops. This is tasty eaten raw, with a sweet anise flavor; it can also be quickly steamed or sautéed, grilled, and even stuffed and baked.

The seeds are used in baking and to flavor sausage; and the feathery tops can be chopped and added to soups or cream sauces —their flavor particularly enhances fish. To retain the bright green color add them just before serving. In Provence, the fennel stalks are dried and used to add fragrance to grilled fish, which is then flamed with Pernod. In Italy, where it is called *finocchio,* raw fennel is often nibbled after meals, to aid digestion.

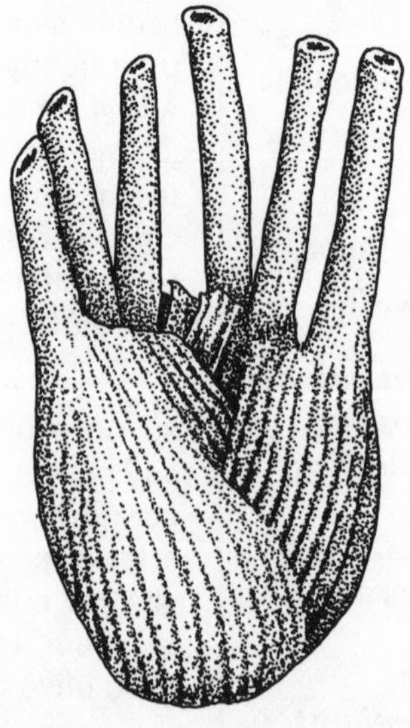

Fennel Stewed with Olive Oil and Garlic

Serves 4

***3** tablespoons olive oil*
***4** garlic cloves, skin on*
***1** medium fennel bulb (about 12 ounces)*
***1/4** teaspoon salt*
***2** tablespoons chopped fennel fronds or parsley*

1. Heat the oil in a medium-size skillet over low heat. Add the garlic and cook slowly for 5 minutes.

2. Trim the bottom of the fennel bulb. Quarter it lengthwise; cut out any hard core. Cut the fennel in 1-inch dice; you should have about 3¼ cups. Add the fennel to the skillet, sprinkle with salt, and raise the heat slightly. Cook uncovered, stirring occasionally, until tender and lightly golden, about 20 minutes. Remove the garlic, sprinkle with the fennel tops or parsley, and serve hot.

Raw Fennel with Lemon Dressing

Serves 4

***1** medium fennel bulb (about 12 ounces)*
***3** tablespoons lemon juice, or more to taste*
***1/4** cup olive oil*
***1/4** teaspoon salt*
***1/4** teaspoon sugar*
Freshly ground black pepper
***2** tablespoons chopped fennel fronds or parsley*

1. Trim the bottom from the fennel bulb. Quarter it lengthwise and cut out any hard core. Slice the quarters crosswise ¼ inch thick and transfer to a mixing bowl. You should have about 3¼ cups sliced fennel.

2. Toss the fennel with the lemon juice; then add the olive oil, salt, sugar, a generous sprinkling of pepper, and feathery fennel fronds or chopped parsley. Toss well to combine; chill for about 30 minutes. Correct seasonings and serve chilled.

GETTING THE MOST OUT OF FENNEL

After trimming the bottom and any tough outer sections from a bulb of fennel, you can use just about the whole vegetable. The slender tops can be thinly sliced, and the feathery fronds on top can be added to dressings, stuffings, or sauces.

OKRA

Are you ready? Okra, which many people grew up hating, is now "in." Thanks to the recent interest in American cooking, more people are willing to try this good vegetable with a bad reputation. The only problem remaining is, few people know exactly how to cook it right, so it emerges just tender (not slimy), and rich with flavor. Here is one of the best ways, stewing the pods whole with onions, chopped ripe tomatoes, and fresh herbs.

Okra with Red Onions, Tomatoes, and Hot Pepper

Serves 4

2 tablespoons olive oil
2 medium red onions, coarsely chopped
1 pound okra, stem ends trimmed without cutting the pods open
4 or 5 ripe plum tomatoes, peeled, seeded, and chopped (1½ to 2 cups)
Salt
Large pinch of dried red pepper flakes

1. Heat the olive oil in a skillet over medium-low heat. Add the onions, tossing to coat. Sweat, covered, until wilted, about 10 minutes.

2. Uncover the skillet and stir in the okra, tomatoes, salt, and pepper flakes. Bring to a boil; then lower the heat to medium-low. Simmer, uncovered, until the okra is tender but not mushy, about 20 minutes. Correct seasonings and serve hot.

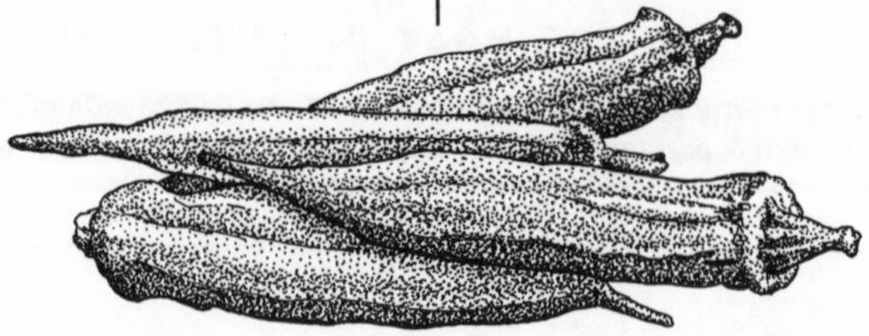

Wild mushrooms are one of the "new foods" that chefs and food enthusiasts are clamoring for—frequently at prices over $20 a pound. The fact that they have only just become so popular is ironic, since wild mushrooms, including morels, chanterelles, and boletes, have long been around in this country. Until recently, only a few people knew how good they were, or where to look for them. Now, shiitake mushrooms are being cultivated commercially, and some are beginning to find their way to farmers' markets in Virginia, North Carolina, Ohio, and Wisconsin.

We spoke to Mark Titus of the Elix Corporation in Virginia, which markets shiitake under the proprietary name Golden Oak mushrooms. Mr. Titus explained that their commercial cultivation is still very new, having started in 1982 with spawn brought from Korea. (Mushrooms begin as spores, the tiny seeds found in the gills; they then grow into spawn, the growing mushroom root system. Shiitake mushrooms are now grown from spawn developed in this country.) Elix uses an outdoor cultivation system, in which the mushrooms grow on oak logs, and has sold the spawn to local farmers in order to help them get started.

Mushroom lovers in Michigan and various areas of the Pacific Northwest enjoy abundant mushroom harvests; Sandy once bought several pounds of chanterelles in Seattle for next to nothing, and brought them back home, "to eat with pasta, of course." (See her recipe on page 90.) James Beard once recalled a mycological congress in Oregon where nearly 100 varieties of wild mushrooms were on display, all gathered locally (not all were edible, and ten of them were hallucinogenic).

Some lucky folks have so many wild mushrooms on hand that they can't use them fast enough. Doris Roncalli, a blue-ribbon cook in Shelton, Washington, told us, "We have such an abundance of the desirable chanterelle mushrooms that we put them up by canning, freezing, and drying for later use." She also manages to use them up by preparing marinated chanterelles, as well as chanterelle frittters and toasted bread rounds topped with creamed chanterelles and ham. We wish we had her problem. . . .

Sautéed Wild Mushrooms with Garlic and Parsley

A quick, basic method for cooking nearly any fleshy wild mushrooms. Here, we've combined the wild mushrooms with cultivated ones; you can use all of either variety if you like.

This cooking method also serves as the basis of a pasta topping; see the recipe on page 90.

Serves 4

- **1/3** ***cup olive oil***
- **6** ***ounces wild mushrooms, e.g., porcini or cèpes, shiitake or Golden Oak, wiped clean and thickly sliced***
- **6** ***ounces cultivated mushrooms, wiped clean and thickly sliced***
- ***Salt and freshly ground black pepper***
- **1 1/2** ***tablespoons minced garlic***
- **2** ***tablespoons dry white wine, if needed***
- **3** ***tablespoons chopped parsley***
- **2** ***tablespoons cold unsalted butter, cut into pieces***

1. Heat the olive oil in a large skillet over medium-high heat. Add both kinds of mushrooms; sprinkle with salt and pepper.

2. Sauté the mushrooms, tossing occasionally, for about 4 minutes. Add the garlic and continue to cook, tossing occasionally, until the mushrooms are tender and have wilted slightly, 8 to 10 minutes in all. (If, after about 4 minutes, the shiitake seem dry, add the wine.) Add the parsley and the butter, tossing to coat. Correct the seasonings and serve immediately. A piece of toasted French or Italian bread, served alongside, will catch the juices nicely.

Mortimer's Chicken Fricassee with Shiitake Mushrooms

From Stephen Atto, chef at Mortimer's, a smart but comfortable hangout on New York's Upper East Side. Stephen created this dish, with a rich, chickeny gravy, especially for shiitake mushrooms, and it shows off their flavor beautifully. Feel free to try this with other wild mushrooms.

Serves 4

1 ***chicken (about 4 pounds), cut into small serving pieces***
Salt and freshly ground white pepper
Vegetable oil, as needed
2 ***ounces fresh shiitake mushrooms, stems removed, stems and caps sliced and kept separate***
½ ***cup sliced cultivated mushrooms***
2 ***shallots, chopped***
1 ***rib celery, trimmed and chopped***
2 ***tablespoons flour***
3 ***ounces dry white wine***
1 ***quart Chicken Broth (page 239)***
Pinch of thyme
1 ***bay leaf***
1 ***cup heavy cream***
3 ***tablespoons unsalted butter***

1. Pat the chicken pieces dry; season with salt and pepper. Heat a thin film of oil in a large heavy casserole over medium-high heat. Brown the chicken pieces lightly, turning each piece once or twice, about 8 minutes in all. Transfer the chicken pieces to a plate.

2. Add the shiitake stems (reserving the sliced caps), cultivated mushrooms, shallots, and celery to the casserole. Sauté, tossing, until the vegetables begin to wilt, about 4 minutes. Sprinkle with the flour and cook, stirring, until the flour has become dry, about 4 minutes.

3. Add the wine and boil until nearly dry. Return the chicken pieces to the casserole; add the broth, thyme, and bay leaf. Bring the mixture to a boil, then lower the heat and simmer, uncovered, until the chicken is tender, 30 to 35 minutes. Transfer the chicken pieces to a plate.

4. Raise the heat and boil the broth, uncovered, until reduced by about three quarters; it should be very syrupy. Add the cream, bring to a boil, and reduce until thickened to a light napping consistency. Strain the sauce into a clean skillet or saucepan, pressing hard on the solids to extract all flavor. Discard solids. Add the chicken to the sauce and simmer briefly, spooning the sauce over the chicken. Correct seasonings.

5. Just before serving, heat the butter in a large skillet. Sauté the reserved shiitake slices over medium-high heat, tossing, until lightly golden, about 4 minutes. Add to the fricassee, or place on top of each serving as a garnish. Serve hot.

Arlene's Summer Vegetable Salad, page 31

Pasta with Wild Mushrooms

A heady toss of buttery noodles and wild mushrooms. The sauce of butter-enriched broth is a nice change from a cream sauce. This is real living.

Serves 4

- ***1/3 cup olive oil***
- ***6 ounces wild mushrooms, e.g., porcini or cèpes, shiitake or Golden Oak, wiped clean and thickly sliced***
- ***6 ounces cultivated mushrooms, wiped clean and thickly sliced***
- ***Salt and freshly ground black pepper***
- ***1 1/2 tablespoons minced garlic***
- ***1 pound fresh pasta (e.g. fettuccine), or 3/4 pound dried***
- ***3/4 cup Chicken Broth (page 239) or water***
- ***6 tablespoons (3/4 stick) cold unsalted butter, cut into pieces***
- ***1/4 cup chopped parsley***
- ***Freshly grated Parmesan cheese***

1. Bring a large pot of water to a boil. Meanwhile, heat the olive oil in a large skillet over medium-high heat. Add both kinds of mushrooms; sprinkle with salt and pepper.

2. Sauté the mushrooms, tossing occasionally, for about 4 minutes. Add the garlic and continue to cook, tossing occasionally, until the mushrooms are tender and have wilted slightly, 8 to 10 minutes in all. Set aside, off the heat.

3. Boil the pasta just until tender. Drain well.

4. Add the chicken broth or water to the mushroom mixture; bring to a boil. Cook the liquid down for about 2 minutes, then lower the heat and add the butter pieces a few at a time, swirling them in until the mixture is smooth. When all the butter has been added, add the parsley and correct seasonings. Add the pasta to the mushroom mixture, tossing with two large spoons to coat the pasta evenly. Serve immediately, passing freshly grated Parmesan cheese and a pepper mill at the table.

Baked Bulgur Pilaf with Mushrooms

A tasty side dish, this can also be prepared with barley, in which case you may need to lengthen the cooking time slightly.

Serves 6

- ***5 tablespoons unsalted butter***
- ***1 large or 2 small-medium onions, coarsely chopped***
- ***2 garlic cloves, smashed and peeled***
- ***1 1/2 cups bulgur (cracked wheat)***
- ***3 1/2 cups Chicken Broth (page 239), Vegetable Broth (page 240) or beef broth***

½ teaspoon fresh thyme leaves, or pinch dried
Salt
3 cups mushrooms (about 6 ounces), stems trimmed, caps quartered
2 tablespoons chopped parsley
Freshly ground black pepper

1. Preheat the oven to 350° F. In a flameproof casserole, melt 2 tablespoons of the butter over medium heat. Add the onions and garlic and cook, stirring occasionally, until lightly golden, 8 to 10 minutes.

2. Add the bulgur, tossing to coat with butter. Cook, stirring to dry out the bulgur, for about 5 minutes. Add 2½ cups of the broth, the thyme, and a pinch of salt, stirring. Bring the mixture to a boil, cover tightly, and place the casserole in the oven. Bake 25 minutes.

3. Meanwhile, heat 2 tablespoons of the butter in a large skillet over medium-high heat. Add the mushrooms and sauté, tossing, until lightly golden, about 5 minutes. Add the mushrooms to the casserole with the remaining cup of broth; stir quickly, and cover tightly. Bake 15 minutes longer.

4. Remove the casserole from the oven. Add the remaining tablespoon of butter, the parsley, a generous sprinkling of pepper, and salt, if needed. Serve immediately.

HOW TO USE DRIED WILD MUSHROOMS

Dried wild mushrooms can be substituted in any of the recipes for fresh—they're available all year and add lots of flavor. About 2 ounces dried will replace 8 ounces fresh. Always use the soaking liquid, too, even when recipes don't specifically tell you to. Here's how:

- *Soak the dried mushrooms in warm water to cover until softened, usually 20 to 30 minutes.*
- *Lift out the mushrooms, draining and reserving soaking liquid (most grit will be left behind). Trim off hard stems.*
- *Strain liquid through a coffee filter or paper towel; use as part of liquid in recipe, reducing if necessary. (Liquid can also be stored, refrigerated, for later use.)*
- *Wash mushrooms to remove any remaining grit; drain well, and proceed to use in recipe.*

Braised Veal Shanks with Wild Mushrooms

A deceptively simple, aromatic stew; serve with noodles or rice.

Serves 4

1 ***ounce dried mushrooms***
2 ***cups warm water***
1 ***veal shank, 2½ to 3 pounds, cut by the butcher in 4 slices, each slice tied compactly***
Flour
Salt and freshly ground black pepper
3 ***tablespoons olive oil***
½ ***cup dry white wine***
½ ***cup Chicken Broth (page 239)***
4 ***garlic cloves, smashed and peeled***
1 ***tablespoon chopped fresh basil, or 1 teaspoon dried***
2 ***sprigs fresh tarragon, or ½ teaspoon dried***
1 ***bay leaf***
8 ***ounces quartered fresh mushrooms (about 2½ cups)***
Juice of ½ lemon
3 ***tablespoons unsalted butter, cut into pieces***
2 ***tablespoons chopped parsley***

1. Place the dried mushrooms in the warm water in a bowl to soak. Set aside while you sauté the veal.

2. Dredge the slices of veal shank in flour seasoned with salt and pepper, shaking off excess. Heat the olive oil in a large flameproof casserole over medium-high heat. Sauté the veal, shaking the pan occasionally and turning once, until golden, 8 to 10 minutes total. Transfer the shanks to a plate; pour off excess fat from the casserole.

3. Preheat the oven to 350° F. Return the casserole to medium heat. Add the white wine, scraping up all the browned bits, and boil for about a minute. Add the chicken broth, garlic, basil, tarragon, and bay leaf; bring to a simmer. Return the veal to the casserole; cover and reduce the heat to low.

4. Lift the mushrooms from the soaking liquid, draining and reserving liquid. Trim off hard mushroom stems. Strain the liquid through a coffee filter or paper towel; add 1½ cups of the liquid to the veal, reserving the rest. Place the casserole in the oven.

5. Wash the soaked mushrooms to remove any remaining grit; drain well. Chop coarsely if large; set aside.

6. Bake the casserole, covered, spooning the juices over the veal occasionally, until the meat is almost tender, 1 to 1¼ hours. Scatter the dried and fresh mushrooms around the veal, spooning the juices over them. (If the stew seems dry, add the remaining mushroom soaking liquid.) Cover and bake until the veal is fork-tender, 30 to 40 minutes longer. Remove the casserole from the oven.

7. Transfer the veal to a warm serving platter; remove the string. Place the casserole on the top of the stove over low heat; skim off all fat. Add the lemon juice to the casserole; then swirl in the butter, a few pieces at a time. Correct seasoning; then stir in the parsley. Pour the juices over the meat and serve immediately.

Members of the genus *Allium* (a bulbous branch of the lily tribe), the family of onions includes Bermuda, Yellow Globe, Sweet Spanish (both white and yellow), Red Globe, and the latest craze, Vidalia onions from Georgia—so sweet, they say, that you can eat one like an apple. Also included are spring onions or scallions, green onions (like scallions, but with rounded bulbs), leeks, the wild leeks that are called ramps, shallots, garlic (and elephant garlic), chives, and several others. All are delicious—the soul of the vegetable kingdom.

David Specca of Mt. Holly, New Jersey, is one of the few farmers in the Northeast who markets his produce fifty-two weeks a year. He learned his trick from "an old-time German farmer down the road" who saved part of his fall harvest for his family to enjoy through the winter by digging an 8-foot-wide trench in the ground and filling it with leeks, which he then covers with soil. Rather than trenching, Dave places his crops in cold storage as soon as they are harvested. Highly regarded for his quality produce, Dave says "I wouldn't sell anything that I wouldn't serve to my own family." Besides such cold-weather crops as onions, leeks, and celery root, Dave specializes in crops that are just becoming widely known, but have long been ethnic favorites: fennel, broccoli rabe, collard greens, and fava beans.

AND ALL BY THEMSELVES....

For surprisingly sweet, mellow flavor, try roasting whole onions, shallots, or garlic—drizzled with olive oil—in a 375° F. oven, just until tender.

LEEKS VINAIGRETTE

While the sweet mild flavor of leeks does wonders for soups, leeks are delicious on their own. Here's a good basic way to enjoy them as an appetizer, or in a salad:

- *Trim the leeks by cutting off the roots and the tough portion of the green tops. Slit the leeks in half lengthwise, keeping the bottoms intact. Wash very carefully by immersing in cold water, to dislodge hidden sand and grit.*
- *Simmer in a skillet, with boiling salted water to cover. When just tender (timing can vary depending on thickness of the leeks), drain, refresh under cold water, and pat dry.*
- *Dress with Basic Creamy Garlic Dressing (page 46), or with any oil and vinegar dressing, and serve at cool room temperature.*

Rice-and-Cheese-Stuffed Onions

The slow cooking of the chopped onion for the filling is what gives this dish its mellow flavor. If you use larger onions, double the quantities for the filling and serve as a main course, with a light tomato sauce (page 138).

Serves 8

8 yellow onions, about 2 inches in diameter (4 ounces each)

FILLING

Reserved onion centers
4 tablespoons (1/2 stick) unsalted butter
Salt
1/3 cup raw long-grain rice
1 2/3 cups Chicken Broth (page 239) or Vegetable Broth (page 240)
2 tablespoons grated Swiss or Gruyère cheese
4 tablespoons freshly grated Parmesan cheese
Freshly ground white pepper

1. Peel the onions; then cut a very thin slice from the bottom of each one. With a sharp paring knife, cut a wide cone shape from the top of each onion, reserving the centers. Cut out and reserve more of the center, leaving a hollow shell with 1/4 inch-thick walls. Take care not to cut through the bottoms. If you do, just plug any torn area with a piece of the reserved centers.

2. Blanch the onion cases in a large pot of boiling salted water until crisp-tender, about 7 minutes. Drain in a co-

lander under cold running water to stop the cooking. Drain well, hollow sides down.

3. *Filling:* Chop the onion centers. Melt 2 tablespoons of the butter in a skillet over medium-low heat. Add 1½ cups of the chopped onion, sprinkle lightly with salt, and sauté, tossing occasionally, until soft and lightly golden, about 20 minutes. Add the rice and stir for 2 minutes. Add 1 cup of the broth and bring to a boil. Lower the heat, cover tightly, and simmer until the rice is tender, about 30 minutes. Remove from heat.

4. Stir the Swiss cheese and 2 tablespoons of the Parmesan into the rice. Season with salt, if needed, and freshly ground pepper. Spoon the filling into the onion cases, mounding it slightly, and place them in a shallow baking dish, such as a 7 x 11-inch rectangular pan. Sprinkle the filling with the remaining 2 tablespoons Parmesan cheese. (Recipe can be prepared ahead to this point.)

5. Preheat the oven to 375° F. Place the remaining 2 tablespoons butter and ⅔ cup broth around the onions in the baking dish. Place a sheet of foil over the onions, folding it tent-fashion. Bake 25 minutes, then raise the heat to 400° F. and remove the foil. Bake until nicely golden and tender, basting frequently with the pan juices, about 20 minutes longer. Serve hot.

Pasta with Sweet Onion Sauce

Based on a Genovese recipe.

Serves 4

5 ***tablespoons unsalted butter***
1½ ***pounds yellow onions, chopped (about 5 cups)***
Salt
2 ***tablespoons Marsala wine***
1¼ ***cups Chicken Broth (page 239)***
1 ***pound fresh flat pasta, e.g., fettuccine, or ¾ pound dried***
Freshly ground black pepper
3 ***tablespoons chopped parsley***
Freshly grated Parmesan cheese

1. In a large heavy skillet, melt 3 tablespoons of the butter over medium heat. Add the onions, sprinkle lightly with salt, and toss to coat. Lower the heat, cover, and cook for 1½ hours, stirring occasionally.

2. Uncover and add the Marsala. Cook, uncovered, for 5 minutes. Add the chicken broth, raise the heat to medium, and cook about 8 minutes longer, or until most of the broth has been absorbed (This recipe can be prepared in advance to this point; moisten with a little extra broth if the mixture seems dry.)

3. Cook the pasta in a large pot of boiling water until *al dente* (just tender, with a slight bite). Drain well.

4. Over low heat, swirl the remaining 2 tablespoons of butter into the hot onion mixture. Season to taste with salt and freshly ground pepper; stir in the parsley. Add the drained pasta and stir gently to combine. Serve immediately. Pass a pepper mill, and grated cheese, if you like.

Onion Pie with Bacon

A new version of the traditional Alsatian onion tart. Sour cream pastry works especially well with this, but regular pie crust is fine, too. Onion Pie makes a satisfying light supper, or can be cut into squares for an easy hors d'oeuvre, served with a glass of white wine or beer.

Serves about 12

SOUR CREAM PASTRY (or substitute Basic Pastry Dough for a Two-Crust Pie, page 241)

3 ***cups flour***
1½ ***teaspoons salt***
1 ***teaspoon sugar***
¾ ***cup (1½ sticks) chilled unsalted butter, cut into pieces***
½ ***cup cold solid vegetable shortening***
¼ ***cup sour cream***
⅓ ***cup cold water, plus more as needed***

FILLING

8 ***ounces thickly sliced bacon, cut in ¼-inch pieces***
2 ***tablespoons unsalted butter***

2½ pounds yellow onions (about 5 medium-large), halved lengthwise and sliced ¼-inch thick
¼ cup flour
Salt and freshly ground black pepper
4 eggs
1½ cups milk
½ cup heavy cream
Pinch each of freshly grated nutmeg and cayenne pepper

1. *Sour Cream Pastry:* Combine the flour, salt, and sugar in a food processor, pulsing on and off. Add the butter and shortening and pulse briefly until the mixture is crumbly. (Or sift the dry ingredients into a mixing bowl and cut in the butter and shortening with your fingers.) Stir together the sour cream and ⅓ cup cold water; add to the flour mixture, processing just until combined. Add just enough cold water until the dough begins to hold together.

2. Transfer the dough to a lightly floured surface; roll into an 8 x 12-inch rectangle. Fold in thirds, as for a business letter. Rotate the dough 90 degrees so the open side is at your right. Repeat the rolling and folding. Wrap the dough in plastic and chill at least 1 hour. (Pastry can be refrigerated or frozen at this point.)

3. *Prebaking the pastry:* On a lightly floured surface, roll out the dough to a 12 x 17-inch rectangle. Fit it into a 10½ x 15½-inch jelly roll pan, preferably one of heavy black steel. Crimp the edge decoratively, prick surface of dough lightly with a fork, and refrigerate 20 to 30 minutes.

4. Preheat the oven to 400° F. Line the pastry with foil and fill with dried beans, rice, or pie weights. Bake 8 minutes. Carefully remove foil and weights. Bake the pastry again, pricking any air bubbles gently with a fork as it bakes, until lightly golden, about 10 minutes longer. Remove from the oven to cool pastry slightly; lower the oven heat to 375° F.

5. *Filling:* Cook the bacon in a large skillet over medium-low heat until browned, about 10 minutes. With a slotted spoon, transfer the bacon to a plate lined with paper towels. Pour off all but about 3 tablespoons of the bacon fat from the skillet; add the butter. Add the onions, tossing to coat. Cover and cook, stirring occasionally, until soft but not browned, 25 to 30 minutes. Sprinkle with flour and cook, uncovered, stirring often, about 4 minutes. Add the reserved bacon; season with salt and pepper.

6. Whisk together the eggs, milk, cream, nutmeg, and cayenne. Spread the onion mixture evenly in the pastry shell and place on the center oven rack. Pour the custard mixture over evenly. Bake until the filling is set and golden, 30 to 35 minutes. Serve the tart warm, cut into squares.

Beer-Braised Beef with Onion Butter-Crumb Dumplings

We love this dish, which is mellow with the flavor of beer and onions. A couple of handfuls of quartered mushroom caps, quickly sautéed in butter, can be added to the stew just before the dumplings.

Serves 6

- ½ ***cup vegetable oil, or as needed***
- 3 ***pounds boneless lean beef, preferably shin, or chuck or bottom round, trimmed and cut in 1½-inch cubes***
- ***Salt and freshly ground black pepper***
- 5 ***medium yellow onions (about 2 pounds), coarsely chopped***
- 3 ***carrots, peeled, trimmed, and thickly sliced***
- 2 ***or 3 garlic cloves, smashed and peeled***
- 2 ***sprigs fresh thyme, or large pinch of dried***
- 2 ***sprigs parsley***
- 1 ***bay leaf***
- 1 ***dried hot chili pepper***
- 8 ***allspice berries***
- 3 ***cloves***
- 1 ***bottle (12 ounces) dark beer***
- 1 ***can (13¾ ounces) beef broth, plus more as needed***
- 2 ***teaspoons tomato paste***

ONION BUTTER-CRUMB DUMPLINGS

- 5 ***tablespoons unsalted butter***
- ⅓ ***cup finely chopped onion***
- 1 ***cup flour***
- 1 ***teaspoon baking powder***
- ½ ***teaspoon baking soda***
- ¼ ***teaspoon salt***
- ½ ***cup buttermilk***
- 2 ***tablespoons chopped fresh dill or parsley***
- ⅓ ***cup fresh bread crumbs***

1. Preheat the oven to 350° F. In a large casserole, heat 2 tablespoons of the oil over high heat. Add enough meat to cover the bottom without crowding; sprinkle with salt and pepper. Sauté, tossing occasionally, until well browned on all sides, 5 to 6 minutes. Transfer to a plate and brown the remaining meat in batches, adding oil as needed. Set the meat aside.

2. Add the onions, carrots, and garlic to the casserole, tossing to coat with oil. Lower the heat to medium and sauté, tossing, until wilted and lightly golden, about 15 minutes. Meanwhile, tie the thyme and parsley sprigs, bay leaf, chili pepper, allspice berries, and cloves in a piece of cheesecloth. Return the meat to the casserole with the spice bag, beer, beef broth, and tomato paste. Bring the mixture to a boil, stirring and scraping any browned bits from the bottom of the casserole into the liquid. Cover the casserole tightly with foil, then with the lid, and place it in the lower part of the oven. Bake, stirring occasionally, until the beef is tender, 1½ to 2 hours.

3. Transfer the casserole to the top of the stove. Remove and discard the spice bag. Degrease the stew thoroughly. Add more beef broth, or water,

if needed, to cover the meat. Correct seasonings. Bring the stew to a simmer.

4. *Onion Butter-Crumb Dumplings:* Melt the butter in a small skillet. Pour all but 1 tablespoon of the melted butter into a small bowl; set aside. Sauté the onion in the remaining tablespoon of butter until wilted but not brown, about 5 minutes. Meanwhile, sift the flour, baking powder, baking soda, and salt into a mixing bowl. In a separate bowl, stir together 2 tablespoons of the melted butter, the buttermilk, dill, and sautéed onion. Make a well in the center of the dry ingredients and add the buttermilk mixture. Stir very gently just until moistened; do not overmix.

5. Combine the remaining 2 tablespoons of melted butter with the bread crumbs. Drop neat spoonfuls of the dumpling mixture into the crumb mixture, gently turning the dumplings to coat. Drop the dumplings onto the simmering stew, spacing them evenly. Cover the casserole tightly and simmer for 20 minutes. Serve immediately.

Sweet-and-Sour Onions with Golden Raisins

Serves 4 to 6

1 pound small white or red onions
3 tablespoons peanut or olive oil
2 garlic cloves, peeled
Small piece of fresh hot chili pepper
2 tablespoons honey
2 whole cloves
1 bay leaf
1/3 cup red wine vinegar
1 cup water
1/4 cup golden raisins
Salt and freshly ground black pepper

1. Blanch the onions in boiling water for 1 minute. Drain, rinse under cold water, and slip off the skins. Set aside.

2. In a heavy skillet, heat the oil over low heat. Add the garlic and chili pepper; cook until the oil is hot, about 2 minutes. Raise the heat to medium; add the onions, tossing to coat. Sauté until lightly golden, 8 to 10 minutes.

3. Add the honey, cloves, and bay leaf. Reduce the heat to low; cook gently 2 minutes. Add the vinegar, water, raisins, and a sprinkling of salt. Cover and simmer about 20 minutes.

4. Uncover the skillet; raise the heat to medium-high, and cook, shaking the pan, until the juices have reduced to a glaze, about 2 minutes. Remove the chili pepper and bay leaf. Season with salt and freshly ground pepper; serve hot.

At one time, it was hard to find any type of pepper at the markets except the green bell variety. Now, other members of the capsicum family, such as sweet red peppers, and the even sweeter yellow ones, are seen more and more frequently. The latter, usually imported from Holland at hefty prices, are beginning to be grown by farmers in New Jersey and elsewhere. We recently found yellow peppers at our local farmers' market for 50 cents per pound—compared to up to $3.99 for the imported ones at fancy food shops. There are even white and purple peppers around, though these are still fairly rare. And with the new interest in southwest American cooking, various kinds of fresh chilies can be found at the markets, too.

Martha Muth, whose family owns a pepper farm in Williamstown, a small town in southern New Jersey, shared some excellent pepper recipes with us, as well as some thoughts about growing peppers:

> *Son Bob, who grew these great peppers, is New Jersey's pepper-growing champ—he used plastic mulch and trickle irrigation and boosted his yields from 200 to 1,500 bushels per acre. Well, Bob's taken a year's leave of absence from here to work as a vegetable specialist in two counties in South Carolina. It's an area that has raised nothing but tobacco since the days of Scarlett O'Hara, and because of a depressed economy, they're trying to introduce vegetable production.*
>
> *In the meantime, we'll have plenty of projects to keep us busy until Bob returns. Actually, on a farm like ours, it's a year-round activity. People don't*

realize when they ride through a snowy landscape and see a plastic-covered greenhouse that inside those walls a farm is greening! I've taken the pepper project from Clorox-treated trays of seed in February, to making mix and planting in March, to "spotting" baby plants in April, to field planting in May, then packing-house work all through the growing season right through October. Actually, that's *when I have the time to make stuffed peppers, after Jack Frost has called a halt to the operation. . . .*

Pierino's Baked Stuffed Pepper Wedges

From Pierino Govene, the generous chef-owner of Ristorante Gambero Rosso in Cesanatico, along Italy's Adriatic coast. Sandy brought this recipe back from a recent trip, and we've both made it often—it's a wonderful (and easy) hors d'oeuvre with drinks or on a buffet, and can be made in advance.

Makes 16 pieces

4 red bell peppers, seeds and ribs removed, cut in 2-inch wedges
10 to 12 oil-cured black olives, pitted and chopped
2 garlic cloves, minced
2 to 3 tablespoons chopped parsley
4 anchovy fillets, chopped
2 tablespoons capers, rinsed
2 or 3 canned tomatoes, drained and chopped
Freshly ground black pepper
Olive oil

1. Preheat the oven to 375° F. Lightly oil a shallow baking dish and arrange pepper wedges in one layer, hollow sides up.

2. In a small bowl, stir together olives, garlic, parsley, anchovies, capers, tomatoes, and freshly ground pepper to taste. Add more of any ingredient to taste; if dry, add a bit more chopped tomato.

3. Spoon a little of the mixture into each hollow. Drizzle with olive oil. Cover the pan with foil and bake 20 minutes. Uncover and bake until the peppers are soft, about 10 minutes longer. Serve at room temperature.

BASIC METHOD FOR ROAST PEPPERS

Roasting peppers gives them a whole new flavor—sweet, mellow, and smoky—that makes them delicious all by themselves, or tossed in salads, stuffings, or with pasta. Roast a few extra and keep them on hand. Here's how:

- ***Place bell peppers on their sides on a foil-lined baking sheet.***
- ***Place under a broiler, 4 to 6 inches from the heat.***
- ***Roast, turning with tongs, until lightly charred on all sides, 8 to 10 minutes total.***
- ***Remove from heat and cover pan with foil (or place peppers in a paper bag, closing the top). Let stand at least 10 minutes to loosen the skins.***
- ***Peel peppers, discarding skins. Remove stems and seeds, reserving juices.***

One Step Further: ***If you'd like to serve the roast peppers as a salad or first course, simply arrange them on a platter with their juices, sprinkle lightly with salt, pepper, and, if you like, a whole peeled garlic clove. Drizzle lightly with balsamic or red wine vinegar and olive oil, and let stand at room temperature at least 1 hour; then remove garlic clove. In season, some chopped basil is a nice touch.***

Red Peppers Stuffed with Sausage and Corn Kernels

From Martha Muth, who recalls:

> *When I was a girl, we used lots of tender sweet corn as the main ingredient in filling peppers, along with sausage and tomato sauce. But there are so many variations. Some people prefer to use large peppers and slice them through the length, stuff them, and lay them lengthwise in a baking dish.*
>
> *And we've had many local folks who stop in at our packing house during the growing season and enthuse about these* gigantic *quart-size peppers, to use for stuffing—and I remind them it would take $5.00 worth of hamburger for each one! I prefer to use medium-size peppers, or even what I call "mini-peps" as the season draws to a close. You can always use two for a serving. I discovered, as my family was growing up (we've had seven grow up on this farm), that a mini-pepper was more attractive to children's appetites than one too large.*
>
> *At the end of the season, I do the stuffed peppers in quantity, making stuffing by the dishpanful, and filling up the whole oven shelf with a roasterful. They are great to put away in the freezer, divide up with my young folks, or give away as gifts.*

If you prefer, the peppers in the following recipe can be halved lengthwise (after parboiling), then arranged in a large baking dish, hollow sides up, and filled "boat" fashion. Prepared that way, you'll need only 3 peppers for this quantity of filling.

Serves 6

5 thin slices firm white bread, crusts removed
6 medium-large red bell peppers
2 tablespoons olive oil

1½ pounds Italian sausage (9 or 10 links), sweet, hot, or a combination, casings split and meat removed
Salt and freshly ground black pepper
2 medium onions, chopped
2 to 2½ cups corn kernels, cut from 3 to 5 ears
¼ cup chopped parsley
2 teaspoons chopped fresh thyme, or pinch of dried (optional)
2 cups tomato sauce (page 138)
½ cup grated Cheddar cheese

1. Bring a large pot of water to the boil. Preheat the oven to 200° F. Place the bread on a baking sheet and bake until the bread is dry but not toasted, 15 to 20 minutes. Set aside. Meanwhile, trim the tops off the peppers; chop the flesh from the tops and set aside. If necessary, shave a thin slice off the bottoms of the peppers, so that they stand upright without wobbling. Trim away all seeds and ribs. Salt the boiling water; parboil the peppers, uncovered, until just crisp-tender, 4 to 5 minutes. Drain under cold water and invert the peppers on a plate to drain.

2. Heat 1 tablespoon of the olive oil in a wide heavy skillet over medium-high heat. Add the sausage meat and sprinkle with salt and pepper. Cook, stirring and breaking up the meat, until it begins to brown, about 5 minutes. Place a flat lid or plate over the skillet and drain off all excess fat. Add the remaining tablespoon of olive oil, the onions, and the reserved chopped pepper tops. Cook, stirring frequently, until the onions are tender, about 8 minutes longer. Remove the skillet from the heat and cool briefly.

3. Raise the oven heat to 375° F. Coarsely crumble the bread into the sausage mixture in the skillet; add the corn, parsley (reserving a little), and thyme. Correct seasonings.

4. Place a layer of tomato sauce in a shallow baking dish that will hold the peppers fairly snug. Spoon the sausage-corn mixture into the peppers, mounding them generously on top and standing each pepper in the baking dish. Top each pepper with a spoonful of tomato sauce and some grated cheese. Spoon the remaining tomato sauce around the peppers.

5. Bake the peppers until the cheese has browned nicely and the sauce is bubbly, 35 to 40 minutes. Serve hot, sprinkling a little of the reserved parsley on each pepper, and spooning the tomato sauce around.

Red Pepper Boats Stuffed with Ricotta, Spinach, and Tomato Sauce

Select large, firm peppers for this recipe; if red ones are unavailable, green can be substituted, but they won't be as sweet. A combination of red and green looks nice. Half a pepper is usually an ample serving, with garlic bread and a crisp green salad. Both of us, however, usually manage to eat two halves.

Serves 4 to 6

- **3** ***large red peppers, halved lengthwise; stems, seeds, and ribs removed***

RICOTTA STUFFING

- **12** ***ounces fresh spinach, stems removed, washed very well; or 1 10-ounce package frozen leaf or chopped spinach, thawed***
- **1** ***container (15 or 16 ounces) ricotta cheese***
- **2** ***eggs***
- **3** ***tablespoons soft bread crumbs***
- **½** ***cup grated Gruyère or Swiss cheese***
- **¼** ***cup freshly grated Parmesan cheese***
- **¼** ***teaspoon salt***
- **½** ***teaspoon freshly ground black pepper***
- **¼** ***teaspoon freshly grated nutmeg***

- **2** ***cups tomato sauce, preferably homemade (page 138)***

1. In a large pot of boiling salted water, blanch the peppers, uncovered, just until crisp-tender, 4 to 5 minutes. Drain and refresh under cold water. Set aside to drain, hollow sides down.

2. *Ricotta Stuffing:* In a large covered saucepan, steam the spinach in just the water that clings to its leaves until wilted, about 3 minutes. Drain under cold water and squeeze as dry as possible. (If using frozen spinach, simply squeeze dry.) Chop coarsely and set aside.

3. In a large mixing bowl, beat the ricotta and eggs until blended. Stir in the spinach, bread crumbs, Gruyère and Parmesan cheeses, salt, pepper, and nutmeg. Correct seasonings and set aside.

4. *Assembly:* Preheat the oven to 400° F. Choose a shallow baking dish just large enough to hold the pepper halves. Spread about ½ cup of tomato sauce in the dish. Arrange the pepper halves, hollows up, in the dish. Spoon about a tablespoon of tomato sauce in each pepper. Fill each with the ricotta mixture, dividing it evenly and smoothing the tops gently. Pour remaining sauce over and around the peppers, and sprinkle each with a little Parmesan cheese.

5. Bake until the tops are set and lightly golden, about 30 minutes. Serve hot, spooning the sauce in the dish around the peppers.

Sausage, Peppers, and Onions with Vinegar

Serves 4

***5** tablespoons olive oil*
***2** pounds Italian sausages (about 12 links), sweet, hot or a combination, links separated*
***2** medium onions, halved and sliced lengthwise*
***3** medium red bell peppers, seeds and ribs removed, cut in thick strips*
***5** garlic cloves, smashed and peeled*
***1/3** cup balsamic or red wine vinegar, plus more to taste*
***1** cup peeled, seeded, and diced ripe tomatoes, or drained canned tomatoes (about 8 ounces)*
***1/2** teaspoon salt*
***1/4** teaspoon dried oregano*
***3** tablespoons chopped fresh basil and/or parsley*
Freshly ground black pepper

1. In a wide heavy skillet, heat 2 tablespoons of the olive oil over medium heat. Add the sausages and brown well on all sides, turning occasionally, 8 to 10 minutes.

2. Meanwhile, in a separate deep skillet or casserole, heat the remaining 3 tablespoons of oil over medium heat. Add the onions, peppers, and garlic, tossing to coat with oil. Cook, tossing occasionally, until the vegetables are slightly wilted, 6 to 8 minutes. Stir in the vinegar, tomatoes, salt, and oregano. Tuck the browned sausages into the pepper mixture, draining off all possible fat.

3. Cook, covered, over medium heat for 15 minutes. Uncover the pan and cook, stirring occasionally, until the sausages are cooked through and the vegetable mixture has thickened slightly, about 15 minutes longer.

4. Stir in the basil and/or parsley, freshly ground pepper, and salt, if needed. Add a few drops more vinegar, if necessary, to give the mixture a slight, pleasant tang. Serve hot, with plenty of good Italian bread.

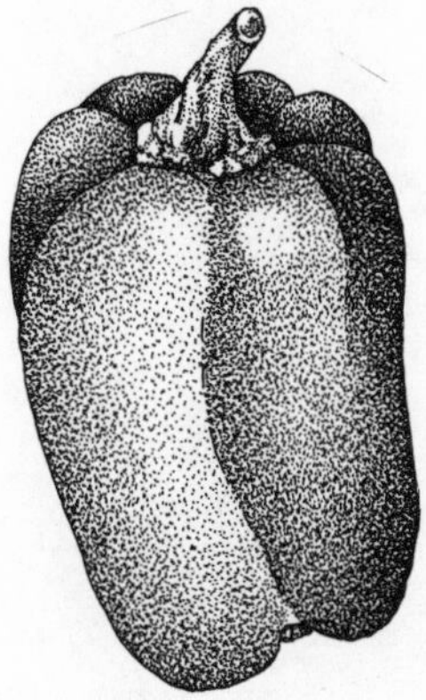

Red Pepper Jam

Another recipe from Martha Muth. This tangy jam has a rich red color; it's excellent on toast or an English muffin, with cream cheese.

Makes 5 half-pints

6 red bell peppers, washed, halved, seeds and ribs removed
3 cups sugar
1 cup apple cider vinegar
1/4 cup lemon juice
2 pouches liquid pectin (3 fluid ounces each)

1. Using the coarse side of a grater held over a mixing bowl, grate the flesh of the peppers. Discard the skins. Measure 2 cups grated pepper flesh and liquid; transfer to a heavy saucepan.

2. Add the sugar, vinegar, and lemon juice and bring to a boil over medium heat, stirring to dissolve the sugar. Raise the heat slightly and bring to a full rolling boil. Stir in the pectin, boil hard 1 minute, and remove from heat.

3. Immediately transfer the jam to sterilized canning jars, top with canning lids and screw bands, and process in a boiling water bath for 10 minutes. Cool.

New Mexican Spoon Bread, page 64
Arlene's Summer Vegetable Salad, page 31
Fresh Tomato-Pepper Salsa, page 138
Baked Zucchini, Pepper, and Tomato Gratin, page 80
Baked Macaroni with Zucchini and Three Cheeses, page 80
Red Pepper-and-Cheese-Stuffed Bread, page 160

Frankly, we could eat nothing but potatoes, bread, and pasta, and never complain. Lately, we've been buying small white new potatoes, and just boiling them, cutting them in halves or quarters, and mashing butter into them right on the plate. Their flesh is so creamy, so full of flavor, that you don't want to do any more to them.

For boiling or in salads (or in other recipes where you want the potatoes to hold their shape), choose firm, waxy potatoes—small red or white new potatoes, or larger ivory-colored potatoes. Mealy-textured potatoes, such as Idaho or Russets, are better suited to baking, where you want dry, fluffy flesh. These high-starch potatoes are also good for mashing, or for homemade french fries. Many potatoes fall somewhere in between, and are considered all-purpose.

BEST OF THE BEST:
A NEW WAY FOR GREAT MASHED POTATOES

While cooking on Time-Life's Good Cook *series, Richard got into the habit of making mashed potatoes using Richard Olney's method. You will, too—here's how:*

- *Boil cut-up, peeled potatoes in salted water until very tender.*
- *Drain well, reserving cooking liquid. Press potatoes through a sieve back into the pan, using a wooden pestle or spoon.*
- *Return pan to moderate heat and add enough reserved cooking liquid to bring mixture to a fairly loose consistency; season with salt, pepper, and freshly grated nutmeg.*
- *Remove from heat, stir in a good-size lump of sweet butter, and serve immediately.*

Even better: a combination of boiled and mashed potatoes and celery root, with a little garlic, if you like.

Roast New Potatoes in Seasoned Oil

Wonderful with roast meats or poultry, these always disappeared quickly from the kitchen during testing. If you have leftover chicken, duck, or goose fat on hand, substitute it for part of the oil and your roast potatoes will be even more irresistible.

Serves 4 to 6

***3** tablespoons corn oil*
***3** tablespoons olive oil*
***1** teaspoon dried rosemary*
***4** garlic cloves, unpeeled*
***2** bay leaves*
***1½** pounds new potatoes, unpeeled, quartered (halved, if small)*
Salt and freshly ground black pepper

1. Preheat the oven to 375° F. Place the oils, rosemary, garlic, and bay leaves in a large baking pan. Put the pan in the oven while you cut up the potatoes. Drop the potatoes in a bowl of water as you cut them to prevent discoloration.

2. When the oil is hot (after about 5 minutes), drain the potatoes, shaking them to dry completely, and carefully place them in the pan with the oil. Salt and pepper lightly and toss to coat.

3. Roast the potatoes until nicely golden, shaking the pan and turning the potatoes occasionally to insure even browning. They should take about 1 hour, and will happily share an oven with a roast or other main course.

Swiss Onion Potato Cake

This first-rate dish is based on recipes by both Frances Smith in Illinois, and Patty Thomsen in Pasco, Washington. It's crusty, cheesy, and easy to prepare. Mrs. Thomsen notes that it's "really tasty, good for brunch, luncheon, or dinner, or for the farm crew." Try it as a side dish with roast meats, or instead of hash browns for breakfast.

Serves 8

1 garlic clove, peeled
4 tablespoons (1/2 stick) unsalted butter
2 medium onions, chopped (about 2 cups)
2 pounds all-purpose or Idaho potatoes, peeled
1 cup grated Swiss cheese
2 eggs
1 tablespoon flour
1/2 cup sour cream
1/2 cup milk
1 1/4 teaspoons salt
1/2 teaspoon freshly ground pepper

1. Preheat the oven to 375° F. Rub a 9 x 13-inch baking pan with the clove of garlic; discard garlic. Butter the pan generously and set aside.

2. Heat 2 tablespoons of the butter in a large skillet over medium heat. Add the onions and sauté, stirring occasionally, until softened but not brown, about 8 minutes. Meanwhile, grate the potatoes into a bowl of cold water. Drain in a colander; squeeze dry. Add the remaining 2 tablespoons butter to the skillet. When melted, stir in the grated potatoes and cook 2 minutes. Remove from heat.

3. Stir half of the grated cheese into the potato mixture; spread the mixture in the prepared baking pan. In a mixing bowl, whisk together the eggs, flour, sour cream, milk, salt, and pepper. Pour the egg mixture over the potatoes and top with the remaining grated cheese.

4. Bake until golden brown, 45 to 50 minutes. Serve hot, cut in squares.

Nippy Potato Salad with Country Ham and Sour Cream

From Celeste Martin, in Gadsden, Alabama.

Serves 6 to 8

- **2** ***pounds new potatoes, washed (unpeeled)***
- **2** ***tablespoons wine vinegar***
- **1/2** ***teaspoon salt***
- ***Freshly ground black pepper***
- **1/2** ***cup cooked ham cut in thin slivers, preferably Smithfield or other country ham***
- **3** ***tablespoons thinly sliced scallions (green and white portions)***
- **2** ***tablespoons finely chopped onion***
- **2** ***tablespoons chopped red bell pepper or pimiento***
- **2** ***tablespoons chopped parsley***
- **2** ***tablespoons chopped dill pickles (optional)***
- **3/4** ***cup sour cream***
- **2** ***tablespoons Dijon mustard***
- **3** ***hard-cooked eggs, shelled and coarsely chopped***

1. Place the potatoes, in their skins, in a pot; add water to cover and bring to a boil. Salt the water and boil the potatoes, uncovered, until they are just tender when poked with a small knife, about 30 minutes. Drain in a colander. Run cold water over the potatoes just until they have cooled to lukewarm. Carefully peel with a paring knife; cut into wedges and transfer to a large mixing bowl.

2. Add the vinegar, salt, and pepper to the potatoes; toss very gently to blend without breaking them up. Add the ham, scallions, onion, pepper, parsley, and pickles; toss very gently. In a small bowl, stir together the sour cream and mustard; add to the potatoes with the eggs, tossing very gently. Let the potato salad stand for 30 minutes before serving at room temperature. (If refrigerating the potato salad, remove from the refrigerator about 30 minutes before serving.)

Potato Doughnuts or Biscuits

From Helen Etheridge, in Perryton, Illinois, a versatile yeast dough that can be used two ways. The potatoes make for especially moist doughnuts ("spudnuts"), and the golden, slightly sweet biscuits are delicious with sweet butter and a cup of strong coffee.

Makes 2 dozen doughnuts or biscuits, or 1 dozen of each

- **8** ***ounces all-purpose potatoes, peeled and cut into pieces***
- **1/2** ***cup (1 stick) unsalted butter, at room temperature***
- **1** ***package dry yeast***
- **1/2** ***cup lukewarm water***
- **1** ***cup milk***
- **1/4** ***cup granulated sugar***

1/4 cup brown sugar
1 tablespoon grated orange zest
1 teaspoon salt
1/8 teaspoon ground cardamom
Pinch of freshly grated nutmeg
4 1/2 to 5 cups flour
Vegetable oil or shortening, for frying doughnuts
Beaten egg mixed with 1 teaspoon cold water, for glazing biscuits

1. Cook the potatoes in boiling water until very tender. Drain well and return to the dry pan. Stir over medium heat for a minute or two to dry them out. Sieve the potatoes into a mixing bowl (or mash in an electric mixer), then work in 2 tablespoons of the butter.

2. Meanwhile, soak the yeast in the lukewarm water for about 5 minutes. Add the yeast mixture to the potatoes with the remaining butter, milk, sugar, brown sugar, orange zest, salt, cardamom, and nutmeg. Stir in enough flour to make a soft, but not sticky dough. Knead on a lightly floured work surface (or in an electric mixer with a dough hook) until smooth and elastic, about 10 minutes. As you knead, work in a little more flour if the dough becomes sticky. Place the dough in a buttered mixing bowl, turning it over to coat. Cover with plastic wrap and let rise until doubled in volume, about 2½ hours (timing can vary).

3. Punch the dough down. On a lightly floured surface, pat the dough into a large rectangle about ¾ inch thick. For doughnuts, cut with a floured cutter and transfer to a lightly floured baking sheet. For biscuits, cut 3-inch pieces of the dough and form into neat pillows by passing each piece back and forth gently between floured palms. Place on a lightly floured baking sheet, pieces touching. Cover the shaped dough and let rise until nearly doubled in volume, about 45 minutes.

4. *To Fry Doughnuts:* Heat oil or shortening in a wide saucepan to a temperature of 375° F. (or until a small piece of dough sizzles when carefully dropped into the oil). Gently lay in doughnuts without crowding. Fry until golden brown, turning once or twice, about 4 minutes total. Drain on paper towels and fry remaining doughnuts. Sprinkle with confectioners' sugar and serve warm.

5. *To Bake Biscuits:* Preheat the oven to 375° F. Brush biscuit dough lightly with beaten egg mixture and bake until golden brown, 20 to 25 minutes. Serve warm or at room temperature.

Zucchini and Potato Pancakes, page 78

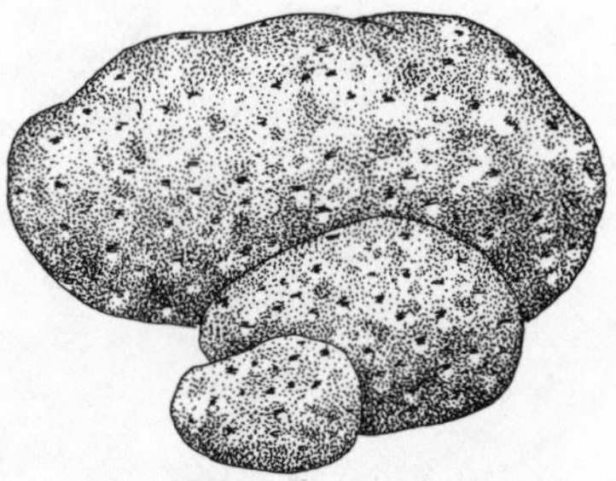

PUMPKIN AND
WINTER SQUASH

There's something exciting about seeing the pumpkins each fall, just waiting to be turned into pies and other home-baked goods. With pumpkins, the variety can make a big difference in cooking. For most purposes, especially pies and baking, you want a pumpkin with firm, sweet, fine-grained flesh. Among the best are Small Sugar (also called Small Sugar Pie) or Cheese pumpkin. The variety called Jack-o'-Lantern is best used for that purpose.

Some of the best pumpkin pies are actually made with winter squash. Varieties you may see in the markets include Early Butternut, with deep, reddish-orange flesh; Green Hubbard, bronze-green and orange-yellow outside, with fine-grained yellow flesh; and Royal Acorn, with sweet, yellow-orange flesh. You can substitute any of these in any of the recipes for pumpkin. (Spaghetti squash, which has recently become popular as a low-calorie substitute for pasta, is too stringy to be pureed.)

If, after cooking, you find that a pumpkin or squash has watery flesh, drain as explained in the box.

BASIC METHOD FOR PUMPKIN PUREE

This baking method results in thick, sweet pumpkin puree. How much will you need? Each pound of raw, untrimmed pumpkin will yield about 1 cup cooked puree (a small pumpkin, weighing 2 to 3 pounds, will yield 2 to 3 cups puree). We usually do 2 or 3 pumpkins in one batch each fall, then freeze the puree in 1-pint containers. (This method can also be used for Hubbard squash.)

- *Break off the pumpkin stem, cut the pumpkin in half crosswise, and scoop out all seeds and stringy material. (Toast the seeds if you like).*
- *Place the halves, cut sides up, on a foil-lined baking sheet. Cover and seal each half with foil.*
- *Bake in a preheated 350° F. oven until the flesh is very tender, about 1½ hours. Cool slightly.*
- *Scoop out flesh and mash with a potato masher, or puree in a food processor or press through a sieve. If puree is very watery, drain in a colander lined with dampened cheesecloth, folding the cheesecloth over the puree and weighting it with a plate.*

This puree keeps refrigerated up to five days, or frozen for up to six months.

Pumpkin-Filled Lasagne Rolls

Sandy brought this recipe back from Italy, where she ate *tortelli di zucca* (pumpkin-filled pasta pockets) at the restaurant Il Cigno in Mantova. Although these *tortelli* are a traditional Italian dish (Giuliano Bugialli has a recipe in *The Fine Art of Italian Cooking,* Times Books), suddenly, pumpkin-filled pasta is being seen all over this country. These lasagne rolls are an easy variation on the theme.

You might be surprised at the slightly sweet flavor combination in the filling—but you'll be even more pleasantly surprised when you taste it. The seasonings for this filling are approximate, and may need to be adjusted according to the pumpkin or squash you use. Add a little more sugar if the pumpkin puree is not naturally sweet.

Makes 10 rolls (serving about 8 as an appetizer, 4 as a main course)

PUMPKIN FILLING

2 cups pumpkin or squash puree (page 113)
1 egg
8 amaretti (crisp Italian macaroons), finely crushed (about 1/4 cup)
1/4 cup bread crumbs
2/3 cup freshly grated Parmesan cheese
2 teaspoons sugar
1/2 teaspoon salt
1/8 teaspoon freshly ground black pepper
1 teaspoon Amaretto liqueur or rum
1/8 teaspoon almond extract

---

1 tablespoon vegetable oil
10 dried lasagne noodles (or 2 x 10-inch strips fresh pasta, cut from whole sheets)
1 cup heavy cream
5 fresh sage leaves, if available, roughly torn (do not substitute dried)
2/3 cup freshly grated Parmesan cheese, plus more for serving
1 1/2 tablespoons cold unsalted butter, cut into bits

1. *Pumpkin Filling:* In a mixing bowl, stir together the pumpkin puree, egg, crushed amaretti, bread crumbs, cheese, sugar, salt, pepper, Amaretto, and almond extract. Correct all seasonings.

2. Bring a large pot of water to a boil. Add the oil and some salt. Cook the lasagne noodles until *al dente* (just tender, with a slight bite). Drain in a colander, rinse under cold water, and drain again thoroughly.

3. Butter a shallow baking dish large enough to hold the rolls compactly. Lay a lasagne noodle flat on a work surface, with a short end toward you. Spread the noodle with a scant 1/4 cup of the pumpkin filling. Roll up the noodle compactly, rolling away from you. Place the roll, seam side down, in the baking dish. Repeat with remaining noodles and filling. (Recipe may be prepared in advance to this point; cover with plastic wrap and refrigerate if not baking immediately.)

4. Preheat the oven to 400° F. Just before putting the lasagne rolls in the oven, pour the cream over the rolls. Scatter the sage and the grated Parmesan over; then dot with butter. Bake until the rolls are bubbly and lightly golden, about 25 minutes. Serve immediately (1 roll per appetizer portion; 2 for a main course), spooning the cream over the rolls, and passing more freshly grated Parmesan cheese and a pepper mill at the table.

Pumpkin Cheese Bread

A yeast bread with a rich golden color. Try this toasted.

Makes two 9 x 5-inch loaves

2 cups lukewarm water
1 tablespoon honey
2 packages dry yeast
1½ cups pumpkin or squash puree, fresh (page 113) or canned unsweetened
7 to 7½ cups bread or all-purpose flour, or as needed
1 rounded tablespoon coarse (kosher) salt (or 2 rounded teaspoons table salt)
¼ teaspoon freshly ground white pepper
2 cups grated Cheddar or Swiss cheese (8 ounces)
1 egg, lightly beaten

1. Place ½ cup of the water and the honey in a mixing bowl; sprinkle with the yeast, stir, and let stand for 5 or 10 minutes to activate the yeast.

2. Beat in the pumpkin puree, remaining 1½ cups water, 6½ cups flour, and the salt and pepper. Knead by hand (or in an electric mixer with a dough hook) until smooth and elastic, about 8 minutes. Work in enough flour so that the dough is no longer sticky.

3. Transfer the dough to a lightly oiled bowl, turning it over to coat with oil. Cover with a clean cloth; let rise in a warm place until doubled in volume, about 1½ hours.

4. Punch the dough down and cut into two equal portions. Knead half the cheese into each portion of dough until it is evenly distributed. Press each portion into a flat rectangle. Roll into a cylindrical shape and place each in a lightly buttered 9 x 5-inch loaf pan, seam side down. Cover with a cloth and let rise until nearly doubled in volume, about 1 hour.

5. Preheat the oven to 375° F. Gently brush the tops of the loaves with beaten egg, then slash the loaves down the center with a razor blade or small sharp knife. Bake until golden and the bottoms of the loaves sound hollow when tapped, about 50 minutes (timing can vary). Remove the loaves from the pans and cool on a wire rack.

Pumpkin Butter

A thick spread, good with toast or on an English muffin.

Makes about 4 half-pints

4 cups pumpkin or squash puree, fresh (page 113) or canned unsweetened
1 cup granulated sugar
1 cup light brown sugar
Juice of 1 small orange (about ¼ cup)
1 tablespoon finely chopped peeled fresh ginger
Pinch of salt

1. Combine the pumpkin puree, white and brown sugars, orange juice, ginger, and salt in a heavy saucepan. Bring to a boil over medium heat, stirring.

2. Lower the heat to medium-low and cook, uncovered, stirring often, until the mixture is very thick and has reduced to about 4 cups, about 1 hour (timing can vary). Cool, then chill. If you wish to can the pumpkin butter, spoon it while still hot into sterilized canning jars, leaving ¼-inch headspace, top with canning lids and screw bands, and process in a boiling water bath for 10 minutes.

Sour Cream Pumpkin Pie

From Normand le Claire, whose Red Rooster Tavern in North Kingstown, Rhode Island, is worth a special journey. A complete reinterpretation of pumpkin pie, and irresistible.

Serves 8

Basic Pastry Dough for a One-Crust Pie (page 241)
¼ cup cold water
1 envelope unflavored gelatin
3 eggs, separated
⅓ cup plus ¼ cup sugar
1¼ cups pumpkin or squash puree, fresh (page 113) or canned unsweetened
½ cup sour cream
½ teaspoon salt
½ teaspoon cinnamon
¼ teaspoon each ground ginger, cloves, and freshly grated nutmeg
Pinch of freshly ground black pepper (optional)
2 cups heavy cream, very cold
1 cup sifted confectioners' sugar
2 teaspoons pure vanilla extract
½ cup chopped pecans

1. Roll out the pastry dough on a floured surface to a thickness of ⅛ inch. Fit it loosely into a 9- or 9½-inch pie pan. Trim excess dough, form a high border, and crimp the edges. Chill briefly.

2. *Baking the Pastry Shell:* Preheat the oven to 375° F. Prick the dough lightly with a fork and line it with foil. Weight the foil with rice or dried beans and bake the shell on a heavy baking sheet until the sides have set, 10 to 15 minutes. Carefully remove the foil and rice and continue to bake, pricking any air bubbles with a fork as the shell bakes, until the pastry is lightly golden and baked through, 10 to 15 minutes longer. Cool the pie shell on a wire rack.

3. Place the cold water in a small bowl and sprinkle the gelatin over it. Set aside.

4. In the top of a double boiler over (but not in) simmering water, whisk together the egg yolks and ⅓ cup sugar until very light and fluffy, about 5 minutes. Add the gelatin mixture and whisk constantly until the gelatin has dissolved, about 1 minutes longer. Remove from heat and transfer the egg mixture to a large metal mixing bowl.

5. Whisk in the pumpkin puree, sour cream, salt, cinnamon, ginger, cloves, nutmeg, and pepper. Chill the mixture, stirring frequently, until it begins to thicken, but is not set. (If you wish to hasten the process, place the bowl in a larger bowl of ice water and stir constantly until mixture begins to thicken but is not set, about 6 minutes.)

6. Beat the egg whites until they form soft peaks. Gradually add the ¼ cup sugar, beating constantly until stiff and shiny. Gently fold the meringue into the pumpkin mixture; set aside briefly at room temperature.

7. Whip the cream until nearly stiff (do not overbeat). Gently whisk in the confectioners' sugar and vanilla; whisk just until stiff. Pour half the pumpkin mixture into the cooled pie shell. Gently top with half the whipped cream mixture. Top with the remaining pumpkin mixture, then with the remaining whipped cream, mounding it in the center. (If you prefer, you can pipe the top layer of whipped cream around the edges, using a pastry bag with a star tip.) Chill the pie at least 2 hours, then sprinkle the edges with the chopped pecans.

Pumpkin Custard Pie

A lighter, more delicately spiced pie than most.

Serves 8

Basic Pastry Dough for a One-Crust Pie (page 241)
1¼ cups pumpkin or squash puree, fresh (page 113) or canned unsweetened
2 eggs
2 egg yolks
1 cup plus 2 tablespoons milk
½ cup heavy cream
¼ cup granulated sugar
¼ cup light brown sugar
¾ teaspoon pure vanilla extract
¼ teaspoon freshly grated nutmeg

1. Roll out the dough on a floured surface to a thickness of ⅛ inch. Fit it loosely into a 9-inch pie pan. Trim excess dough, form a high border, and crimp the edges. Chill briefly.

2. *Partially Baking the Pastry Shell:* Preheat the oven to 400° F. Prick the dough lightly with a fork and line it with foil. Weight the foil with rice or dried beans and bake the shell on a heavy baking sheet until the sides have set, about 8 minutes. Carefully remove the foil and rice and bake until the pastry is very faintly golden, about 6 minutes longer. Prick any air bubbles with a fork as the pastry bakes. Remove the pie shell from the oven and lower the heat to 350° F.

3. In a mixing bowl whisk together the pumpkin puree, eggs, egg yolks, milk, cream, sugars, vanilla, and nutmeg. Pour the mixture into the pie shell and bake until the filling has just set in the center, 40 to 45 minutes. Do not overbake. Cool on a rack; then serve at cool room temperature.

Pumpkin Roll with Cream Cheese Filling

This is a free adaptation of a recipe from pastry chef Alain Roby, of the American Harvest Restaurant in New York City's Vista International Hotel. Chef Roby's pastry cart makes the end of the meal a wonderful bout with indecision.

10 to 12 servings

4 eggs, at room temperature
¾ cup sugar, plus more as needed
1 tablespoon honey
¾ cup flour
1¼ teaspoons cinnamon
1 teaspoon baking soda
¾ teaspoon salt
1 cup pumpkin puree, fresh (page 113) or canned unsweetened
4 tablespoons (½ stick) unsalted butter, melted and cooled slightly

CREAM CHEESE FILLING
9 ounces cream cheese, softened slightly

6 tablespoons unsalted butter ($3/4$ stick), softened slightly
1 cup sifted confectioners' sugar, plus more for garnish
1 teaspoon pure vanilla extract

1. Preheat the oven to 375° F. Grease a $10\frac{1}{2}$ x $15\frac{1}{2}$-inch jelly roll pan. Line the bottom of the pan with a sheet of wax paper; butter the paper. Flour the pan, shaking out excess. Set aside.

2. In an electric mixer at medium-high speed, beat the eggs, sugar, and honey until very pale, fluffy, and tripled in volume, about 8 minutes. Meanwhile, sift the flour with the cinnamon, baking soda, and salt onto a sheet of wax paper; set aside.

3. When the egg mixture is ready, lower the speed and beat in the pumpkin. Remove the mixture from the electric mixer. Gently fold in the flour mixture, adding it in two or three additions. Work fairly quickly and do not overmix once you add the flour. Fold a little of the cake batter into the melted butter; then gently fold the butter mixture into the batter without overmixing. Transfer the batter to the prepared cake pan, smoothing it gently with a spatula.

4. Bake until the sides shrink slightly from the edges of the pan and the surface of the cake is set and slightly springy when pressed gently, about 15 minutes.

5. Transfer the cake to a wire rack and cool about 3 minutes. Sprinkle the surface of the cake with a fine layer of granulated sugar. Lay a large sheet of wax paper on the surface of the cake. Top with the back of a large baking sheet; invert the cake quickly but carefully onto the baking sheet. Lift off the baking pan and carefully peel away the wax paper and discard. Starting with a long side, gently roll the cake around the clean wax paper while still warm, using the wax paper to help you roll. Cool completely.

6. *Cream Cheese Filling:* In an electric mixer, beat together the cream cheese and butter until light; add the confectioners' sugar gradually, beating until smooth. Beat in the vanilla and set aside.

7. Very carefully unroll the cake. With a spatula, spread the exposed surface of the cake with the cream cheese filling, leaving a slight border all around. Reserve a few spoonfuls of the filling. Gently roll the cake into a compact cylinder, using the wax paper to help you roll (but this time, don't roll the paper into the cake). As you finish rolling, transfer the cake to a serving platter, seam side down. Spread the ends of the cake with reserved filling; chill the pumpkin roll.

8. With a serrated knife, neatly trim off the ends of the cake roll, cutting on a slight diagonal. Sprinkle with confectioners' sugar, then cut in 1-inch-thick slices and serve.

SPINACH AND GREENS

We've come a long way from the days when Popeye had to convince kids to eat their spinach. Today, they might even be willing to try some of the other types of greens; collards, mustard greens, beet greens, turnip greens, dandelion greens, arugula, escarole, broccoli rabe, kale, and Swiss chard. All of these are very nutritious; and when cooked according to the recipes that follow, their slightly bitter flavor makes them very tasty.

ONE OF OUR FAVORITE WRITERS HAS HER SAY ON GREENS:

From* Cross Creek*, by Marjorie Kinnan Rawlings (Scribner paperback, originally published in 1942):

Greens probably save more backwoods lives than the doctors, for they are the one vegetable, aside from cowpeas, for which country folk have a passion. Spinach as a green is unheard of, although it is raised for the northern market. Beet greens are not relished. But turnip greens, mustard greens and above all, collard greens, cooked with white bacon, with cornbread on the side, make an occasion. Pot liquor and cornbread have their adherents and have even entered into southern politics, a man addicted to the combination being able to claim himself a man of the people.

BASIC METHOD FOR COOKING GREENS

When not cooked right, greens can be bitter and soggy. But if you follow this method, you'll be surprised at how fresh and sweet they can be.

Serves 4

- **1 pound kale or other greens, e.g. collard greens, mustard greens, Swiss chard, beet greens**
- **3 tablespoons unsalted butter**
- **¼ teaspoon salt**
- **¼ teaspoon sugar**

1. De-rib the greens by holding onto the stem and ripping the leafy portion away from you; discard stems and ribs. Blanch the greens, uncovered, in a large pot of boiling salted water until just crisp-tender, about 1 minute (tougher greens may take slightly longer). Drain under cold running water; squeeze out all possible moisture.

2. Heat the butter in a large skillet over medium heat. Add the drained greens and sprinkle with salt and sugar. Toss gently until heated through, about 2 minutes. Serve immediately.

Kale or Broccoli Rabe with Bacon and Hot Oil

Based on a Sicilian recipe, this way of cooking greens sets off their slight bitterness with sweet golden raisins.

Serves 4

- ***¼ cup olive oil***
- ***½ cup bacon cut in ½ x 1-inch chunks or strips***
- ***3 garlic cloves, smashed and peeled***
- ***½ medium dried hot chili pepper, seeds and ribs removed***
- ***12 ounces fresh kale or broccoli rabe, washed well, stems trimmed, and well drained***
- ***2½ tablespoons balsamic or red wine vinegar***
- ***3 tablespoons golden raisins***

1. Place the olive oil, bacon, garlic, and chili pepper in a heavy skillet over medium-low heat. Cook, stirring occasionally, until the bacon has rendered its fat and the bacon and garlic are lightly golden, 8 to 10 minutes.

2. Meanwhile, blanch the greens, uncovered, in a large pot of boiling salted water for 1 minute. Drain and squeeze out all possible liquid. Transfer to a warm serving dish.

3. Add the vinegar and raisins to the skillet, raise the heat to high, and boil for 2 minutes, stirring to combine. Pour the mixture in the skillet over the greens and serve immediately.

Herbed Spinach and Rice Bake

From New Jersey's Mercer County Farm Bureau Women.

Serves 8

- ***2** pounds fresh spinach, washed well, stems removed and discarded, leaves chopped*
- ***4** tablespoons (1/2 stick) unsalted butter*
- ***1/3** cup chopped onions*
- ***1/2** teaspoon salt*
- *Pinch of sugar*
- ***3/4** cup milk*
- ***3** eggs, lightly beaten*
- ***1/2** teaspoon Worcestershire sauce*
- ***1/2** teaspoon fresh thyme leaves, or 1/4 teaspoon dried*
- ***1** cup cooked rice*
- ***1** cup grated sharp Cheddar cheese*

1. Preheat the oven to 350° F. Be sure the spinach is well washed; shake dry. Heat the butter in a large skillet over medium heat. Add the onions and cook until slightly wilted, 3 to 4 minutes. Add the spinach to the onions, sprinkle with the salt and sugar, and toss until the spinach is wilted, 3 to 4 minutes longer.

2. Transfer the spinach mixture to a colander or large sieve set over a bowl. Press, draining and reserving liquid. Add the milk, eggs, Worcestershire, and thyme to the spinach liquid, whisking to blend. Stir in the spinach, rice, and all but 2 tablespoons of the cheese. Pour the mixture into a buttered shallow baking dish, such as an 11 x 7-inch rectangular dish, or a 9-inch round pan. Sprinkle with the remaining 2 tablespoons of cheese.

3. Bake until the mixture is set, 20 to 25 minutes. Serve hot, cut into squares or wedges.

Arugula and Potato Soup

An unusual and delicious use for this peppery green.

Serves 6

- ***3** tablespoons unsalted butter*
- ***2** medium onions, sliced*
- ***2** leeks, trimmed, halved lengthwise, washed well, and sliced*
- ***1** garlic clove, sliced*
- ***1/4** teaspoon salt, plus more to taste*
- ***1 1/2** pounds boiling potatoes (about 4 medium), peeled, quartered lengthwise, and sliced*
- ***2 1/2** cups Chicken Broth (page 239) or Vegetable Broth (page 240), plus more as needed*
- ***1/8** teaspoon ground ginger*
- ***1/8** teaspoon freshly grated nutmeg*
- ***1/3** cup heavy cream or milk*
- ***2** bunches coarsely chopped arugula leaves (about 2 1/2 cups)*
- *Freshly ground black pepper*

1. Melt 2 tablespoons of the butter in a heavy saucepan over medium-low heat. Add the onions, leeks, garlic, and salt, tossing to coat. Cover and sweat the vegetables, tossing occasionally, until softened, about 20 minutes.

2. Add the potatoes, broth, ginger, and nutmeg, stirring to combine. Raise the heat and bring the mixture to a boil, skimming off all froth from the surface. Simmer, partially covered, until the potatoes are tender, 30 to 40 minutes.

3. Remove half the solids with a slotted spoon and puree until smooth in a food processor or blender. Return the puree to the soup and add the cream or milk. Bring to a boil, then thin the soup, if desired, with additional broth. (The soup can be prepared in advance to this point, then returned to a boil at serving time.)

4. Scatter the chopped arugula over the surface and cover the pan. Cook until the arugula has wilted, about 2 minutes. Stir, add salt and pepper to taste, then swirl in the remaining tablespoon of butter. Serve immediately.

Mary's Escarole Soup with Tiny Meatballs

This recipe comes from my (R.S.'s) good friend (and surrogate Italian mother) Mary Codola. Mary and her husband, Pat, live in Rhode Island, and no matter what time of day you stop by, Mary manages to throw together some "little snack." I'll never forget the first time I visited the Codolas. "Don't put your coats on the bed!" Mary shouted from the kitchen. The entire expanse of a huge double bed was covered with tender, homemade fettuccine, which she had just set out to dry.

This soup is traditionally served at weddings and holiday feasts, but it can also serve as a meal in itself at any time of the year.

Serves 10

- ***1*** ***large chicken, preferably a 5- to 6-pound fowl***
- ***2*** ***meaty beef shankbones***
- ***2*** ***medium onions, quartered***
- ***2*** ***carrots, peeled and trimmed***
- ***1*** ***celery rib, trimmed and cut up coarse***
- ***1*** ***leek, trimmed, halved lengthwise, washed well, and chopped coarse***
- ***1*** ***bay leaf***
- ***6*** ***peppercorns***
- ***Salt***
- ***1½*** ***to 2 cups escarole leaves (about 4 ounces), trimmed and well washed***
- ***½*** ***cup uncooked small pasta (e.g. tiny shells, orzo, or acini de pepe)***
- ***½*** ***pound ground beef chuck***
- ***Freshly ground black pepper***
- ***Freshly grated Parmesan cheese***

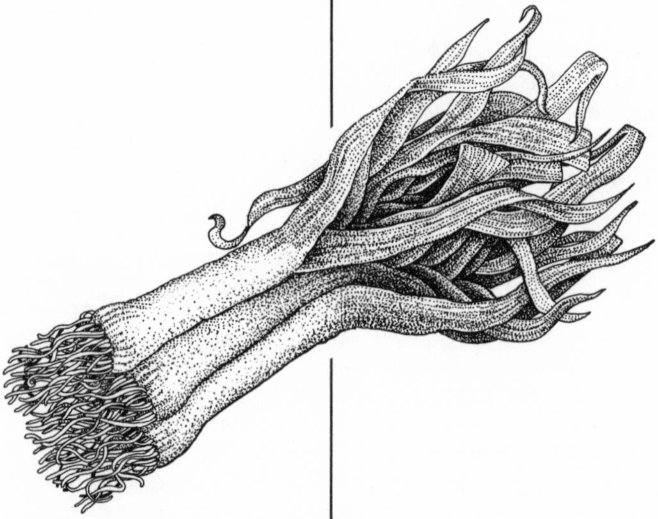

1. In a large stockpot or kettle, place the fowl (including all giblets except liver) and the beef shankbones. Add enough cold water to cover generously and bring slowly to a boil, partially covered. Skim off all froth; lower heat to a simmer. Add the onions, carrots, celery, leek, bay leaf, peppercorns, and salt to taste. Simmer, partially covered, until the chicken is tender, about 1½ hours. Remove the chicken and the carrots, reserving them, and continue to simmer until the beef is very tender, 2 hours longer, or more. Remove the beef shankbones, but continue to simmer broth. When the shanks are cool enough to handle, trim the meat from the bones; set meat aside, return shankbones to the pot, and simmer until the broth is nicely flavored, 1 to 2 hours longer.

2. Degrease the broth; strain, cool thoroughly, then chill. (The broth can be prepared in advance to this point and refrigerated or frozen.) Lift the fat from the chilled broth, leaving a few small pieces of fat on the surface for flavor. Cut the beef and some of the chicken meat into bite-size pieces (reserve remaining chicken for another use). Thickly slice the carrots; set meat and carrots aside, covered and refrigerated.

3. Cook the escarole, uncovered, in a pan of boiling salted water until just tender, about 10 minutes. Drain, rinse under cold water, drain well, and cut in bite-size pieces. Set aside. In a separate small pan of boiling salted water, cook the pasta just until *al dente;* drain under cold water, drain again, and set aside.

4. Season the ground chuck with a little salt and freshly ground pepper. Roll into tiny ½-inch meatballs. Set aside on a plate, cover, and refrigerate.

5. At serving time, bring the broth to a boil and correct seasonings. Drop in the meatballs and simmer briefly, just until cooked through. Add the reserved beef, chicken, carrots, escarole and pasta; stir. Serve hot, passing freshly grated Parmesan cheese separately.

Red Pepper Boats Stuffed with Ricotta, Spinach, and Tomato Sauce, page 104

What's a sweet potato and what's a yam? Good question. The best explanation we've found is from *The Victory Garden Cookbook* by Marian Morash (Knopf), one of our favorite cookbooks ever:

> *Sweet potatoes by any other name are not yams—regardless of what the labeling at the supermarket might be. True yams are starchy tropical vegetables rarely seen outside of Latin markets because they require 8–11 months of warm weather to reach maturity. The "yams" or "Louisiana yams" you see at the store are sweet potatoes. No one knows for sure where this custom of nicknaming sweet potatoes "yams" originated, but the practice is widespread and has led to much confusion.*

Elizabeth Schneider, a colleague and friend currently at work on a guide to specialty fruits and vegetables called *Uncommon Fruits and Vegetables: A Commonsense Guide,* notes that the confusion may have arisen when African slaves, who were familiar with the yam *(dioscoreaceae),* gave their name to the sweet potato *(convolvulaceae)* when they found them in the southern states. She also notes that yams, which are totally different in texture from sweet potatoes —dry and starchy—"can range from the size of a kneecap to that of a baby elephant."

DON'T BE CAUGHT UNPREPARED....

When cooking sweet potatoes, put on a few more than you'll need. You'll have the leftovers on hand to make any number of goodies in this chapter: sweet potato biscuits, corn bread, chocolate cake, or burnt custard.

Candied Sweet Potatoes with Rum Glaze

Not too sweet, silky smooth—and no marshmallows.

Serves 6

2½ pounds sweet potatoes (7 to 8 medium)
2 tablespoons unsalted butter
¼ teaspoon salt

RUM GLAZE
2 tablespoons unsalted butter
½ cup light brown sugar
1 tablespoon lemon juice
3 tablespoons dark rum

1. Preheat the oven to 400° F. Wrap the sweet potatoes together in foil, making one large, flat package, and place it on a baking sheet. Bake until tender, about 1 hour. Unwrap and cool. Lower the oven temperature to 375° F.

2. When the sweet potatoes are cool enough to handle, peel them and transfer the flesh to a bowl. Mash coarsely with a potato masher or a ricer (do not use a food processor), add butter and salt, and transfer to a buttered 1-quart casserole, smoothing the surface with a spatula.

3. *Rum Glaze:* Melt the butter in a wide heavy skillet. Stir in the sugar and lemon juice and cook over medium-high heat until bubbly, 3 to 5 minutes. Add the rum, return the mixture to a boil, and pour it over the sweet potatoes.

4. Bake until the glaze has become slightly crusty and nicely golden, about 40 minutes. Cool about 5 minutes; then serve.

Sweet Potato and Apple "Pancake"

This was suggested by several farmers' recipes for casseroles that combine sweet potatoes and apples. Though they tested well, we found them a bit sweet. Based on her recollections of a dish cooked by a fine southern cook named Miss Ednita Quick, Sandy converted the combination into a layered "pancake" that bakes to a gloriously golden brown. Try this along with ham or turkey at your next holiday feast.

Serves 8 to 10

- ½ ***cup (1 stick) unsalted butter, melted***
- 5 ***medium sweet potatoes (about 1 pound 10 ounces), peeled and thinly sliced***
- ½ ***teaspoon salt, or to taste***
- ***Freshly ground black pepper***
- 1 ***pound tart apples (about 3 medium; e.g. Granny Smith), peeled, halved, cored, and thinly sliced***
- 3 ***tablespoons pure maple syrup***

1. Preheat the oven to 400° F., with a rack in the lower third of the oven.

2. Lightly brush a 9-inch cake or pie pan with melted butter (a Pyrex pie pan lets you see how the bottom layer is browning). Arrange a layer of sliced sweet potatoes in the pan, overlapping them slightly in a neat pattern. Gently press the layer with your hands to flatten it slightly. Sprinkle with salt and pepper, and drizzle with a little more melted butter.

3. Top with one third of the apple slices, sprinkling them with 1 tablespoon maple syrup and more butter. Continue layering, pressing gently and seasoning as directed, ending with a layer of sweet potatoes. Drizzle the top with the rest of the melted butter. Cover the pan with foil, then with a lid.

4. Bake in the lower third of the oven for 40 minutes. Remove the lid and the foil and bake until tender and lightly golden, about 25 minutes longer. If you'd like to glaze the "pancake" further, place the pan directly on the floor of the oven for about 5 minutes (watch carefully to prevent overbrowning).

5. Remove the pan from the oven and cool for about 5 minutes. Carefully invert the pan onto a large round platter and let the pancake settle. Remove the baking pan carefully (replace any slices stuck to the pan). Serve hot, cut into wedges.

Chicken and Chips

A combination of fried chicken breast morsels and golden rounds of sweet potato, inspired by English fish and chips. The chicken is soaked in seasoned buttermilk and fried in a light, cornmeal-crunchy coating; the sweet potatoes fry up thin and crisp. A frying thermometer helps insure precise temperatures.

Serves 4

1½ pounds boneless chicken breast, trimmed of all skin, fat, and tendons
1 cup buttermilk
2 teaspoons honey
1 teaspoon salt
¼ teaspoon cayenne pepper
¾ cup flour
1½ teaspoons cornmeal
Vegetable oil or shortening for frying
4 sweet potatoes (1¼ to 1½ pounds), washed, unpeeled, and sliced ⅛- to ¼-inch thick (or cut in french-fry size strips)
Coarse salt

1. *The Chicken:* Cut the chicken in 1-inch chunks. In a shallow dish, stir together buttermilk, honey, ½ teaspoon of the salt, and ⅛ teaspoon of the cayenne pepper. Add chicken pieces, turning them to coat. Cover and soak the chicken for 1 hour at room temperature (refrigerate if you wish to hold the chicken longer).

2. In a shallow dish, stir together the flour, cornmeal, and remaining ½ teaspoon salt and ⅛ teaspoon cayenne pepper. Lift the chicken pieces from the buttermilk mixture and dredge in the flour mixture, coating them evenly and shaking off excess. Place on a baking sheet lined with wax paper and chill at least 30 minutes.

3. Place oil or shortening in a wide saucepan, to come to a depth of 2 inches. Heat to 375° F. (or until a small cube of bread sizzles when gently placed in the fat). Carefully place the chicken pieces in the oil and fry until golden brown, about 5 minutes, turning the pieces once or twice. Transfer to a platter lined with paper towels and keep warm.

4. *Sweet Potatoes:* Let the oil cool to 350° F. Add the sweet potatoes and fry 2 minutes. With a slotted skimmer or spoon, transfer the potatoes to a plate lined with paper towels. Raise oil heat to 400° F. Return the sweet potatoes to the oil and fry again until crisp and golden brown, about 2 minutes longer. Drain on a paper towel. Sprinkle the sweet potatoes with salt and serve chicken and chips immediately.

A SWEET POTATO BY ANY COLOR...

At some local markets, you can find sweet potatoes in three different colors, with flesh ranging from ivory to deep reddish-orange. Though they are interchangeable in these recipes, we both like the variety with creamy, pale yellow flesh.

Sweet Potato Biscuits

Sweet potatoes make these tender biscuits moist and flavorful.

Makes 1 dozen

2 small sweet potatoes (10 to 12 ounces)
2 cups flour
1 tablespoon baking powder
2 teaspoons light brown sugar
1/4 teaspoon freshly grated nutmeg
Large pinch each of salt and freshly ground black pepper
6 tablespoons (3/4 stick) cold unsalted butter, cut into pieces
Heavy cream, as needed
1 egg, well beaten

1. Preheat the oven to 400° F. Wrap the sweet potatoes in foil in a single package and bake until tender, about 1 hour. Remove from the oven, unwrap, and cool. Raise the oven heat to 425° F.

2. When the sweet potatoes are cool enough to handle, peel and mash with a potato masher or ricer. You should have 1 cup.

3. Sift the flour, baking powder, brown sugar, nutmeg, and salt into a mixing bowl. Stir in the pepper and butter and cut the mixture together until it is coarsely crumbled. Make a well in the center and add the cup of mashed sweet potatoes. Stir the mixture together gently with a fork, stirring in enough cream to make a sticky but manageable dough.

4. Transfer the dough to a floured surface and pat to a thickness of 3/4 inch. Use a floured 2 1/4- to 2 1/2-inch biscuit cutter to cut out rounds of the dough; transfer to a well-buttered baking sheet. Re-roll the remaining dough as necessary. Lightly brush the tops of the biscuits with beaten egg.

5. Bake until the biscuits are golden brown, 14 to 16 minutes. Serve hot, with sweet butter.

Chicken and Cheese Hash with Sweet Potato Corn Bread Squares

We've allowed a generous amount of sauce, so you can sop it up with the corn bread.

Serves 4 to 6

6 cups Chicken Broth (page 239)
1 medium onion, coarsely chopped
1 small carrot, peeled, trimmed, and coarsely chopped
6 parsley stems
3 whole chicken breasts, halved, fat and excess skin removed
6 tablespoons (3/4 stick) unsalted butter, or as needed
2 cups thickly sliced mushrooms (about 6 ounces)

- 1 ***medium onion, quartered through the root end, and cut crosswise into ¼-inch-thick slices***
- ⅓ ***cup flour***
- ***Pinch of freshly grated nutmeg***
- ⅓ ***cup heavy cream***
- ***Sweet Potato Corn Bread (recipe follows)***
- ¼ ***cup grated Italian Fontina or Swiss cheese***
- 2 ***to 3 tablespoons freshly grated Parmesan cheese***
- 2 ***tablespoons chopped parsley***
- 1 ***tablespoon chopped fresh chives (if available)***
- ***Few drops of lemon juice***
- ***Pinch of cayenne pepper***
- ***Salt and freshly ground black pepper***

1. Place the broth, chopped onion, carrot, and parsley stems in a large skillet; bring to a boil over medium heat. Arrange chicken breasts in the broth in a single layer, overlapping them slightly. Lower the heat; simmer, covered, until the chicken is just firm when pressed lightly, 10 to 15 minutes. Transfer the chicken to a plate to cool briefly. When cool enough to handle, cut the flesh from the bones, discarding the skin and adding the bones to the broth.

2. Simmer the broth, uncovered, until reduced by about one-third. Meanwhile, cut the chicken into ½-inch dice; set aside, covered. Strain the broth, pressing the solids to extract liquid. There should be about 4 cups of broth. Degrease and set aside.

3. Heat 3 tablespoons of the butter in a clean skillet over high heat. When the foam subsides, add the mushrooms; sauté, tossing frequently, until lightly golden, 3 to 4 minutes. Transfer mushrooms to a plate with a slotted spoon.

4. Add 3 tablespoons butter to the skillet and heat. Add the onion slices; sauté over medium heat until softened but not browned, about 5 minutes. Sprinkle the onions with flour and cook, stirring constantly, about 3 minutes. Do not brown. Add the stock and the nutmeg. Bring to a boil, whisking. Reduce the heat and simmer uncovered, whisking occasionally, until the sauce is lightly thickened, about 10 minutes. Stir in the cream and any juices exuded by the mushrooms and continue to simmer, uncovered, until lightly thickened, 7 to 8 minutes. Remove from heat and cover the skillet.

5. Make the corn bread.

6. Reheat the sauce in the skillet. Add the cheeses and simmer gently, stirring, until smooth, 2 to 3 minutes. Fold in the diced chicken, mushrooms, parsley, chives, lemon juice, cayenne pepper, and salt and black pepper to taste. Simmer until heated through, 3 to 5 minutes. Cut the corn bread into squares, place on individual serving plates, and spoon the hash, with plenty of sauce, over the cornbread.

Sweet Potato Corn Bread

Serves 4 to 6

***12** ounces sweet potatoes (2 to 3 medium), peeled and cut into chunks*
***3/4** cup yellow cornmeal*
***2** tablespoons flour*
***1** tablespoon baking powder*
***3/4** teaspoon salt*
***1/2** teaspoon baking soda*
***1/4** teaspoon ground allspice*
Pinch of freshly ground black pepper
***1** egg, lightly beaten*
***3/4** cup buttermilk*
***3** tablespoons unsalted butter*

1. Boil or steam the sweet potatoes until tender, 15 to 20 minutes. Drain thoroughly; press through a sieve into a medium bowl. Set aside to cool slightly.

2. Preheat the oven to 400° F. Sift together the cornmeal, flour, baking powder, salt, baking soda, and allspice into a small bowl. Stir in the pepper.

3. Add the egg and buttermilk to the sweet potato puree and mix until blended.

4. Heat the butter in a 9-inch square baking pan in the oven until sizzling but not brown, about 2 minutes. Pour excess butter into the sweet potato mixture, leaving a generous coating in the pan. Quickly add the dry ingredients to the sweet potato mixture and stir just until blended. Pour the batter into the baking pan. Bake until lightly golden and the bread has shrunk from the sides of the pan, about 25 minutes. Cut into squares and serve hot.

Sweet Potato Chocolate Cake

Dark, dense, and delicious. Our colleague Jean Anderson brought back a chocolate potato cake recipe from Gladys Rasmussen's Idaho potato farm. We liked the cake so much that we thought it would work well with sweet potatoes. It does.

Makes 12 to 16 pieces

***1** medium sweet potato (about 5 ounces)*
***3/4** cup (1 1/2 sticks) unsalted butter, softened*
***3** ounces unsweetened chocolate, cut into pieces*
***1** cup finely chopped pecans (about 4 ounces)*
***2** cups sifted flour*
***3/4** teaspoon baking soda*
***1/4** teaspoon salt*
***1 1/4** cups granulated sugar*
***1/2** cup light brown sugar*
Grated zest of 1 orange
***4** eggs*
***1** tablespoon orange juice*
***2/3** cup buttermilk*

CHOCOLATE FROSTING (OPTIONAL)

***6** tablespoons (3/4 stick) unsalted butter, melted*
***1/3** cup milk*
***1** teaspoon pure vanilla extract*
***3** tablespoons unsweetened cocoa powder*
***2 2/3** cups confectioners' sugar*
Pecan halves, for garnish

1. Preheat the oven to 400° F. Generously butter a 9 x 13-inch baking pan; set aside.

2. Wrap the sweet potato in foil and bake on the center rack of the oven until tender, 45 minutes to 1 hour. When cool enough to handle, peel the sweet potato and mash the flesh with 2 tablespoons of the butter; you should have about ¾ cup. Set aside. Melt the chocolate over hot water; set aside.

3. Adjust the oven heat to 350° F. In a small bowl, toss the pecans with ¼ cup of the flour; set aside. Re-sift the remaining flour onto a sheet of wax paper with the baking soda and salt; set aside.

4. In an electric mixer, cream the remaining butter with the sugar, brown sugar, and orange rind at medium speed until light and fluffy. Beat in the eggs, one at a time. Lower the mixer speed slightly; beat in the melted chocolate and sweet potato mixture.

5. Add the sifted flour mixture alternately with the buttermilk, beginning and ending with the dry ingredients; do not overmix. Add the pecan mixture, mixing just until incorporated. Spread the batter in the prepared cake pan, smoothing the surface evenly.

6. Bake just until the cake pulls away from the sides of the pan and springs back lightly when touched, 40 to 45 minutes. Transfer to a wire rack and cool for about 20 minutes.

7. *Chocolate Frosting (optional):* Stir together the melted butter and milk until blended. Stir in the vanilla; set aside. In a mixing bowl, stir together the cocoa powder and confectioners' sugar. Pour in the butter mixture, stirring until smooth. Add more milk, if needed, to bring the frosting to a spreadable consistency. Spread the frosting evenly over the cake with a spatula. Garnish with pecan halves. (If you don't want to frost the cake, just dust with confectioners' sugar.) Cut in rectangles and serve from the pan.

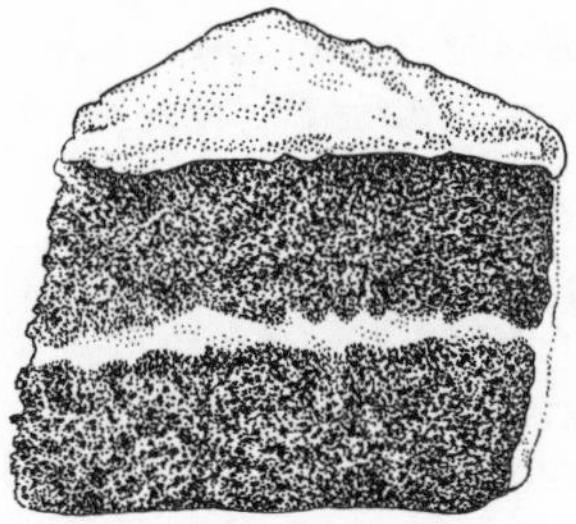

Sweet Potato Pie with Pecan Crunch Topping

A real winner from Merras Brown.

Serves 8

Basic Pastry Dough for a One-Crust Pie (page 241)

FILLING
- ***1½ pounds sweet potatoes (about 5 medium)***
- ***⅓ cup maple syrup***
- ***½ teaspoon ground ginger***
- ***¼ teaspoon cinnamon***
- ***¼ teaspoon freshly ground nutmeg***
- ***⅛ teaspoon ground cloves***
- ***¼ teaspoon salt***
- ***Few grinds of black pepper***
- ***3 eggs***
- ***1½ cups half-and-half***
- ***¼ cup bourbon or dark rum***

PECAN CRUNCH TOPPING
- ***¼ cup flour***
- ***¼ cup dark brown sugar***
- ***2 tablespoons cold unsalted butter, cut into pieces***
- ***Few gratings of fresh nutmeg***
- ***¼ cup coarsely chopped pecans***

Whipped cream flavored with bourbon or rum (optional)

1. Preheat the oven to 375° F. Wrap the sweet potatoes in two foil packages; bake until tender, about 1 hour. Cool; then peel and mash with a potato masher, or press through a coarse sieve. You should have 2½ cups mashed sweet potatoes. Set aside.

2. Roll out the pastry dough on a lightly floured surface and fit it into a deep 9½-inch pie dish, forming a high fluted border. Chill the pastry while you prepare the filling.

3. *Filling:* In a large bowl or electric mixer, combine the mashed sweet potatoes, maple syrup, ginger, cinnamon, nutmeg, cloves, salt, pepper, eggs, half-and-half, and bourbon or rum, whisking until smooth. Pour the filling mixture into the pie shell.

4. Bake the pie in the preheated 375° F. oven until the custard is just set in the center, about 35 minutes. Do not overbake, as the pie will be baked longer.

5. *Pecan Crunch Topping:* In a mixing bowl or food processor, combine the flour, brown sugar, butter, and nutmeg until the mixture is crumbled to the size of peas. Gently stir in the chopped pecans.

6. When the pie is just set, scatter the crunch topping over the surface. Bake until lightly browned, about 15 minutes longer. Cool the pie on a wire rack. Serve at room temperature, with bourbon- or rum-flavored whipped cream.

Sweet Potato Burnt Custard

It took us many tries to get this one perfected; it was worth it.

Serves 8

1 medium sweet potato (about 5 ounces)
2 cups milk
1 cup heavy cream
Zest of 1 small orange, in strips
1 vanilla bean, split lengthwise
2 eggs
4 egg yolks
⅓ cup sugar
Pinch of salt
⅓ cup or more light brown sugar

1. Preheat the oven to 400° F. Wrap the sweet potato in foil and bake until tender, 45 minutes to 1 hour. Unwrap and cool slightly. Turn off the oven.

2. When the sweet potato is cool enough to handle, peel it and press the flesh through a sieve. Measure ½ cup into a mixing bowl.

3. Place the milk, cream, strips of orange zest, and the vanilla bean in a heavy saucepan and bring slowly to a boil. Let stand 1 hour.

4. Preheat the oven to 325° F. Bring a kettle of water to the boil; set aside. If necessary, reheat the milk mixture until nearly boiling. Whisk together the eggs, egg yolks, sugar, and salt until smooth, about 1 minute. Pour a little of the hot milk mixture into the egg mixture, whisking constantly. Repeat. Pour the egg mixture into the pan of milk and return to low heat.

5. Stir the custard constantly with a wooden spoon, taking care to stir in the "corners" of the pan, until the custard thickens enough to coat the back of the spoon evenly, about 7 minutes. Do not boil. Immediately remove from the heat and strain the mixture into the bowl of mashed sweet potato, stirring gently until smooth but not frothy.

6. Place eight 5-ounce ramekins or custard cups in a large roasting pan (you can also bake this custard in one large shallow baking pan, such as a 9-inch square or 11 x 7-inch rectangular pan). Carefully pour the custard mixture into the ramekins and place the pan on the center rack of the oven. Carefully pour hot water into the roasting pan to come about 1 inch up the sides of the ramekins or smaller pan. Lay a sheet of foil over them.

7. Bake until the custard is set but still slightly wobbly, 50 to 60 minutes. (Timing varies depending on the depth of the ramekins; do not overcook. A larger baking pan may take over an hour.) Transfer the ramekins from their water bath to a wire rack and cool to room temperature. Chill well.

8. Shortly before you wish to serve the custards, preheat the broiler until very hot. Sieve a ⅛-inch-thick layer of brown sugar over the surface of the custards, smoothing the sugar very gently with a spatula.

9. Place the custards on a baking sheet and broil until the sugar has caramelized to a rich brown, about 1 minute. Watch almost constantly; the sugar can burn easily. Cool briefly; then serve as soon as possible. Each person cracks the crisp burnt surface of his custard with the back of a spoon.

Probably more than any other fruit or vegetable, a good, ripe tomato is the most sought-after item at farmers' markets. There have already been enough laments about the sorry state of commercially grown tomatoes, so we'll just be thankful that, for a few weeks each summer, we can get the real article—bright red, bursting with juice, and still warm from the sunshine when you pick it up.

Several varieties of tomatoes are available. The old-fashioned, meaty beefsteak tomato is still around, as is Burpee's Delicious (which, their catalog informs us, is "the seed which produced the world's largest tomato—a whopping 6 lb. 8 oz. beauty grown by Clarence Dailey of Monona, Wisconsin, and listed in *The Guinness Book of World Records.*" See the box on page 143 for the saga of the attempt to outdo Mr. Dailey). Besides the other standard tomato varieties, several hybrids can usually be found in the markets, e.g. Big Boy, Better Boy, and Early Pick.

Other categories of tomatoes are cherry tomatoes, which are good for more than just salad (see opposite page); plum tomatoes, our choice for tomato sauces, homemade ketchup, and chutney; and low-acid tomatoes, including tiny, sweet yellow ones.

BEST OF THE BEST: RIPE TOMATO SALAD

When ripe tomatoes are at their peak, the less that's done to them, the better. In tomato season, we eat this salad just about every day:

- ***Core tomatoes; then slice thick with a serrated knife.***
- ***Sprinkle with coarse salt, then with chopped fresh basil, if you like (thyme, tarragon, or chives are also good).***
- ***Arrange the slices in a shallow dish, layering if necessary. You can also drizzle them with olive oil.***
- ***Let the tomatoes stand at room temperature for at least an hour, then dig in.***

Sautéed Cherry Tomatoes with Fresh Herbs

We usually think of cherry tomatoes only for salads, but they also make a quick, attractive side dish with meats or fish. Here's how:

Serves 4

1 tablespoon unsalted butter
1 pint cherry tomatoes, stems removed, rinsed quickly and drained well
1/4 teaspoon salt
2 tablespoons chopped fresh parsley, basil, or chives, or a combination; or 2 teaspoons chopped fresh tarragon or thyme, or a combination

1. Heat the butter in a large skillet over medium-low heat. Add the tomatoes and salt, tossing to coat. Cook, tossing frequently, just to heat through and soften slightly, about 4 minutes (if the tomatoes are overcooked, their skins will split).

2. Toss with herbs and serve immediately.

Note: The tomatoes can also be cooked in the oven, if you are using it to roast or bake another dish. Just place a shallow baking dish in the oven with the butter, then add the tomatoes and bake, tossing occasionally, until heated through, about 5 minutes.

TO PEEL AND SEED FRESH TOMATOES

Many recipes call for fresh tomatoes that are peeled, seeded, and chopped. Here's how:

- ***Core the tomatoes; then blanch in boiling water and count to 10.***
- ***Lift out with a skimmer and run under cold water.***
- ***Slip off the skins with a paring knife or your fingers.***
- ***Halve crosswise and gently squeeze out the seeds.***

BASIC CHUNKY TOMATO SAUCE

You can make this sauce with fresh or canned tomatoes, or a combination. Prepare a big batch in late summer, and freeze it in small containers.

Makes about 3 pints

- 5 to 6 pounds ripe fresh tomatoes (or use canned tomatoes in thick puree, or a combination)
- 2 tablespoons olive oil
- 2 medium onions, chopped
- 4 garlic cloves, minced
- 1½ teaspoons salt, plus more to taste if needed
- ½ teaspoon sugar
- ½ cup shredded fresh basil leaves, or ¾ teaspoon dried
- ½ teaspoon dried oregano
- Freshly ground black pepper
- ¼ cup chopped fresh parsley

1. If the tomatoes are fresh, peel them, core, seed as directed on page 137. Chop coarsely; set aside.

2. Heat the oil in a large heavy saucepan over medium heat. Add the onions and sauté until wilted, about 8 minutes. Add the garlic and cook 2 minutes longer.

3. Add the tomatoes, salt, sugar, about 3 tablespoons of the fresh basil or all of the dried, and the oregano. Raise the heat slightly and bring to a boil. Boil uncovered, stirring frequently, until the liquid has reduced to a thick puree, 20 to 25 minutes. Add the pepper, parsley, remaining fresh basil, and salt, if needed, and remove from heat. This sauce keeps for several days in the refrigerator, or can be frozen or canned.

Note: *The parsley will stay bright green if added to the hot sauce just before serving.*

Fresh Tomato–Pepper Salsa

Tasty with corn chips, or with grilled meats or fish.

Makes 2½ to 3 cups

- *1 pound ripe tomatoes (about 3 medium, or 6 to 7 plum tomatoes)*
- *2 fresh jalapeño peppers (or use pickled jalapeños, available in jars)*
- *2 garlic cloves, thinly sliced*
- *1 teaspoon coarse (kosher) salt*
- *1 tablespoon balsamic or red wine vinegar*
- *½ cup finely shredded basil leaves*
- *Juice of ½ lime*
- *¼ cup fruity olive oil*
- *Freshly ground black pepper*

1. Core the tomatoes, then halve and gently remove seeds. Dice tomatoes coarsely and place in a glass serving dish. Halve jalapeños lengthwise and remove seeds and ribs carefully (wash hands immediately after handling). Halve again lengthwise and cut crosswise into thin strips. Add to tomatoes with garlic, salt, vinegar, basil, and lime juice; toss gently. Place a sheet of plastic wrap on the surface of the mixture and let stand at room temperature 1 to 2 hours, stirring occasionally.

2. Holding a plate over the dish, drain off almost all of accumulated liquid. Add the olive oil and pepper to taste; stir to combine. This sauce will keep, refrigerated, for one day.

Homemade Barbecue Sauce

Try basting pieces of chicken or ribs with this not-too-sweet sauce; then cook on a charcoal grill, or in the oven on a foil-lined baking sheet.

Makes 2 to 3 cups

2 tablespoons vegetable oil
1 medium onion, chopped
3 garlic cloves, minced
2 tablespoons chopped fresh basil leaves, or large pinch of dried
Large pinch of dried thyme
2 pounds ripe fresh tomatoes, peeled, seeded, and chopped (page 137; or use 2 pounds canned tomatoes in puree, whole or crushed)
3 tablespoons Worcestershire sauce, or as needed
3 tablespoons honey
1/3 cup red wine vinegar
2 teaspoons Dijon mustard
1/2 teaspoon salt
1/4 teaspoon ground allspice
1/4 teaspoon Tabasco sauce

1. Heat the oil in a heavy saucepan over medium heat. Add the onion, garlic, basil, and thyme and sauté until the onion is softened slightly, 5 to 7 minutes.

2. Add the tomatoes, Worcestershire sauce, honey, vinegar, mustard, salt, allspice, and Tabasco. Bring to a boil and lower the heat slightly. Simmer uncovered, stirring frequently, until thickened, 20 to 30 minutes. Correct the seasonings and cool completely. Store refrigerated, in tightly covered containers. This sauce will keep for several weeks.

Fresh Tomato and Vegetable Chutney

Makes about 5 half-pints

- ***2** pounds ripe fresh tomatoes (5 or 6 medium), peeled, seeded, and chopped (page 137; or use a combination of fresh and canned)*
- ***2** leeks (white portions, with a little green), trimmed, halved lengthwise, washed well, and sliced crosswise 3/4 inch thick*
- ***2** large carrots, peeled, trimmed, and cut in 1/4-inch dice, blanched in boiling salted water 5 minutes, then drained*
- ***1** rib celery, trimmed and diced*
- ***1** small onion, chopped medium-fine*
- ***1** teaspoon grated orange rind*
- ***1 1/2** teaspoons salt, or as needed*
- ***1/2** teaspoon cayenne pepper, or as needed*
- ***1 3/4** cups red wine vinegar*
- ***1** cup granulated sugar*
- ***1/2** cup (packed) brown sugar*
- ***1/2** teaspoon ground allspice*
- ***3** garlic cloves, minced*
- ***1** tablespoon minced peeled fresh ginger*
- ***1** cup golden raisins*

1. Place the tomatoes in a heavy nonaluminum saucepan. Add the leeks, carrots, celery, onion, orange rind, salt, and cayenne. Cover the pan and heat over medium heat until the vegetables start to sizzle. Toss the vegetables. Cook covered, stirring occasionally, until the vegetables begin to soften, about 5 minutes.

2. Uncover the pot and stir in the vinegar, granulated and brown sugars, allspice, garlic, and ginger. Cook uncovered, stirring, until the sugar has dissolved. Adjust the heat to maintain a steady simmer and cook uncovered, stirring often to prevent scorching, until the chutney has thickened, about 1½ hours. Timing can vary; the chutney is done when the vegetables are tender and the syrup coats a spoon evenly. Stir in the raisins; correct seasonings with salt and cayenne as needed.

3. If you like, can the chutney by pouring it while hot into sterilized canning jars, leaving ¼-inch headspace. Top with canning lids and screw bands and process 15 minutes in a boiling-water bath. Cool and store.

Scalloped Tomatoes and Corn

Scalloped dishes, layered with cracker crumbs, butter, and milk, are a delicious, old-fashioned way of cooking corn, tomatoes, and other vegetables, and sometimes seafood. Traditional in Midwestern, New England, and southern kitchens, they are well worth reviving.

Here's a tasty combination of ripe tomatoes and corn; try it at the height of summer, when both are at their peak.

Serves 4

***2** cups corn kernels, cut from 3 to 4 ears*
***1/3** cup finely chopped red onion*
Salt and freshly ground black pepper
***1** generous cup coarsely crumbled pilot crackers (6 crackers), or other bland white crackers*
***4** tablespoons (1/2 stick) cold unsalted butter, cut into bits*
***1 1/4** pounds ripe tomatoes (about 3 medium), cored and thickly sliced*
***1 1/2** cups milk*

1. Preheat the oven to 400° F. In a mixing bowl, combine the corn kernels, onion, and a generous sprinkling of salt and pepper. Set aside. Scatter about one quarter of the cracker crumbs in a buttered shallow baking dish (an 11-inch oval gratin dish, 8-inch square pan, 9-inch pie pan all work fine). Dot with 1 tablespoon of the butter. Top with half the corn mixture. Arrange about half the tomato slices on top; season generously with salt and pepper.

2. Scatter another quarter of the cracker crumbs over the tomatoes; dot with another tablespoon of the butter. Top with the remaining corn mixture, then the remaining tomatoes. Season the tomatoes; then pour on the milk, being careful not to cover the top layer of tomatoes. Scatter the remaining cracker crumbs on top; dot with the remaining 2 tablespoons butter.

3. Bake until golden and bubbly, about 30 minutes. Serve immediately.

Tomato and Cheese Strata

A puffy layered casserole with plenty of cheese—perfect for a Sunday night family supper. If you like, stir a little chopped fresh basil, thyme, or oregano into the tomato sauce.

Serves 4 to 6

- ***12 to 16 slices white or Italian bread (with crusts), or as needed***
- ***2 cups milk, or as needed***
- ***2½ cups tomato sauce, preferably homemade (page 138)***
- ***12 ounces mozzarella cheese, thinly sliced***
- ***8 ounces Italian Fontina cheese, thinly sliced***
- ***4 eggs, lightly beaten***
- ***¾ teaspoon salt***
- ***¼ cup freshly grated Parmesan cheese***
- ***2 tablespoons cold unsalted butter, cut into bits***

1. Preheat the oven to 375° F. Butter a 2-quart soufflé dish or casserole; set aside.

2. Cut the bread slices in half if large. Place the milk in a shallow pan or dish; place a few slices of the bread in the milk until softened but not falling apart. Lift the bread from the milk; place a layer of the bread slices in the buttered baking dish. Top with a layer of tomato sauce, then with a thin layer each of mozzarella and Fontina cheese.

3. Continue layering as above, ending with a neat layer of overlapping bread slices, and reserving a little tomato sauce and several neat slices of mozzarella for the top. Beat the eggs with the salt. Poke the casserole in several places with a small sharp knife; then pour the beaten eggs over. When the eggs have been nearly absorbed, top with a layer of tomato sauce. Arrange a layer of mozzarella slices evenly over the top.

4. Sprinkle the surface of the casserole with Parmesan cheese and the bits of butter. Bake the strata until it is puffed and nicely golden, 50 to 60 minutes. Serve hot.

Stewed Corn and Tomatoes, page 70
Baked Zucchini, Pepper, and Tomato Gratin, page 80

"The tomato is to New Jersey what the potato is to Idaho."

—a New Jersey gardener

THAT'S SOME B.L.T....

Each year, tomato growers gather in an attempt to outdo the record for the world's largest tomato (see page 136). In 1978, Joseph Heimbald established a contest that brings farmers and home gardeners to Eatontown, New Jersey, on the last Saturday in August.

This exciting event is actually just the final stage of a long competition. Weigh stations in eight states each select a winner who will go to Eatontown in the hopes of winning the $1,000 grand prize, and exceeding the 6½-pound world tomato record.

Great care is taken to insure that the hefty candidates will be at their ripe prime on that August weekend. Last year's winner, a beefy 4.41- pound Delicious, almost didn't get to compete. When it looked as if the tomato might ripen too early, its owner pitched a tent around it, in which he installed air conditioning. It cost him $200, but his beauty won the prize. (Mr. Heimbald, whose entry did not win, was quick to point out that "Delicious was the winner's variety, not necessarily its taste.")

Another contestant wasn't as lucky. When his tomato had ripened fully by the Tuesday before the big Saturday, he placed it in the refrigerator, and then went away on a business trip. When he returned, he found that houseguests had eaten the would-be prizewinner, which he swears weighed in at well over 5 pounds.

The seeds of each year's winner are distributed to the farmers and gardeners, to aid in their continuing quest for increased tomato size. Having planted the winning seeds, which are dubbed "Champs of New Jersey," Mr. Heimbald kicks off each tomato season in his own special way. "It's a tradition in our family that the first vine-ripened tomato is eaten by no one other than myself. I eat it on a bacon, lettuce, and tomato sandwich."

PART II
Herbs AND More

1 PT.
MASON'S

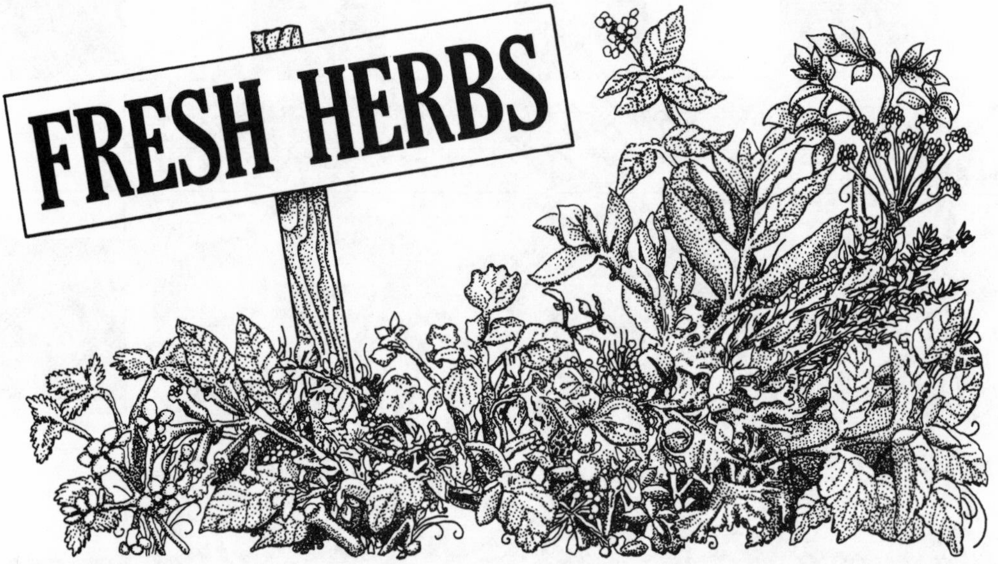

FRESH HERBS

One of the most exciting developments in the current "food revolution" is the increasing availability of fresh herbs. For those of us who grew up believing that herbs came in little bottles, looking like some kind of dried hay, the flavors of fresh herbs in cooking came as a revelation.

If you're lucky enough to have an herb garden, or even a couple of small pots on a sunny windowsill, you can snip off what you need and add them to whatever is simmering on the stove. But when you bring fresh herbs home from the farmers' market, it's good to know the best ways to keep them fresh, as well as the various methods that preserve them for longer storage. This way, you can have the lively flavors of fresh herbs all year long.

We've included several hints on herbs from Marilyn Hampstead, owner of Fox Hill Farm, "a small family-owned herb nursery that is nestled in the softly rolling countryside at Parma, Michigan, about 85 miles west of Detroit." Marilyn supplies fresh herbs to many fine chefs, and has become well known as the founder of an annual basil festival. Her book, *The Basil Book,* available in paperback (Pocket Books), has eleven different recipes for pesto! Marilyn also makes wonderful herb vinegars, which you can order directly from her farm, along with dried herbs, herb plants, and seeds. She has also written several helpful booklets on growing and using fresh herbs. For mail-order information, write to Fox Hill Farm, 444 West Michigan Avenue, Box 7, Parma, MI 49269.

KEEPING FRESH HERBS FRESH

Stored properly, parsley, thyme, rosemary, marjoram, and sage will keep for quite a while. Others, such as chives, tarragon, and chervil, are more delicate, and should be used as soon as possible.

To prolong the refrigerator life of fresh herbs:

■ For 1–5 Days:
Wrap herbs in a dampened paper towel; then place in a plastic bag in the crisper drawer of the refrigerator. Check occasionally, discarding any wilting leaves, and keeping the paper towel damp. (For parsley, wash first and shake as dry as possible.)

■ For up to 10 Days:
For parsley, basil, mint, or other very leafy herbs, place bunches of herbs in a glass of water (as you would flowers). Now place a plastic bag over the herbs and store on a refrigerator shelf. Change the water every couple of days and discard any discolored leaves.

HOW TO FREEZE HERBS

Freezing preserves the flavors of herbs fairly faithfully, though they'll never look quite as good as when they are fresh. There's no sense freezing parsley, as it's always available. For other herbs, here's how:

- *If necessary (and always for basil), wash herbs and shake dry. Remove leaves and soft stems, discarding hard stems. Arrange on a baking sheet and freeze.*
- *Gently gather herbs in plastic bags; seal, label and date, and return to freezer. Remove herbs as needed, using them in their frozen state.*

Another convenient method is to make herbed ice cubes:

- *Chop fresh herbs (wash first, if necessary) and pack in an empty ice cube tray, filling compartments about two-thirds full. Fill the tray with cold water and freeze. When frozen, transfer the cubes to a plastic bag, label and date, and keep frozen. Pop an herbed ice cube directly into soups, stews, and sauces as needed.*

Note: *If you have combinations of herbs that you use frequently, they can be frozen together, using either of these methods.*

PRESERVING HERBS IN OIL

This is a method we particularly like, since you get not only the preserved herbs, but also nicely flavored oils. Here's how:

- *Chop the leaves and soft stems of any fresh herb. (Wash first if necessary, as with basil; then shake dry.)*
- *Pack in jars; then add enough olive or vegetable oil to cover completely.*
- *Cover tightly; label and date, and store at cool room temperature.*
- *Simply spoon out a little of the herb as you need it. Add oil, if necessary, so that the herbs are always covered.*
- *When you've used up the herbs, use the oil in salad dressings, marinades, quick sautés, or drizzled over vegetables or pizza.*

Herbed Mayonnaise

Try this on cold fish, vegetables, or meats. For a light variation, stir in about ½ cup sour cream or plain yogurt to the finished mayonnaise; add a squeeze of lemon juice and correct all seasonings.

Makes about 1½ cups

2 ***egg yolks, at room temperature***
1 ***teaspoon Dijon mustard***
¾ ***teaspoon salt***
Pinch of cayenne pepper
Juice of ½ lemon, plus more as needed
1 ***tablespoon wine vinegar***
⅔ ***cup corn or peanut oil***
½ ***cup olive oil***
⅓ ***cup mixed chopped fresh herbs, e.g. parsley, chives, tarragon, dill, chervil***

1. Place the egg yolks, mustard, salt, cayenne pepper, lemon juice, and vinegar in a food processor. Process for about 10 seconds.

2. With the machine running, gradually add the oils in a very thin stream. Fold in the chopped herbs and correct all seasonings, adding additional mustard, salt, cayenne, lemon juice, and vinegar to taste. Transfer to a bowl, cover tightly with plastic wrap, and refrigerate for an hour or so before serving, to let the flavors blend. This keeps for about 3 days, tightly covered, in the refrigerator.

Herb Butter Glaze for Fish or Chicken

A quick sauce, beautifully glossy. You can use this procedure any time you sauté a piece of fish or chicken.

Serves 4

- ¾ ***cup (1½ sticks) cold unsalted butter, cut into pieces***
- 2 ***garlic cloves, finely chopped***
- ***Juice of 1 lemon, plus more as needed***
- 3 ***tablespoons chopped fresh herbs, e.g. parsley, chives, sage, tarragon, dill***

1. Heat 1 tablespoon of the butter over medium heat in a medium-size saucepan (or in an empty skillet, after sautéing fish or chicken). Add the garlic and sauté for about 2 minutes. Squeeze in the lemon juice and lower the heat to medium-low.

2. Add the butter 2 pieces at a time, swirling the pan constantly. The butter should become white and smooth. Continue to add more butter just before the previous pieces have melted. When all the butter has been incorporated, remove the pan from the heat and swirl in the herbs. Add more lemon juice to taste; serve immediately.

OTHER PRESERVING METHODS

■ **Drying Your Own:**

You can also dry your own herbs, which will have much more flavor than the dried products you can buy. There are various methods: hanging them in bunches, leaves downward, or drying them on racks or screens, one layer deep, in a very slow oven with the door ajar, in a slow convection oven, or in the open air.

Here are some details from Marilyn Hampstead: "Most herbs take from 4 to 10 days to dry, depending on the temperature, humidity, and the succulence of the plant material.

"When dry to a crisp, place leaves, flowers, and tender stems in an opaque, air-tight container. Label [and date]. Store containers in a cool [dark] place. Check in a few days for any signs of condensation. Re-dry, if necessary, until absolutely crisp."

■ **Herbal Vinegars:**

Herbal vinegars are also a good method, though better for flavoring the vinegar than for actually preserving the herbs. Again, advice from Marilyn Hampstead: "Quickly rinse [and dry] herbs. Cut off hard stems and roots. Crush the remaining soft stems with foliage and flower buds in your hands and loosely fill two-thirds full a [wide-mouth] container.

"Fill container with [cider or wine] vinegar, making sure [the herb] is completely covered. Seal and shake. Age for 3 to 4 weeks in a cool place out of direct sunlight, which can bleach herb colors."

HERB BUTTERS

This is one of the best ways to enjoy the flavor of fresh herbs. Made in advance and frozen, the butter can be sliced off in thick pats to add instant flavor to grilled or broiled fish, poultry, steaks, or other meats. Here is a basic formula; use less of overpowering herbs like rosemary, mint, or thyme. For a* fines herbes *butter, try a combination of parsley, chives, and tarragon.

Makes about 1 cup

- **1 cup (2 sticks) unsalted butter, at room temperature**
- **¼ cup any chopped fresh herb (choose from parsley, chives, tarragon, dill, basil, chervil, sage, thyme, rosemary, mint, or a combination)**
- **2 tablespoons lemon juice, or to taste**
- **Salt and freshly ground black pepper**

1. Mash the butter in a bowl or food processor with the herb, lemon juice, salt, and pepper. Correct all seasonings.

2. Place the butter down the length of a sheet of plastic wrap. Fold the wrap over and shape the butter into a smooth log shape. Label and freeze. To use, slice off thick pats directly from the frozen log.

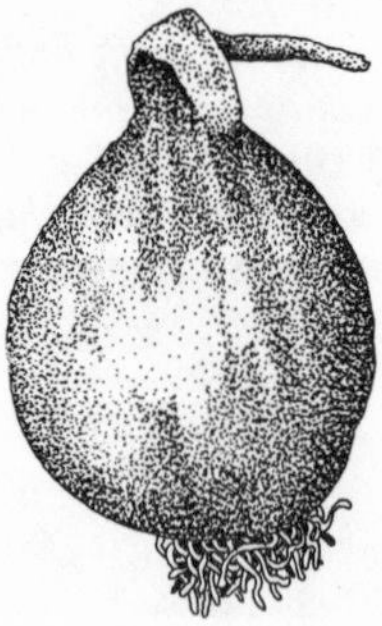

Renita's Herb Bread

A tender loaf, first tasted with cocktails and cheese at a fishing lodge in Alaska. When asked for the recipe, Renita warned, "Do Not Use Dried Basil!!"

Makes two 9 x 5-inch loaves

- ***2 packages dry yeast***
- ***⅔ cup lukewarm water***
- ***2 tablespoons sugar***
- ***2⅔ cups buttermilk***
- ***½ cup olive oil***
- ***1 tablespoon salt***
- ***6½ to 7 cups flour, or as needed***
- ***¼ cup thinly sliced scallion greens***
- ***¼ cup chopped parsley***
- ***¼ cup chopped fresh basil***
- ***1 tablespoon chopped fresh dill***
- ***2 tablespoons snipped fresh chives (optional)***
- ***1½ tablespoons finely chopped shallots (optional)***
- ***Beaten egg, for glaze***

1. In a cup or small bowl, stir together the yeast, lukewarm water, and sugar. Set aside for 5 minutes. Heat the buttermilk over low heat until lukewarm (don't worry if the buttermilk separates slightly).

2. Place the buttermilk, olive oil, and salt in a mixing bowl or an electric mixer with a dough hook. Add the yeast mixture, 6½ cups flour, the scallions, parsley, basil, dill, chives, and

shallots. Work the ingredients together; the dough will be very soft. Knead on a lightly floured surface (or with the dough hook), adding enough flour until the dough is very soft, but no longer sticky. Knead until very smooth and elastic, 8 to 10 minutes. Place the dough in a greased bowl, turn over to coat with grease, and cover with a kitchen towel. Let the dough rise until doubled in volume, 1½ to 2 hours.

3. Punch the dough down; divide in two pieces. On a lightly floured surface, pat each portion of dough into a neat rectangle about 9 inches wide. Roll each piece of dough into a compact cylinder and transfer to a buttered 9 x 5-inch loaf pan, seam down. Cover with a towel and let rise until the dough reaches the rims of the pans, about 45 minutes.

4. Preheat the oven to 375° F. Brush the dough lightly with beaten egg and bake until nicely golden brown, about 40 minutes. Remove the loaves from the pans and return to the oven. Bake until the loaves sound hollow when tapped on the bottoms, 5 to 8 minutes longer. Cool completely on a wire rack.

Cheese Popovers with Fresh Herbs, page 159
Red Pepper-and-Cheese-Stuffed Bread, page 160

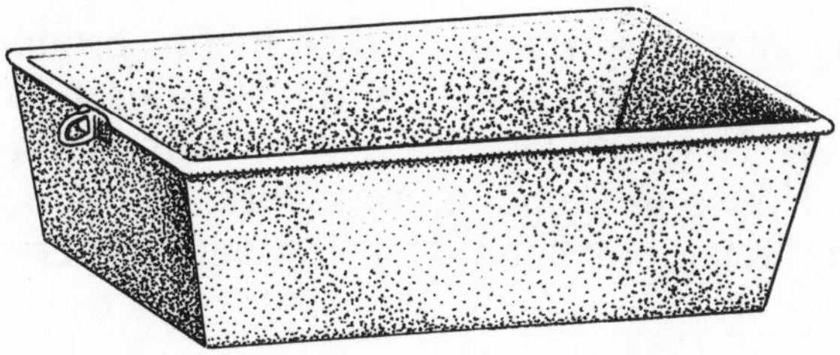

HERBED CROUTONS

Nice in a salad, or on soup. Here's how:

- ***Cut a loaf of French or Italian bread, with crust, into ¾-inch cubes.***
- ***Place on a baking sheet and bake in a preheated 375° F. oven until lightly golden, about 8 minutes.***
- ***While the bread is toasting, melt 3 tablespoons butter in a small saucepan with 3 tablespoons olive oil.***
- ***Remove the pan from the heat and stir in about 3 tablespoons chopped fresh herbs —basil, parsley, chives, tarragon, dill, and sage are all good, and a touch of chopped garlic doesn't hurt.***
- ***Drizzle this mixture over the toasted bread cubes, toss to coat, and return to the oven until fragrant and golden, about 3 minutes longer. These are especially good served warm.***

Top-quality maple syrup and other maple products are often available at farmers' markets in the Northeast. To learn about how syrup is produced, we spoke with John Mahardy of Wright's Sugar House in Camden, New York, which produces Little Chief Maple Products. John shared his first-hand experience at maple sugaring:

Ours is a moderate-size maple syrup operation, presently with between 4,000 and 5,000 taps. Several crews of two persons each gather the sap from roadside and woods trees, of which half are tapped with buckets, and the rest with plastic tubing.

We process the sap with a reverse osmosis machine and two oil-fired evaporators, making somewhere in the neighborhood of 15 gallons of syrup every hour. (When it comes from the tree, maple sap is clear and watery, with only 2 to 3 percent sugar. Only once the sap is boiled down in special evaporating pans does it become concentrated [66 percent sugar], with its amber color and pure maple flavor. It takes an average of 40 gallons of maple sap to produce a single gallon of pure maple syrup.)

We also make maple cream (a thick spread) and maple sugar. We offer tours of the operation, and also operate a pancake kitchen in connection with the Sugar House during March and April, and again in October, serving pancakes, fruit pancakes with blueberries, strawberries, and bananas, French toast, and all sorts of omelets. Of course, everything is served with pure maple syrup.

We use maple syrup for canning our fruits and berries. Keep in mind that maple syrup enhances the flavor of whatever food it is used with. It makes an excellent topping on ice cream or fruit, or on cereals. (Little Chief maple syrup can be mail-ordered; write to 28 Liberty Street, Camden, NY 13316; telephone [315] 245-1519.)

If you've bought only commercial "breakfast syrups," you'll be surprised at how rich-tasting pure maple syrup is. Incidentally, the pure syrup should be stored refrigerated (or frozen) once opened. And although it's generally used for making bulk syrups, we're both fond of Grade B maple syrup, which is darker and has a deeper, more pronounced maple flavor than Grade A.

Apple Upside-Down Corn Bread

From John Tjenos and Posey Tibbon in northern California. Serve warm, for breakfast, with lots of real maple syrup. One of the first recipes we tested, and one of our favorites.

Serves 6 to 8

2 tablespoons unsalted butter
2 tablespoons maple syrup, plus more for serving
2 apples (about 12 ounces), peeled, cored, and sliced 1/4 inch thick

BATTER
3/4 cup cornmeal
3/4 cup flour
1 teaspoon baking powder
1/2 teaspoon salt
1/4 teaspoon baking soda
1 egg, lightly beaten
1 cup buttermilk
1/4 cup maple syrup
3 tablespoons unsalted butter, melted

1. Preheat the oven to 375° F. Heat the butter and maple syrup in a heavy 10-inch skillet over medium-high heat. Add the apple slices and sauté, tossing occasionally, until softened slightly, about 5 minutes. Use two spoons to arrange the apple slices in a neat pattern, fanning them out from the center.

2. *Batter:* Combine the cornmeal, flour, baking powder, salt, and baking soda in a mixing bowl. In a separate bowl, beat the egg, buttermilk, maple syrup, and melted butter. Make a well in the center of the dry ingredients, pour in the egg mixture, and stir together with a wooden spoon just until combined.

3. Spread the batter gently over the apples. Bake until a knife inserted in the center of the corn bread comes out clean, 30 to 35 minutes. Cool, in the skillet, on a wire rack for about 5 minutes. Invert the corn bread onto a serving platter and serve immediately, passing additional maple syrup at the table.

French Canadian Maple Sugar Pie

Like a pecan pie, but with a nice tart edge. From the late Regina Menard of Plaisance, Quebec, the cousin of our friend and colleague Ruth Cousineau.

Serves 8

Basic Pastry Dough for a One-Crust Pie (page 241)
3 eggs
3/4 cup plus 2 tablespoons light brown sugar
3/4 cup pure maple syrup
6 tablespoons (3/4 stick) unsalted butter, melted
1/4 cup brewed tea
2 tablespoons plus 1/2 teaspoon apple cider vinegar
Pinch of salt
3/4 cup coarsely chopped walnuts

Lightly whipped cream or vanilla ice cream

1. Roll out the pastry dough on a lightly floured surface to a large circle about 1/8 inch thick. Transfer it to a 9-inch pie dish and trim excess pastry dough, leaving a 3/4-inch border. Fold the border under the pastry and crimp the edge. Chill the pastry shell.

2. Preheat the oven to 450° F. In a mixing bowl, whisk together the eggs and brown sugar. Add the maple syrup, butter, tea, vinegar, and salt, whisking until smooth. Stir in the walnuts. Place the pastry shell on a heavy baking sheet and place on the center rack of the oven. Pour in the filling.

3. Bake the pie for 10 minutes; then reduce the heat to 350° F. and continue to bake until the center is set, about 25 minutes longer. Cool on a wire rack; then serve warm or at room temperature, with lightly whipped cream or vanilla ice cream.

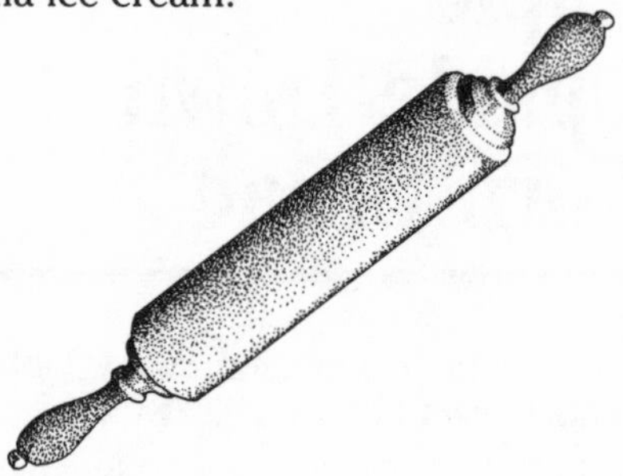

Maple Refrigerator Ice Cream

Based on a recipe from the Vermont Department of Agriculture.

Serves 6

1 cup pure maple syrup
2 egg yolks
1 cup milk
2 cups heavy cream

1. Bring the maple syrup to a boil in a small saucepan. Boil, uncovered, for 5 minutes.

2. In a mixing bowl, whisk together the egg yolks and milk. Whisk in the maple syrup until smooth. Cool to room temperature. Whip the cream until it forms soft peaks. Gently fold the cooled custard mixture into the whipped cream. Pour the mixture into a shallow pan, such as a 9-inch square baking pan.

3. Freeze the ice cream until the sides have set but the center is still fluid, 45 minutes to 1 hour. With a wooden spoon, stir the mixture, combining firm and soft portions. Return to the freezer. When the mixture has partially frozen again, after about 45 minutes, stir again. Return the ice cream to the freezer and freeze just until firm. Soften the ice cream briefly in the refrigerator before serving.

Maple–Walnut Sauce for Ice Cream

Makes about 1 cup

1/3 cup chopped walnuts (pecans can be substituted)
1 cup pure maple syrup

1. Preheat the oven to 350° F. Toast the chopped walnuts in a small baking pan until fragrant and lightly colored, about 6 minutes (watch carefully). Set aside.

2. While the walnuts are toasting, bring the maple syrup to a boil in a small, heavy saucepan. Boil gently, uncovered, until the syrup has thickened slightly (it should be reduced to about 3/4 cup, or slightly less if the syrup was very thin). Stir in the walnuts and remove from heat. Serve warm over ice cream. Store refrigerated, in a tightly closed jar. To reheat, place the jar in a pan of cold water and reheat slowly.

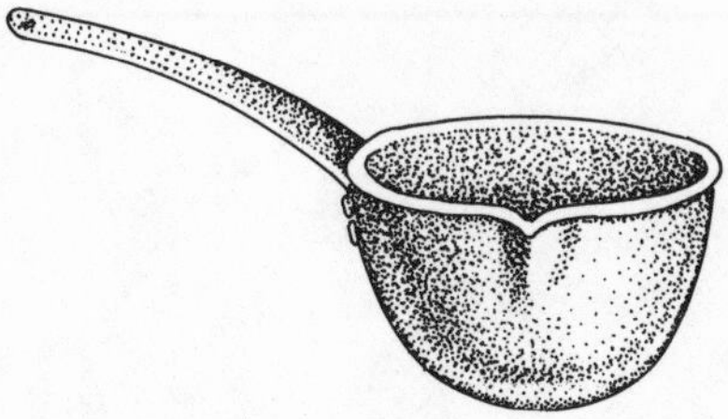

More and more, Americans are becoming interested in a wider variety of cheeses, many of which can now be seen at farmers' markets. Small farms are using old artisan methods to produce cheeses ranging from sharp Cheddars to a wide variety of goat cheeses. People like Laura Chenel of California Chèvre; Gail LeCompte of Goat Works in Washington, New Jersey; and Goat Folks of Interlaken, New York, offer soft, fresh goat cheeses, as well as firmer aged ones and cheeses flavored with garlic and herbs. You can also make your own white cheese, using the instructions below.

HOMEMADE FROMAGE BLANC (FRESH WHITE CHEESE)

Without much trouble, you can make your own soft, white cheese, which has a remarkably sweet flavor. Here's how:

1. Place a large pot on a rack within a larger pot or casserole. Pour enough cool water into the larger pot to come three-quarters of the way up the sides of the smaller one. Pour 3 quarts of milk into the smaller pot and heat gently until the milk reaches a temperature of 72° to 80° F. Remove from heat.

2. Stir in 3 tablespoons buttermilk until well combined; cover the smaller pot. Leave the milk, still in its water bath, at room temperature until the curd (the milk solids) separates from the liquid whey (if your kitchen is very cool, place the pots in the oven with only the pilot light on. The coagulation can take up to about 24 hours).

3. Line a colander with several thicknesses of cheesecloth that have been rinsed in hot water, then wrung out. Leave a generous overhang of cheesecloth over the sides. Gently ladle in the curd and cover the colander. Let the curd drain for at least 2 hours, or until somewhat firm, spooning together wet and dry portions if necessary. (If you like, save the whey and use in making biscuits or breads.)

4. Gather the edges of the cheesecloth and tie together with string to form a compact bag. Hang the string over a bowl and let the curd drain off excess liquid. Scrape the cheese into a bowl; cover and refrigerate. Makes about 2 cups (1 pound). This cheese keeps about 3 days, refrigerated.

Now that you've made your own cheese, it can be eaten as is, lightly salted if you like, with crisp raw vegetables, or lightly sweetened and eaten with fruit, or used in cooking anywhere a soft curd cheese (e.g. ricotta) is called for. Or try:

HERBED FROMAGE BLANC

Concoct your own boursin-type mixtures by beating a little cream into the fromage blanc, *then flavoring the cheese with minced garlic, salt and pepper, and any fresh herbs you choose. Laura Chenel, founder of California Chèvre, uses whatever is in season, usually chives, rosemary, and thyme, plus summer savory, marjoram, or oregano. If you like, after about two days of refrigeration, the cheese will be firm enough to form into small balls or cylinders, which can then be rolled in herbs, or marinated with them, with plenty of fruity olive oil poured over.*

SWEETENED FROMAGE BLANC

To serve the cheese with fruit, beat in a little cream or sour cream (or crème fraîche), *sweeten with sugar to taste, and add a tiny pinch of salt. The cheese can now be sprinkled with a little cinnamon or freshly ground coffee, and can also be flavored with a little vanilla or a fruit brandy or* eau-de-vie. *It's best, though, just by itself, letting its own sweet flavor come through.*

MAKE YOUR OWN...

If you'd like to go further into cheesemaking, contact Bob and Ricki Carroll at the New England Cheesemaking Supply Company, P.O. Box 85, Ashfield, MA 01330; telephone (413) 628-3808. They offer cheesemaking equipment, booklets, and a newsletter, as well as one-day cheesemaking workshops.

Quesadillas

These cheesy wedges are terrific with drinks—almost a Tex-Mex grilled cheese sandwich. Note that the recipe is a basic formula—each 8-inch tortilla sandwich will make 8 wedges; 6-inch ones are cut into 6. Count on 2 or 3 wedges per person. You can vary the ingredients according to what's on hand.

FOR EACH TORTILLA "SANDWICH"

- ***2** 6- or 8-inch flour tortillas*
- ***3/4** cup grated cheese (use a combination of Cheddar and Monterey Jack; or Italian Fontina or Gruyère); use 1 cup for 8-inch tortillas*
- ***2** or 3 pickled jalapeño peppers (available in jars; or use canned jalapeños), thinly sliced*
- ***Optional: Slivers of ham, sopressata, chorizo, pepperoni, or prosciutto; shredded cooked chicken or shrimp; strips of roasted red bell pepper***

1. Preheat the oven to 350° F. Lightly butter a baking sheet. Place one tortilla on the sheet and top with grated cheese. Scatter the sliced jalapeños and any optional ingredients over the cheese. Top with a second tortilla, then cover loosely with foil.

2. Bake until the cheese melts, about 6 minutes. Cut into wedges and serve hot.

Cheese Pancakes

These not-too-sweet pancakes were suggested by the Russian *syrniki,* and by the Hungarian curd cheese dumplings called *túrós gombóc.* Try them for brunch, sprinkled with confectioners' sugar and passing sour cream separately. Or, even better, with fresh strawberries and/or blueberries that have been tossed with sugar until they form their own light syrup.

Makes about 20 small pancakes

- ***1** pound farmer cheese*
- ***1** tablespoon sour cream*
- ***1** egg*
- ***1** egg yolk*
- ***3** tablespoons sugar*
- ***1/2** teaspoon salt*
- ***1/4** teaspoon pure vanilla extract*
- ***Large pinch of cinnamon***
- ***1/2** cup flour*
- ***4** tablespoons (1/2 stick) unsalted butter, plus more if needed*
- ***Confectioners' sugar***
- ***Sour cream***

1. In a mixing bowl, combine the farmer cheese, sour cream, egg, yolk, sugar, salt, vanilla, and cinnamon,

beating with a wooden spoon until smooth. Sprinkle on the flour and stir just until blended. Smooth the surface of the mixture; cover and chill well, at least 30 minutes.

2. Generously film with butter the bottom of the skillet (preferably nonstick). Place the skillet over medium-high heat; when the butter stops sizzling, spoon 2 to 3 tablespoons of the cheese mixture into the skillet, then flatten the mixture lightly to form a round patty about 2½ inches in diameter. Repeat, forming as many pancakes in the skillet as you can without crowding them (they shouldn't touch).

3. Cook the pancakes until lightly golden, 2 to 2½ minutes, shaking the pan occasionally to prevent sticking. Turn the pancakes over gently with a spatula and cook the other sides. Regulate the heat as needed; you may have to turn it down to medium occasionally so the pancakes are evenly golden, but not dark brown. Transfer the cooked pancakes to a platter and keep warm while you fry the remaining pancakes. Add butter to the pan as needed, and replace the butter if it becomes dark brown.

4. Serve the pancakes immediately, sprinkled with confectioners' sugar. Pass a bowl of sour cream separately.

Cheese Popovers with Fresh Herbs

Makes 1 dozen popovers

- ***3** tablespoons unsalted butter, melted*
- ***3** eggs*
- ***1½** cups milk*
- ***1½** cups sifted flour*
- ***¾** teaspoon salt*
- *Few grinds of black pepper*
- ***1** tablespoon chopped fresh chives*
- ***1** tablespoon chopped parsley*
- ***⅔** cup freshly grated Parmesan cheese*

1. Preheat the oven to 450° F. Use half the butter to grease a muffin tin, preferably one of heavy metal.

2. In a mixing bowl, whisk together the remaining 1½ tablespoons melted butter, the eggs, and the milk. Gradually add the flour, whisking until smooth. Whisk in the salt, pepper, chives, parsley, and all but 2 tablespoons of the grated Parmesan.

3. Place the buttered muffin tin in the preheated oven until it is very hot and the butter is sizzling but not browned, about 3 minutes. Pull out the oven shelf and carefully pour about ¼ cup of the batter in each indentation; sprinkle the batter with the reserved Parmesan cheese. Bake 15 minutes (no peeking!), then lower the heat to 350° F. and continue to bake until puffed and golden brown, about 15 minutes longer. Serve hot, with sweet butter.

Red Pepper-and-Cheese-Stuffed Bread

Serve wedges of this gutsy bread as an appetizer or snack, with a glass of wine. It also transports well on a picnic.

Makes one 11-inch round loaf (10 to 16 wedges)

HERBED WHOLE WHEAT BREAD DOUGH

- ***4** teaspoons dry yeast (a little less than 2 envelopes)*
- ***1¼** cups lukewarm water*
- ***2⅔** cups all-purpose flour, plus more as needed*
- ***1** cup whole wheat flour*
- ***1** tablespoon cornmeal*
- ***1** tablespoon coarse (kosher) salt*
- ***1½** tablespoons olive oil*
- ***2** tablespoons chopped parsley*
- ***1½** teaspoons chopped fresh rosemary leaves, or ½ teaspoon dried*

PEPPERS

- ***4** red bell peppers (or 2 red and 2 yellow)*
- ***3** medium onions, quartered lengthwise, then sliced*
- ***2** tablespoons olive oil*
- ***2** tablespoons chopped parsley*
- *Salt and freshly ground black pepper*

HERBED CHEESE

- ***6** ounces fresh goat cheese* (**chèvre frais**), *or other soft cheese (e.g. ricotta, homemade* **fromage blanc**, *page 157)*
- *Milk or cream, if needed*
- ***1** garlic clove, minced*
- ***3** tablespoons mixed chopped fresh herbs, such as parsley, basil, rosemary, thyme, and/or chives*
- *Salt and freshly ground black pepper*

ASSEMBLY

- *Olive oil*
- *Corn meal*
- ***1¼** pounds mozzarella cheese, thinly sliced*
- ***1** egg yolk beaten with 1 teaspoon cold water (for glaze)*

1. *Bread Dough:* Stir together the yeast and lukewarm water in a cup and set aside for about 5 minutes. Place the flours, cornmeal, and salt in the bowl of a food processor and pulse on and off briefly. When the yeast is ready, stir the olive oil into it, and with the processor running, add the liquid mixture to the dry ingredients. The dough should be soft but cohesive, and just slightly sticky; add more all-purpose flour as needed. Process the dough for 1 minute, adding the parsley and rosemary for the last few seconds only.

2. Turn the dough out onto a floured surface and knead for about 2 minutes, or until smooth and elastic, kneading in a bit more flour until the dough is no longer sticky. Place the dough in an oiled bowl, turn over to coat with oil, and cover the bowl with a dampened towel. Let stand in a warm place until the dough has doubled in volume, about 1½ hours.

3. *Peppers:* Roast the peppers (page 102). Peel; then halve the peppers and remove stems, ribs, and seeds. Cut the pepper halves in half crosswise, then in wide strips. Drain any juices from the peppers (you can add these juices to salad dressings). Set aside. In a wide skillet, sauté the onions in olive oil over moderate heat, stirring occasionally, until softened but not browned, about 10 minutes. Remove from heat and stir in the reserved peppers, parsley, salt, and pepper. Set aside.

4. *Herbed Cheese:* Place the cheese in a small mixing bowl and beat lightly with a fork. If it is not creamy, stir in some milk or cream. Stir in the garlic, herbs, and salt and pepper. Set aside.

5. *Assembly:* Oil an 11-inch fluted porcelain quiche pan, or another similar shallow baking dish, with olive oil; then sprinkle the bottom with a little cornmeal. Punch the risen dough down and divide it with a sharp knife into two slightly unequal pieces. Roll the larger piece of dough on a floured surface to a circle about 2 inches larger than the pan; the edges of the dough should be rolled quite thin. Fit the dough gently into the pan, with about an inch of dough overhanging on all sides.

6. Arrange half the mozzarella slices over the dough, overlapping them slightly. Gently spoon about half the pepper mixture over, then carefully spoon the herbed cheese mixture over. Top with the remaining pepper mixture, then with remaining mozzarella slices.

7. Roll the smaller piece of bread dough into a circle to fit the top, rolling the edges quite thin. Lay it gently over the mozzarella slices. Brush the circle of dough with the egg yolk glaze. Gently roll the overhanging dough up and onto the surface of the top layer of dough. Glaze the edges, cut a series of curved slashes in the top, and let the dough rise for 10 or 15 minutes.

8. Preheat the oven to 400° F. Bake the bread until golden brown and the dough sounds hollow when tapped, 40 to 50 minutes. Let cool 15 to 20 minutes before serving directly from the baking dish.

Pasta with Broccoli and Two Cheeses, page 44
Baked Macaroni with Zucchini and Three Cheeses, page 80
Pecan Cheese Crackers, page 163
Tomato and Cheese Strata, page 142

DRIED FRUITS AND NUTS

Nuts have long been a significant American crop. Although the California almond industry is less than a century old, we now produce over half the world's almonds. And the U.S. is the world leader in walnut production, with most grown in California, and a small amount in Oregon. The pecan is our all-American contribution to the nut world, grown in at least twelve states, chiefly Georgia, Texas, Oklahoma, and North Carolina.

In the 1877 *Kettner's Book of the Table,* E. S. Dallas called the almond "the most versatile and the most poetical" of fruits. The word fruit here is no accident; almonds are, in fact, a fruit related to peaches and plums. Their scientific name, *Prunus amygdalus,* means "tonsil plum," and the almond does resemble a peach pit.

The peanut, which has been called "the nut that isn't a nut," is a pea, or a legume, and thus a rich source of protein. No less than 50 percent of the huge peanut crop is used to make peanut butter.

But if you really want good peanut butter—or any nut butter, for that matter—try making your own (page 164). And once you've bought any nuts, be sure to keep them fresh by storing them in tightly wrapped plastic bags in the freezer. Label and date the packages, and rotate your stock carefully, using the oldest first. You'll be surprised at the difference in flavor really fresh nuts can make.

You'll also be pleased with the difference in freshness of dried fruits found at farmers' markets—which haven't been subjected to chemical preservatives or long storage. They're plump, moist, and bursting with concentrated fruit flavor.

TO KEEP NUTS FRESH ...

Wrap tightly in plastic bags and keep frozen until needed, up to one year. Stored at room temperature, nuts can quickly become rancid.

Pecan Cheese Crackers

From Mrs. F. P. Wetherbee, Jr. in Georgia, one of the principal pecan-growing states. These crackers are very rich with pecans and sharp cheese flavor, with a nice bite of cayenne—addictive with a glass of wine or beer.

Makes about 100 small crackers

- ***1 cup (2 sticks) unsalted butter, at room temperature***
- ***1 pound extra-sharp Cheddar cheese, grated***
- ***3 cups flour***
- ***1 teaspoon baking powder***
- ***½ teaspoon baking soda***
- ***½ teaspoon cayenne pepper***
- ***2 cups finely chopped pecans***
- ***2 teaspoons cold water or beer, if needed***

1. In an electric mixer, cream together the butter and grated cheese until well blended. Meanwhile, sift together the flour, baking powder, baking soda, and cayenne onto a sheet of wax paper. Lower the mixer speed and add the flour mixture, beating just until blended. Do not overmix. Add the chopped nuts. If the mixture is too dry to come together, add cold water or beer, a little at a time, just until it coheres. Shape the mixture into 3 or 4 cylinders about 1½ inches thick, wrapping each one in wax paper and smoothing the cylinders neatly. Refrigerate until firm, at least 1 hour. (If you like, freeze some of the dough; then defrost and bake at another time.)

2. Preheat the oven to 350° F. Slice the dough about ¼ inch thick and place the slices on ungreased cookie sheets. Bake until starting to set and the edges are pale gold, 15 to 17 minutes. Cool the crackers on the baking sheets for about 2 minutes, then transfer to a wire rack and cool completely while you bake the remaining crackers. Serve within two to three days; store airtight.

Chocolate Peanutters

Loaded with chopped peanuts and chocolate chips, these cookies are based on a favorite family recipe from Melba Melton of Montgomery, Alabama.

Makes 4 dozen

1¾ cups sifted flour
1 teaspoon baking soda
¼ teaspoon salt
½ cup (1 stick) unsalted butter, softened
¾ cup smooth peanut butter, preferably homemade (see box on this page)
½ cup sugar
½ cup brown sugar
1 egg
1 teaspoon pure vanilla extract
½ cup chopped peanuts
½ cup semisweet chocolate bits

1. Preheat the oven to 375° F. Resift the flour with the baking soda and salt onto a sheet of wax paper; set aside.

2. Cream the butter and peanut butter until well combined. Gradually add the sugar and brown sugar, beating until fluffy. Add the egg and the vanilla, beating until well blended. Stir in the flour mixture just until blended; do not overmix. Add the peanuts and chocolate chips and mix briefly, just until well distributed.

3. Roll the dough into walnut-size balls and place on greased baking sheets, spacing them apart slightly. Flatten the balls gently with the palm of your hand. Bake 8 minutes, or until set and very lightly browned. Cool cookies on a wire rack.

HOMEMADE NUT BUTTERS

You can make your own nut butters with peanuts, hazelnuts, cashews, almonds, or any other nuts. They'll be fresher and have lots more flavor than those you can buy (and no sugar or preservatives, either). Here's how:

- ***Process any amount of whole nuts with a little salt in a food processor until smooth. (Toasting them first—for about 10 minutes in a preheated 350° F. oven—will add flavor.) If you like, leave a few crunchy pieces by pulsing the machine on and off, instead of processing continually.***
- ***If necessary, add a spoonful of vegetable oil for smoothness. Store the nut butter refrigerated, in a tightly sealed container.***

Peanut Butter Bread

A moist quick bread, delicious with Cheddar cheese, or toasted, topped with bacon and cheese, and quickly broiled.

Makes one 9 x 5-inch loaf

- ***2 cups sifted flour***
- ***1½ teaspoons baking powder***
- ***½ teaspoon baking soda***
- ***1¼ teaspoons salt***
- ***4 tablespoons (½ stick) unsalted butter, softened***
- ***¾ cup smooth peanut butter, preferably homemade (see box, opposite page)***
- ***¾ cup light brown sugar***
- ***¼ cup honey***
- ***2 eggs***
- ***1¼ cups milk***
- ***1 cup roasted peanuts***

1. Preheat the oven to 350° F. Butter a 9 x 5-inch loaf pan and set aside. Resift the flour onto a sheet of wax paper with the baking powder, baking soda, and salt. Set aside.

2. In an electric mixer, beat the butter and peanut butter at medium speed until smooth. Add the brown sugar and beat until the mixture is smooth and light. Add the honey, beating until blended, then the eggs, one at a time. Add the milk in a thin stream and mix until smooth, scraping the batter down from the sides of the bowl as needed.

3. Lower the mixer speed and add the dry ingredients, mixing just until combined. Stir in the peanuts. Pour the mixture into the loaf pan and bake for 40 minutes. Lower the heat to 325° F. and continue to bake until the bread is golden brown and a toothpick inserted in the center emerges clean, about 30 minutes longer. (If, during the baking time, the surface of the bread is becoming too brown before the inside has baked through, cover the loaf lightly with foil.)

4. Cool the bread, in the pan, on a wire rack for about 10 minutes; then turn it out to cool completely. Store tightly wrapped in plastic wrap. Slice with a serrated knife.

Molasses Date and Nut Bars

A moist, chewy bar, loosely based on a molasses cookie recipe from Mr. and Mrs. Travis Kuykendall of Zapata, Texas. The pepper added to the spice mix is an old American touch, frequently found in early gingerbread recipes.

Makes 25 bars

- ***1 cup molasses***
- ***1⅓ cups sugar***
- ***1 jumbo egg (or 1½ large eggs), lightly beaten***
- ***2¾ cups sifted flour***
- ***2 teaspoons baking powder***
- ***1 teaspoon baking soda***
- ***1½ teaspoons cinnamon***
- ***¼ teaspoon allspice***
- ***½ teaspoon salt***
- ***½ teaspoon freshly grated nutmeg***
- ***¼ teaspoon freshly ground black pepper***
- ***½ cup (1 stick) unsalted butter, melted and cooled slightly***
- ***⅔ cup buttermilk***
- ***1 teaspoon pure vanilla extract***
- ***½ cup chopped pitted dates***
- ***½ cup golden raisins***
- ***¾ cup chopped pecans or walnuts***

1. Preheat the oven to 375° F. Butter a 10½ x 15½-inch jelly roll pan and set aside.

2. In an electric mixer, beat together the molasses, sugar, and egg for 5 minutes. Resift the flour with the baking powder, baking soda, cinnamon, allspice, and salt. Stir the nutmeg and pepper into the flour mixture; set aside.

3. Add the melted butter, buttermilk, and vanilla to the molasses mixture. Lower the mixer speed and add the flour, mixing until not quite blended. Add the dates, raisins, and nuts, stirring with a large rubber spatula just until blended. Scrape the mixture into the prepared pan, spreading it to the edges of the pan.

4. Bake until the edges are deep golden brown, 30 to 35 minutes. Cool on a wire rack, then cut into 2 x 3-inch bars. Serve with a tall glass of cold milk.

Caramel Pecan Sticky Buns

Loosely based on a recipe from Stahmann Farms, Las Cruces, New Mexico.

Makes 12 buns

- ***6 tablespoons lukewarm water***
- ***1½ teaspoons dry yeast (slightly more than ½ envelope)***
- ***2½ cups all-purpose flour, plus more as needed***
- ***3 tablespoons sugar***
- ***½ teaspoon salt***
- ***¼ cup lukewarm milk***
- ***1 teaspoon pure vanilla extract***
- ***2 eggs***
- ***4 tablespoons (½ stick) unsalted butter, softened slightly***

CARAMEL TOPPING

1/2 cup sugar
1/2 cup heavy cream
1/3 cup hot water
3/4 cup pecan halves

FILLING

4 tablespoons (1/2 stick) unsalted butter, melted
3/4 cup chopped pecans
1/4 cup sugar
1/2 teaspoon cinnamon

1. Place the lukewarm water in a small cup or bowl; sprinkle with the yeast and let stand until bubbly, about 5 minutes.

2. In an electric mixer with a flat paddle attachment, combine the flour, sugar, and salt. Add the yeast mixture, the milk, and the vanilla. Add the eggs and begin to mix at low speed until the ingredients are combined. Add the butter a few pieces at a time; raise the mixer speed to medium and continue to beat until the dough becomes silky and smooth, about 5 minutes. The dough will be very sticky.

3. Scrape the dough off the paddle and sprinkle lightly with flour. Cover the bowl with plastic wrap, then with a kitchen towel, and let rise until doubled in bulk (1 to 2 hours, though timing can vary).

4. *Topping:* While the dough is rising, prepare the baking pan. In a wide heavy skillet, heat the sugar over moderately high heat, stirring constantly with a wooden spoon. As it begins to caramelize, break up any lumps with the spoon. When the caramel is a medium-amber color, remove from heat and carefully add the cream and hot water (mixture will sputter), swirling the pan to combine the ingredients. Immediately pour the caramel mixture into a 10-inch pie pan (a 9 x 13-inch baking pan can be substituted), tilting the pan to coat evenly. Scatter the pecan halves over the caramel; set aside.

5. Punch the dough down and turn it out on a lightly floured work surface. Pat or roll the dough into a 12 x 16-inch rectangle.

6. *Filling:* Brush the dough with melted butter. In a small bowl, combine the chopped pecans, sugar, and cinnamon; sprinkle the mixture over the dough. Starting with a short end, roll the dough into a compact cylinder. Pinch the seam to seal. Cut the cylinder in 12 neat slices.

7. Preheat the oven to 350° F. Arrange the slices neatly in the prepared pan, cut sides down. Leave a little space between slices. Cover the pan with a kitchen towel and let rise until doubled in bulk. Bake until golden brown, 25 to 30 minutes.

8. Invert the pan onto a serving platter; carefully lift off the pan. Cool the sticky buns to warm and serve, pulling them apart.

Dried Fruit Mincemeat Pie

Mincemeat was traditionally prepared with beef and generous quantities of suet, all doused with plenty of brandy and allowed to macerate for weeks. This recipe is based on one in Marion Harland's *Common Sense in the Household* (New York, 1871). The suet and beef have been omitted.

Serves 8

CREAM CHEESE PASTRY DOUGH

***1** cup (2 sticks) unsalted butter, at room temperature*
***8** ounces cream cheese, at room temperature*
***3** tablespoons sugar*
Pinch of salt
***1/2** teaspoon pure vanilla extract*
***2** cups flour*

Dried Fruit Mincemeat Filling

***2** tart apples, peeled, cored, and cut in 1/4-inch dice*
***1** firm-ripe pear, peeled, cored, and cut in 1/4-inch dice*
***1** cup dried currants*
***1/2** cup chopped dates*
***1/2** cup chopped dried figs*
***1/2** cup golden raisins*
***3** tablespoons chopped candied citron (optional)*
***6** gingersnaps, broken up*
Grated zest and juice of 1 orange
***1** tablespoon lemon juice*
***1** cup light brown sugar*
***1/4** cup brandy, or more as needed*
***1** tablespoon dry white wine*
***1** teaspoon cinnamon*
***1/2** teaspoon mace*
***1/2** teaspoon allspice*
***1/4** teaspoon cloves*
***3/4** teaspoon salt*

***1** tablespoon cold unsalted butter, cut into bits*
Granulated sugar

Vanilla ice cream (optional)

1. *Cream Cheese Pastry Dough:* In an electric mixer or food processor, cream together the butter, cream cheese, sugar, and salt until light and fluffy. Add the vanilla extract, mix briefly, then lower the speed and mix in the flour just until blended. Gather the dough into a ball. Flatten slightly, dust with flour, and chill, wrapped in plastic wrap, for at least 30 minutes, or until the dough is just firm.

2. Divide the chilled dough into two slightly unequal portions. On a lightly floured surface (or between two sheets of wax paper), roll out the larger piece to a thickness of ⅛ inch. Fit the pastry into a deep 9-inch pie dish. Roll the remaining dough into a circle ⅛ inch thick and transfer it to a pastry sheet. Chill the pastry.

3. *Dried Fruit Mincemeat Filling:* In a mixing bowl, combine the apples, pear, currants, dates, figs, raisins, citron, gingersnaps, orange zest and juice, lemon juice, brown sugar, brandy, wine, cinnamon, mace, allspice, cloves, and salt, stirring gently until everything is combined and moistened. If the mixture seems dry, stir in another splash of brandy.

4. Preheat the oven to 350° F. Cut the chilled circle of pastry into 1-inch-wide strips, using a rippled pastry cutter or a sharp knife. Moisten the edge of the bottom crust with cold water. Pour the filling into the bottom crust and dot with butter. Lay half the pastry strips across the top of the pie at even intervals, pressing them into the edges of the bottom crust. Lay the remaining strips of pastry across the top, placing them at a sharp angle to the strips already in place and pressing them into the edge of the bottom crust. Trim off the ends of the strips; then fold the overhanging edge of the bottom crust over onto the rim of the pie plate, pressing gently to form an even rim. Form a decorative border, if you wish. Sprinkle the pastry with sugar.

5. Place the pie in the lower third of the oven and bake until the filling is bubbly and the crust is golden brown, about 1 hour (timing may vary). Cool on a rack to room temperature. Serve with ice cream, if you wish.

Dried Apple "Pour-Through" Pie

The "pour-through" crust is an old farm tradition, as is making pies with apples that have been dried for storage. The apples in this pie have a slightly firmer texture than fresh, with intense, concentrated flavor.

Serves 8

Basic Pastry Dough for a Two-Crust Pie (page 241)
1 quart apple cider
3/4 pound dried apples
1/4 cup plus 1 tablespoon sugar, or more to taste
1 tablespoon cornstarch
1/2 teaspoon cinnamon
1/4 teaspoon freshly grated nutmeg
1 tablespoon lemon juice
2 tablespoons cold unsalted butter, cut into bits
1 tablespoon milk
3 tablespoons heavy cream

Vanilla ice cream or sharp Cheddar cheese

1. Divide the dough into two slightly unequal portions. Roll out the larger piece on a floured surface to a thickness of 1/8 inch. Fit it into a deep 9- or 9½-inch pie dish. Roll the smaller piece of dough to a circle 1/8 inch thick and transfer it to a foil-lined baking sheet. Place the pastry dough in the refrigerator while you prepare the filling.

2. Bring the cider to a boil in a large saucepan. Add the dried apples and simmer, covered, until they are softened but not mushy, 25 to 30 minutes (timing may vary; add water to keep the apples covered with liquid, if necessary). Drain the apples, reserving the cider.

3. Preheat the oven to 425° F. Sift into a mixing bowl the 1/4 cup sugar, cornstarch, cinnamon, and nutmeg. Add the drained apples and toss gently. Add 1/4 cup of the reserved cider (chill the remainder for drinking) and the lemon juice, and toss again. Add more sugar to taste. Pour the mixture into

the pastry-lined pie dish, mounding the apples in the center. Dot with butter; then lay the top crust over loosely. Trim off excess pastry, leaving a ¾-inch border. Turn the edges under the edges of the bottom crust, forming a smooth border on the rim of the pie plate. Crimp or flute the border.

4. Brush the pastry lightly with milk, then sprinkle with 1 tablespoon sugar for a light glaze. Cut several slashes in the top crust to release steam.

5. Place the pie on a baking sheet and bake for 15 minutes. Lower the heat to 400° F. and continue to bake until golden brown, about 30 minutes longer. About 5 minutes before the pie is done, dribble the cream into the slashes of the top crust, then bake 5 minutes longer.

6. Cool on a wire rack. Serve warm with vanilla ice cream or wedges of sharp Cheddar.

Maple–Walnut Sauce for Ice Cream, page 155
Prune Batter Pudding, page 202
(Substitute for the cherries ¾ cup coarsely chopped pitted prunes that have soaked in ⅓ cup Armagnac or other brandy for at least 20 minutes.)

PART III
Fruits

"Who in hell," I said to myself, "wants to try to make pies like Mother makes, when it's so much simpler to let Mother make 'em in the first place?"

—H. Arnow, quoted by John Thorne in "Simple Cooking"

We've included more recipes for apples in this book than any other single item—not surprising, because, having been grown in many parts of the country from the earliest Colonial days, apples are just about our official American fruit. John Thorne, who we think is the most interesting—and opinionated—food writer in this country today, writes that by the late nineteenth century, apple pie had become the "emblem of our nation's cooking: not because we invented it but because we love it—and made it—so well."

Helen Kent of Locust Valley Farm in Milton, New York, can often be seen at the Greenmarkets of New York City, slicing an apple and chatting with customers as she encourages them to taste some of the farm's forty apple varieties:

My generation sticks to Red Delicious and McIntosh. But it's changing now—you younger people are showing more interest in other varieties—Northern Spy, Black Twigs, Jonathans, Baldwins. When I'm selling, I give samples, and if they ask me, I'll talk about how to use them, too. There was one girl who wanted an apple for her grandmother who couldn't eat coarse food or sugar. I told her to make applesauce with Golden Delicious, because you don't need any sugar with them. And she loved it.

We stick mostly with the older varieties on our farm. They don't look as good, but they sure taste good. I'm having a Golden Delicious right now. We've got six or seven new varieties this year, by grafting branches onto older trees. You have to grow those trees seven to ten years before you can pick the apples.

One of our most popular apples is called the Chipper, named after my oldest son. That one just grew wild, we didn't graft it. That's how the McIntosh started. It was a wild tree that originated in Canada. They used to be called Grandmother apples, but then, because they were on the McIntosh family farm, they named them McIntosh. Now there's *a good apple! One year, we had a cold summer, and they were beautiful! They don't like it too hot.*

Several recipes in this chapter come from the Aamodt family of Stillwater, Minnesota. Visitors to Aamodt's Apple Farm stop by for a taste of cider or home-baked pie in the farm's restored century-old barn. "During the harvest season," Jo Ann Aamodt told us, "it is possible for the apples to be picked in the morning, graded, and on the sales floor by that afternoon—that's orchard fresh! We raise twenty-six different varieties. For the pies in our bake shop, we adhere closely to old family recipes and use two or more varieties for a blend of flavor, aroma, and texture. If you ask one of our employees, 'What kind of apples are in the pies this week?', they will probably be able to tell you."

APPLES: WHICH ONES FOR WHICH USE?

There are dozens of different varieties of apples available, so you'd do well to ask the farmers in the market which ones they recommend for which uses in cooking. Some apples, e.g. McIntosh, are rich in flavor, but their texture doesn't hold up when baked (they make great applesauce, though). Many are considered all-purpose, but may need a little more or less sweetening than we've indicated in the recipes.

Baldwin—*Mildly sweet-tart, fairly crisp, all purpose.*

Black Twig—*Sweet-tart, extremely crisp, an eating apple.*

Cortland—*Sweet-tart, crisp and juicy, good for pies.*

Golden Delicious—*Sweet, fairly crisp, best for eating. Some of those available in farmers' markets have a lot more flavor than the commercial variety.*

Granny Smith—*Tart, crisp, all-purpose.*

Ida Red—*Spicy, crisp, all-purpose.*

Jonathan—*Sweet-tart, spicy, all-purpose.*

McIntosh—*Tart-sweet, fairly crisp, all-purpose, though disintegrates quickly when cooked.*

Northern Spy—*Sweet-tart, crisp, excellent all-purpose, great for pies.*

Roast Loin of Pork with Apples and Cider

During testing, we found that Gorgonzola polenta (page 71) was a perfect accompaniment to this juicy roast.

Serves 8, with leftovers

***1** loin of pork, about 4 pounds, bone-in*

DRY MARINADE

***1½** tablespoons coarse (kosher) salt*
***¼** teaspoon ground ginger*
***¼** teaspoon dried thyme*
***10** grinds black pepper*
***1** bay leaf, crumbled*

***1** cup apple cider*
***⅔** cup dry vermouth*
***3** tart apples (e.g. Northern Spy or Granny Smith), peeled, quartered, cored, each quarter cut in 3 wedges*
***1** tablespoon sugar*

1. Ask your butcher to crack the chine bone on the roast, and then hinge the bones (the bones are partially separated from the meat in one flat piece, but left attached, so that they add flavor to the roast, but can then be removed easily after roasting).

2. *Dry Marinade:* Several hours before cooking, combine the salt, ginger, thyme, pepper, and bay leaf in a small bowl. Rub the mixture all over the meat, massaging it into the flesh. Cover loosely and refrigerate at least 2 hours.

3. Preheat the oven to 450° F. Place the pork loin in a large roasting pan, bones down. Place in the oven and roast for 35 minutes.

4. Lower the oven heat to 350° F. Roast 15 minutes longer, then pour off rendered fat into a large shallow roasting pan (such as a 9 x 13-inch rectangular pan, or large gratin dish). Pour the cider and vermouth around the roast and return to the oven. Continue to roast the pork, basting the meat occasionally, until the meat reaches an internal temperature of 170° F. on a meat thermometer or until a skewer, after being inserted into the center of the roast, feels hot to the touch, about 45 minutes from the time the temperature is lowered. Remove the pork roast from the oven and let the meat rest about 15 minutes before carving.

5. While the pork is resting, place the shallow roasting pan with the pork fat into the oven. Heat until the fat is sizzling, about 5 minutes. Scatter the apple wedges in the pork fat, sprinkle with the sugar, and toss to coat. Continue to cook, tossing the apples very gently once or twice. Remove the pan of apples from the oven as soon as they are tender, about 10 minutes. Keep warm.

6. Remove the bones from the pork and set aside (the meaty ribs are delicious; save them for yourself). Transfer the pork to a carving board or work surface. Skim off all fat from the pan juices and place the roasting pan on the stove over two burners. Bring to a boil; then cook over medium-high heat

until the juices have reduced slightly. Turn off the heat.

7. Meanwhile, slice the pork loin in ¼-inch-thick slices. Serve hot, 2 or 3 slices per portion, with a few apple wedges alongside, and the pan juices spooned over.

ABC Sandwich

A favorite recipe from Jo Ann Aamodt, and an excellent combination of flavors. Serve for lunch or a simple supper, or cut each muffin half in pieces and serve as an hors d'oeuvre.

FOR EACH SANDWICH

2 slices Canadian bacon or cooked ham
1 teaspoon unsalted butter, if needed
1 English muffin, split (or 2 slices whole wheat, French, or white bread)
Dijon mustard
2 thick slices cored unpeeled apple
2 slices Gouda cheese, about 2 ounces

1. Preheat the broiler. If you are using Canadian bacon, sauté it in butter until lightly golden on both sides (the ham does not need to be sautéed).

2. Toast the English muffin; spread each cut side with mustard. Lay the bacon or ham on top. Cover with the apple slices, then with the cheese. Broil until the cheese melts and browns slightly. Serve immediately.

Apple Cider Jelly

Most apple jelly recipes call for liquid pectin, which allows a greater yield for the amount of fruit. In this one, apple cider is boiled down until the natural pectin forms a firm jelly, and the flavor is very, very concentrated. This version is more expensive, but the flavor is worth it. The jelly is delicious with sweet apple muffins (page 187), and it also makes a good glaze for roast poultry.

Makes about 1 cup

2 quarts apple cider

1. Boil the cider, uncovered, over moderate heat, until it reaches the jelling point (see box on page 178). This will take over an hour, so test the jelly frequently. There should be about 1 cup reduced liquid.

2. Store the jelly, tightly covered, in the refrigerator, up to one year.

SETTING POINT FOR JAMS AND JELLIES

There are three ways to test whether a jam or jelly has reached the setting point:

- **With a Thermometer:** *Place a jelly or candy thermometer in the boiling mixture. When the jam or jelly reaches 220° F. (or 8 to 9 degrees higher than the boiling point of water where you live), it is ready.*
- **The "Sheeting" Test:** *Dip a large spoon into the boiling mixture; then hold it up and let the jam or jelly drip back into the pot. If 2 drops join together (in a "sheet") as they fall, the jam is ready.*
- **The Saucer Test:** *Place two or three saucers in the freezer as you begin to cook your jam or jelly. When you think it is ready, spoon a small amount of the mixture onto a chilled saucer; return to the freezer briefly until chilled. (Remove the pan of jam from the heat while you test.) The mixture is ready when it forms a semisolid mass and wrinkles when pushed gently with a fingertip.*

Golden Delicious Sour Cream Pie

Joyce Cowin, who grows apples in Yakima Valley, Washington, sent us this recipe. Both her family farm and this tasty pie go back for generations:

> *My husband's grandparents, both college graduates, came west from Cleveland, Ohio, in 1909 for health reasons. Earle and Elsie Cowin knew nothing about farming, and they struggled with the inexperience and lack of funds and Earle's health for several years.*
>
> *They learned every aspect of farming from tilling the soil to planting the trees to working with bankers, and they eventually ended up with over 250 acres of orchard and a fruit packing and cold storage warehouse.*
>
> *Their son Bob took over many of the duties as he grew older and now his two sons, Dick and Don, are running the orchards along with three of Dick's grown sons. The family still believes college is important, and encourages all the family to attend, even though they know that ex-*

FUN FOOD FACTS....

Oliver Cromwell, a fanatical Puritan, is said to have banned apple pies in England in the mid-1600s—because they gave too much pleasure.

perience cannot be replaced by all book learning. Since Earle, there have been three generations graduated from W.S.U. in horticulture.

During the early years, Earle and Elsie had one of the first large plantings of Golden Delicious that were sent to New York to be sold. Earle developed and modified a paper carton with corrugated dividing cells for packing each Golden Delicious apple individually to protect them from bruising. They were the first to switch from the wooden boxes to this method of packing and shipping.

Because the Golden Delicious has been such an important fruit in the Cowin history, I am sending my favorite pie recipe using Goldens. It is a prize-winner in our valley. It has won at the fair, and last year I won a prize for being in the top twelve of a pie contest where there were over 200 pies entered. This is the pie:

Serves 8

Basic Pastry Dough for a One-Crust Pie (page 241)
1 egg, lightly beaten
1 cup sour cream
1 teaspoon pure vanilla extract
1 cup (scant) sugar
2 tablespoons flour
Pinch of salt
2½ cups grated peeled Golden Delicious apples (4 medium, about 1½ pounds)
2 teaspoons lemon juice

CRUMB TOPPING

⅓ cup flour
5 tablespoons cold unsalted butter, cut into pieces
3 tablespoons sugar
1 teaspoon cinnamon

1. Roll out the pastry dough and fit it into a 9- or 9½-inch pie pan, forming a fluted edge if you like. Chill the pie shell while you prepare the filling.

2. Preheat the oven to 400° F. In a mixing bowl, stir together the egg, sour cream, and vanilla until smooth. Add the sugar, flour, and salt, mixing until blended. Stir together the grated apples and the lemon juice; stir in the sour cream mixture. Pour the filling into the pie shell and place the pie pan on a baking sheet.

3. *Crumb Topping:* In a small bowl, cut together the flour, butter, sugar, and cinnamon until crumbly. Sprinkle the mixture over the filling and bake the pie until nearly set, 40 to 45 minutes (the filling will still be somewhat wobbly in the center). Cool the pie on a wire rack and serve at room temperature.

Margaret's Apple Cake

From Margaret Stieber of Sheboygan, Wisconsin, this is one of our favorites in this collection. A moist, spicy apple cake with a crunchy nut topping, it's the kind of simple, delicious cake that has long been baked in farm kitchens. It keeps well for about three days, so you'll be able to cut yourself a thick square with a glass of cold milk, or a cup of coffee, any time you like. Margaret makes this cake with a good baking apple: Cortlands, Golden Delicious, or any early summer apples.

Serves 12 to 16

***1** cup (2 sticks) soft unsalted butter*
***1** cup sugar*
***½** cup dark brown sugar*
***2½** cups flour*
***1** teaspoon baking powder*
***1** teaspoon baking soda*
***2** teaspoons cinnamon*
***¾** teaspoon salt*
***2** eggs*
***1** cup buttermilk*
***2** cups diced peeled apple, in ½-inch chunks (4 small-medium apples, about 14 ounces)*

NUT CRUNCH TOPPING
***½** cup sugar*
***3** tablespoons flour*
***1½** teaspoons cinnamon*
***3** tablespoons cold unsalted butter, cut into bits*
***¾** cup coarsely chopped pecans, hazelnuts, or almonds*

1. Preheat the oven to 350° F. Butter a 9 x 13-inch baking pan; set aside.

2. Beat the butter until creamy; gradually add the white and brown sugars and cream the mixture until light and fluffy. Meanwhile, sift the flour, baking powder, baking soda, cinnamon, and salt onto a sheet of wax paper; set aside.

3. Add the eggs, one at a time, to the creamed butter mixture. Add the dry ingredients alternately with the buttermilk, beginning and ending with the dry ingredients. Stir in the apples just until blended; do not overmix. Pour the mixture into the prepared pan.

4. *Nut Crunch Topping:* Cut together the sugar, flour, cinnamon, and butter until crumbly. Stir in the nuts; scatter the topping over the cake batter in an even layer.

5. Bake the cake until a toothpick inserted in the center emerges clean, about 50 minutes. Cool on a wire rack, then serve directly from the pan, cut into squares.

Apple Bread Pudding

Adapted from a recipe of Merras Brown of Phoenix, Arizona, who for many years cooked and baked for weddings and other parties. Puddings that combined apples, bread, and custard were seen more often in old American recipes than they are now. This one, with a smooth custard and crisp glazed sugar topping, is another of our favorite recipes in this book.

Serves 6 to 8

2 cups crustless 1-inch bread cubes (use Italian, French, or a good white bread)
2 tablespoons unsalted butter
2 tart apples (about 12 ounces), peeled, quartered, cored, and cut in ½-inch dice (about 2 cups)
1 tablespoon plus ¾ cup sugar
6 eggs, lightly beaten
3 egg yolks
Pinch of salt
3 cups milk
1½ teaspoons pure vanilla extract
2 to 3 tablespoons confectioners' sugar

1. Preheat the oven to 350° F. Bring a kettle of water to a boil; remove from the heat and set aside.

2. Place the bread cubes on a baking sheet; toast in the preheated oven until lightly golden, about 10 minutes. Set aside.

3. Heat the butter in a wide heavy skillet over medium-high heat. Add the apples and toss until slightly softened, 2 to 3 minutes. Sprinkle with 1 tablespoon of sugar and continue tossing until lightly golden, about 2 minutes longer. Remove from heat.

4. In a mixing bowl, whisk together the ¾ cup sugar, eggs, egg yolks, salt, milk, and vanilla until smooth. Stir in the apples. Gently stir in the bread cubes; let stand until the bread is very slightly softened, about 3 minutes.

5. Place a shallow baking dish, such as an 11-inch oval gratin dish or an 8-inch square pan, into a larger baking pan. Pour the custard mixture into the baking dish; then place the pan on the center rack of the oven. Carefully pour enough hot water into the larger pan to come about halfway up the sides of the custard.

6. Bake until the custard is set but still slightly wobbly in the center, 50 to 55 minutes. Take the pan out of the oven; carefully remove the baking pan from its water bath. Cool on a wire rack to lukewarm, or refrigerate until chilled.

7. *To Serve:* Preheat the broiler. Place the bread pudding on a baking sheet; sift an even layer of confectioners' sugar over the surface of the custard. Broil until the surface is lightly caramelized (watch carefully to prevent burning), about 1 minute. Serve.

Apple–Almond Deep-Dish Pie

A single-crust pie, piled high with apples. This is a family recipe of Mrs. Harold Cozart, who lives, she tells us, with her husband "in the beautiful Chelan Valley [in the State of Washington] along 55-mile Lake Chelan, surrounded by acres and acres of apple orchards. We own 25 acres of apples and pears on Howard Flat, north of Chelan—and also are in partnership with two other couples in 40 acres of Granny Smiths along the Columbia near Orondo."

Mr. Cozart was manager of the Blue Chelan Apple Warehouse for thirty-seven years. Although he retired recently, he is still involved in the apple industry in several capacities, including serving as current chairman of the Washington Apple Commission.

"So," Mrs. Cozart concludes, "I guess you could say we *live* apples."

Serves 8

ALMOND CRUST

1½ cups flour
2 tablespoons sugar
½ teaspoon salt
¼ cup fine-ground almonds
¼ cup (½ stick) cold unsalted butter, cut into pieces
¼ cup solid vegetable shortening, chilled
⅛ teaspoon almond extract
2 tablespoons cold milk, or as needed

FILLING

8 cups sliced peeled apples (8 medium apples; about 2½ pounds)
½ cup sugar
3 tablespoons unsalted butter, cut into bits
3 tablespoons cider, applejack, or brandy
Cream (optional)

1. *Almond Crust:* In a mixing bowl or food processor, cut together the flour, sugar, salt, ground almonds, butter, and shortening until crumbled to the size of peas. Mix the almond extract with 1 tablespoon of the milk; stir this into the crumbled mixture. Add just enough additional cold milk to hold the dough together. Gather the dough into a ball; flatten into a disk, wrap in plastic, and chill at least 1 hour.

2. *Filling:* In a mixing bowl, toss together the apple slices, sugar, and butter. Transfer the mixture to a deep 9½-inch pie dish, mounding the apples in the center.

3. Preheat the oven to 425° F. Roll out the almond dough on a lightly floured surface to a neat 12-inch round. Fold the dough in half and quickly but gently transfer it to the pie dish, unfolding it over the apples. Roll the overhanging edges of the pastry up and over toward the surface, forming a thick border around the edges of the dough. Flute the edges and cut several slashes in the center of the dough.

4. Bake the pie for 15 minutes; then lower the heat to 350° F. and continue to bake until the pastry is nicely golden and the apples are tender when checked with a fork, 35 to 40 minutes longer.

5. Remove the pie from the oven. Using a funnel, pour the cider, applejack, or brandy through one of the steam vents in the pastry. Cool the pie on a wire rack; then serve warm or at room temperature in deep bowls, passing a pitcher of cream separately, if you like.

Applesauce Cake

Another recipe from Mrs. Harold Cozart. Using homemade applesauce, made with such apples as McIntosh, Spy, Rome Beauty, or Cortlands, will make the cake even better. Adding the baking soda to hot liquid is an old trick to activate the soda quickly; it still works well.

Serves 12 to 16

3 cups cake flour
½ teaspoon cinnamon
½ teaspoon freshly grated nutmeg
½ teaspoon allspice
1 cup vegetable oil
2 cups sugar
2 cups unsweetened applesauce, preferably homemade (page 184)
2 teaspoons baking soda
½ cup hot water
1 cup dark or golden raisins
1 cup chopped pitted dates
1 cup chopped walnuts or other nuts

1. Preheat the oven to 325° F. Butter and flour a 9 x 13-inch baking pan; set aside. Sift together the cake flour, cinnamon, nutmeg, and allspice onto a sheet of wax paper; set aside.

2. In a large mixing bowl or an electric mixer, combine the oil and sugar until blended. Stir in the applesauce. In a small bowl, combine the baking soda and hot water; add to the applesauce mixture.

3. Add all but ¼ cup of the sifted dry ingredients, stirring until nearly but not quite blended. Toss the raisins, dates, and nuts with the reserved flour mixture; fold gently into the batter until blended. Pour the batter into the prepared pan.

4. Bake until a toothpick inserted in the center of the cake emerges clean, 1 to 1¼ hours. Cool on a wire rack. Serve in large squares, directly from the pan.

HOMEMADE APPLESAUCE

When the farmers' market is overflowing with apples, put up a big batch of your own applesauce. Here's how:

Makes about 3 cups

- **8 tart apples, e.g. McIntosh, peeled, cored, and diced**
- **¾ cup sugar, or less to taste**
- **Juice of 1 lemon, plus more as needed**

1. In a heavy saucepan, combine the apples, sugar, and lemon juice over medium heat. Cover and cook, stirring occasionally, until the apples start to give off their juices.

2. As the apples soften, mash some of them lightly against the side of the pan. Continue to cook until the applesauce reaches the desired consistency: for chunky applesauce, cook until there are still some chunks bound with a thick puree. To use in cooking (as in Applesauce Brownies, page 186, and Applesauce Cake, page 183), cook until the apples have broken down to a puree. Add more sugar and/or lemon juice to taste.

Dutch Apple Bars

Makes 20 bars

COOKIE CRUST

- ***¾ cup (1½ sticks) unsalted butter, softened***
- ***2 tablespoons sugar***
- ***1 egg, lightly beaten***
- ***1 teaspoon pure vanilla extract***
- ***2 cups flour***
- ***¼ teaspoon salt***

FILLING

- ***10 cups sliced peeled apples (10 medium apples, 3½ to 4 pounds)***
- ***2 tablespoons lemon juice***
- ***¼ cup sugar (or slightly more, if apples are very tart)***
- ***3 tablespoons flour***
- ***1 teaspoon grated lemon zest***
- ***½ teaspoon cinnamon***

STREUSEL TOPPING

- ***1 cup flour***
- ***⅔ cup sugar***
- ***Pinch of cinnamon***
- ***½ cup (1 stick) cold unsalted butter, cut into pieces***

1. *Cookie Crust:* In an electric mixer or a mixing bowl, combine the butter, sugar, egg, and vanilla. Stir in the flour and salt just until combined; do not overmix. Press the dough into a buttered 10½ x 15½-inch jelly roll pan. Prick the dough gently with a fork and refrigerate while you prepare the filling. Preheat the oven to 400° F.

2. *Filling:* Toss the apple slices with the lemon juice in a mixing bowl. In a small bowl, combine the sugar, flour, lemon zest, and cinnamon. Add to the apples and toss to combine; set aside.

3. *Streusel Topping:* In a mixing bowl or food processor, combine the flour, sugar, cinnamon, and butter until crumbled to the size of large peas.

4. Place the apple mixture evenly over the dough. Scatter the topping over the apples. Bake until lightly golden and the apples are tender, 25 to 30 minutes. Cool on a wire rack, then trim the edges and cut into 2 x 3-inch bars.

Apple and Cheese Pizza

The old New England combination of apple and Cheddar cheese, in a new form. From Jo Ann Aamodt, this is unusual, attractive, and great for kids.

Serves 8 to 10

Basic Pastry Dough for a Two-Crust Pie (page 241)
6 ***medium apples (about 2¼ pounds), peeled, quartered, cored, and sliced ¼ inch thick***
1 ***teaspoon sugar***
¼ ***teaspoon cinnamon***
Pinch of freshly grated nutmeg

STREUSEL
⅓ ***cup flour***
2 ***tablespoons dark brown sugar***
2 ***tablespoons cold unsalted butter, cut into pieces***

8 ***ounces sharp Cheddar cheese, grated (about 3 cups, very loosely packed)***

1. Preheat the oven to 450° F. Roll out the pastry on a lightly floured surface to a large round about 13 inches in diameter and ⅛ inch thick. Trim off excess dough, forming a neat circle (chill excess dough and reserve for another use). Transfer the dough to a 12-inch pizza pan or a heavy baking sheet. Gently fold the edges of the dough over onto the surface of the circle to form a neat border.

2. Arrange the apple slices over the dough in concentric circles, overlapping them slightly. In a small cup or bowl, toss together the sugar, cinnamon, and nutmeg; sprinkle this mixture over the apples.

3. *Streusel:* In a mixing bowl or food processor, combine the flour, brown sugar, and butter until crumbled to the size of large peas. Scatter the streusel mixture over the apples.

4. Bake the pizza until the apples are lightly golden and the pastry is crisp, 20 to 25 minutes. Scatter the grated cheese over the apples and bake until the cheese just begins to melt, about 1 minute longer. Serve hot, cut into wedges.

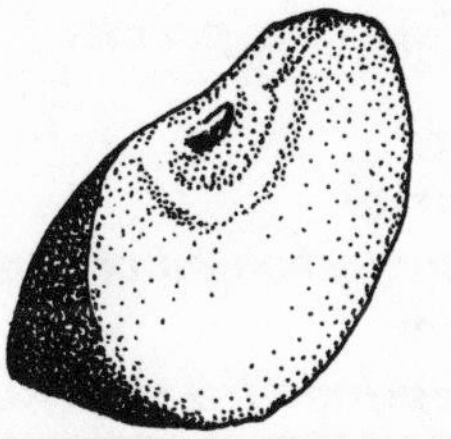

Applesauce Brownies

Cakelike brownies with a deep cocoa glaze; the applesauce keeps them nice and moist. From Jo Ann Aamodt.

Makes 16 brownies

- ***2 squares (1 ounce each) unsweetened chocolate, cut up***
- ***½ cup (1 stick) unsalted butter***
- ***1 cup sifted flour***
- ***½ teaspoon baking powder***
- ***¼ teaspoon baking soda***
- ***¼ teaspoon salt***
- ***2 eggs***
- ***1 cup sugar***
- ***⅔ cup applesauce, preferably homemade (page 184)***
- ***1 teaspoon pure vanilla extract***
- ***½ cup chopped walnuts, hazelnuts, or pecans***

COCOA GLAZE

- ***1 cup sugar***
- ***⅓ cup unsweetened cocoa powder***
- ***4 tablespoons (½ stick) unsalted butter, cut into pieces***
- ***¼ cup milk***

1. Preheat the oven to 350° F. Butter an 8-inch square baking pan; set aside. Melt the chocolate and butter in a double boiler over hot water, stirring until smooth. Remove from heat and set aside to cool slightly.

2. Resift the flour with the baking powder, baking soda, and salt; set aside.

3. In an electric mixer, beat the eggs and sugar at medium speed until light and foamy, about 5 minutes. Lower the mixer speed and add the applesauce, vanilla, and the chocolate mixture, mixing until only partially blended. Use a large rubber spatula to fold in the flour gently; quickly fold in the nuts just until the mixture is blended. Pour the batter into the prepared pan, smoothing it to the edges of the pan.

4. Bake until a toothpick inserted in the center of the brownies emerges just clean, about 35 minutes (do not overbake). Cool on a wire rack.

5. *Cocoa Glaze:* Combine the sugar, cocoa, butter, and milk in a saucepan over moderate heat, stirring until blended. Bring to a boil; boil 1 minute. Remove from heat and transfer to an electric mixer bowl. Beat the frosting until cool and thick; then spread on the cooled brownies. Cut into squares and serve directly from the pan with a tall glass of cold milk.

Sweet Apple Muffins

Try these warm, with sweet butter and apple cider jelly (page 177).

Makes 1 dozen

2¼ cups sifted flour
¾ cup sugar
2 teaspoons baking powder
1 teaspoon baking soda
¾ teaspoon salt
1 egg
1 egg yolk
¾ cup buttermilk
⅜ cup vegetable oil
1½ cups grated peeled apples (2 medium)

TOPPING

2 teaspoons sugar
¼ teaspoon cinnamon

1. Preheat the oven to 400° F. Generously butter a muffin tin and set aside.

2. Resift the flour into a large mixing bowl with the sugar, baking powder, baking soda, and salt. Make a well in the center.

3. In a smaller mixing bowl, beat together the egg, egg yolk, buttermilk, and vegetable oil until well blended. Stir in the grated apples; pour the mixture into the well in the dry ingredients.

4. With a large wooden spoon, combine the ingredients just until thoroughly moistened (the mixture will still be lumpy; do not overmix). Spoon the batter into the muffin tins; they should be quite full.

5. *Topping:* Stir together the sugar and cinnamon; sprinkle this over the batter.

6. Bake until the muffins have risen and are golden brown, about 25 minutes. Turn out onto a wire rack and serve warm.

Puree of Root Vegetables and Apples, page 54
Sweet Potato and Apple "Pancake," page 128
Apple Upside-Down Corn Bread, page 153
Dried Apple "Pour-Through" Pie, page 170
Spiced Pear Butter, page 229
(Substitute an equal weight of apples for the pears.)
Fresh Pear Cake, page 225
(Substitute an equal weight of apples for the pears.)
Edna Lewis's Peach Chutney, page 218
(Substitute an equal weight of apples for the peaches)
Preserved Spiced Seckel Pears, page 230
(Substitute Lady apples for the pears.)
Pear Crisp with Vanilla Custard Sauce, page 227
(Substitute an equal weight of apples for the pears.)

BERRIES

We've both traveled to the Pacific Northwest, and were amazed by the berries there. Not only are they growing along the side of the road, in empty parking lots, and everywhere else you look, but there are varieties most of us have never seen. Besides the raspberries, blackberries, and strawberries that we know well, there are also juicy huckleberries, marionberries, olallieberries and even golden raspberries.

At Seattle's Pike Place Market, we saw entire flats of beautiful berries on sale for not much more than the cost of a single pint in expensive shops back East, and were frustrated for lack of a kitchen —the raspberries were just crying out to be made into jam. (Since that time, we've tried some canned blackberries and boysenberries from Oregon Fruit Products in Salem, Oregon, that were surprisingly fresh tasting. While there's no real substitute for fresh, these products are a good out-of-season alternative.)

We recently spoke to Doug Miller of Cascade Conserves in Portland, Oregon, a fourth-generation berry wholesaler who produces remarkable jams and conserves with all the varieties of fresh berries that are available in the Northwest. Doug works closely with berry growers in the area, and told us a great deal about the different varieties available:

> *One interesting thing about berries in the Northwest is the volcanic ash that came from Mount St. Helens when it erupted in 1980. A lot of growers find that the ash enriched the soil, and that the berries are not only larger, but seem to have more flavor. Of course, many growers would disagree—especially the ones whose berries are* not *grown in volcanic ash. . . .*
>
> *There's some confusion about what is a wild berry. The most common are the Evergreen and the Himalaya blackberries—they grow everywhere. The Evergreen are smaller, with more seeds. And the Himalayas have larger sections, big and plump, very, very juicy, with less seeds. A lot of large jam manufacturers will use both of these blackberry varieties, and they make good pies. They're so abundant along the sides of the roads that they're almost considered a nuisance, a weed. But they're very good, and tasty.*
>
> *Technically, these varieties are real wild blackberries. But when people here say "wild blackberries," they usually mean the smaller wild mountain blackberries. Those make* great *pies and jam.*
>
> *It's difficult to find these berries—there's a lot of hiking involved. Usually, people who find a patch will guard it jealously, just like people who know a place to gather morels.*
>
> *We've got some obscure and unknown varieties of berries here in the Willamette Valley. Like Chehalem and Cascade blackberries. The Cascade might be my favorite—it tastes like a wild mountain blackberry. We've got*

boysenberries, loganberries, and nectarberries. Those are similar to boysenberries, but a bit larger, and a little juicier, without losing their full flavor.

Marionberries were developed as a crossbreed of blackberries and loganberries. Anybody who likes wild blackberries is in love with the marionberries. They have such great flavor—intense, with a slightly tart acid base. They make great pies, and make one of our most popular jams.

And olallieberries—they're also similar to boysenberries. They were developed at Oregon State, as an answer to California growers who wanted to grow boysenberries, which were difficult because of the warm climate. They work well there.

With berries, the variety is extremely important. And the climate is important, too. For strawberries, you need mostly cool temperature. They really need a lot of overcast days, so they don't get red too fast. Then, just when they're ready, they need sun. They get ready very quickly, and you have to pick them right away, or they'll go bad.

Marshall strawberries have become just about extinct. They're softer than most, so some people aren't crazy about them, but they have excellent flavor. They're the ones we use in our strawberry jam, as much as we can. Also, Hood strawberries have very good flavor, and are a little bit firmer. Rainier and Shukson strawberries are more prominent varieties. They're large and beautiful, but in my opinion, their flavor doesn't measure up.

The raspberries flourish in June and July. The Willamette raspberries are the tastiest. They were James Beard's favorite [Beard was a Portland native], and they're mine, too.

We've got quite a few black raspberries here, too; they're real popular. They're called Black Caps, because they're as small as little thimbles. In the past, the U.S. Government bought most of them; they found they could use the juice as ink, to stamp meat. It had a good red color, and was edible. They bought so many of them that they kept them out of the market, because the price, in the early '70s, was about twice as much as other berries. But now, the price of the black raspberries has come down. They're extremely delicious.

The Golden raspberries, which are sometimes called Golden Queen raspberries, look just like raspberries, but have a pale gold color. They're similar to cloudberries in Scandinavia, and they're sometimes called that, too. We'll be making them into jam this summer.

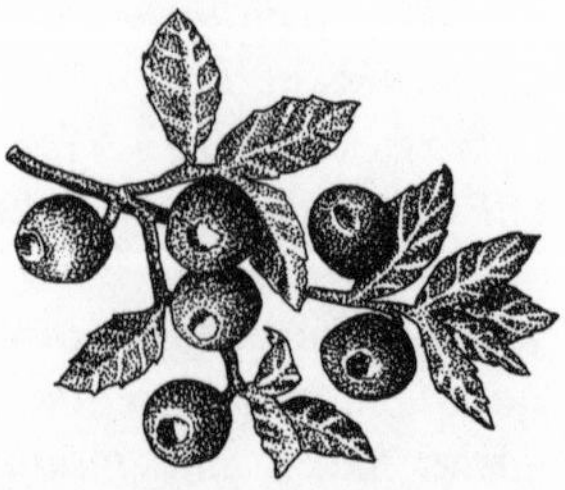

Double Blueberry Tart

A nice change from the all-American berry pie. The combination of cooked and raw fresh berries, piled high in a buttery pastry shell, gives this tart an interesting play of contrasting textures. The same procedure can be used with blackberries, boysenberries, huckleberries, raspberries, marionberries, or a combination.

Serves 8

Rich Tart Pastry Dough (page 240), or Basic Pastry Dough for a One-Crust Pie (page 241)
3 ***pints fresh blueberries, picked over***
1/4 ***cup cold water***
2/3 ***cup sugar, or less if the berries are very sweet***
3 ***tablespoons cornstarch***
1/2 ***teaspoon ground cinnamon***
1 ***lemon***
Small pinch of freshly ground black pepper (optional)
Lightly sweetened whipped cream, flavored with vanilla

1. Roll out the pastry dough on a lightly floured surface. Fit it loosely into a 9-inch tart pan with a removable bottom; trim excess dough. Form a high border and flute the edge. Chill the pastry dough for 30 minutes.

2. *Baking the Pastry Shell:* Preheat the oven to 400°F. Line the pastry dough with a sheet of aluminum foil; weight the foil with rice or dried beans. Place the tart pan on a heavy baking sheet and bake until the sides have set, 8 to 10 minutes. Carefully remove the foil and rice and continue to bake the pastry shell until the pastry is golden and baked through, 10 to 13 minutes longer. Prick any air bubbles gently with a fork as the pastry bakes. Remove the shell from the oven and cool on a wire rack.

3. Place about 2 cups of the blueberries in a heavy saucepan with the cold water. Bring to a boil, covered. Meanwhile, in a small bowl, use a fork to stir together the sugar, cornstarch, and cinnamon. Use a zester or vegetable peeler to remove the zest from the lemon; reserve a few long, thin strands of zest for garnish. Finely chop the remaining zest and add it to the sugar mixture. Juice the lemon; stir it into the sugar mixture, and add this mixture to the boiling berries. Boil, uncovered, stirring constantly, until thickened. (Adding a hint of pepper is a nice touch.) Remove from heat, place a sheet of plastic wrap or wax paper on the surface, and cool completely, stirring occasionally.

4. Set aside about 1 cup of the nicest remaining blueberries. Stir the remaining raw berries into the cooled cooked berry mixture. Shortly before serving, pile the blueberry mixture into the cooled pastry shell, mounding it carefully. Top with an even layer of reserved raw blueberries and garnish with a few strands of lemon zest. Chill, if not serving immediately.

5. Remove the tart from the rim of the pan. To serve, top each slice with a large dollop of lightly whipped cream, and pass the remaining cream separately.

Black and Blue Compote

A berry-studded sauce for waffles, pancakes, ice cream, or custards, rich with fresh fruit flavor. It's also delicious stirred into yogurt. This is from Clarissa Metzler Cross of Canter-Berry Farms in Auburn, Washington.

Makes about 4½ cups

***3** cups blueberries, picked over*
***3** cups blackberries (or boysenberries), picked over*
***1** cup plus 2 tablespoons cold water*
***1½** cups brown sugar*
***1** cup granulated sugar*
***½** cup light corn syrup*
***¼** teaspoon salt*
***1** tablespoon cornstarch*
Fresh lemon juice

1. Place the blueberries, blackberries, and 1 cup cold water in a heavy saucepan. Cover and bring to a boil. Lower the heat and simmer, covered, until the berries are softened slightly, 5 to 10 minutes.

2. Uncover and add the brown and white sugars, corn syrup, and salt. Return the mixture to a boil. Meanwhile, in a cup or small bowl, stir together the cornstarch and 2 tablespoons cold water until smooth. Add this mixture to the saucepan, stirring.

3. Simmer until the compote has lightly thickened and the berries are tender, about 5 minutes longer. Remove from heat. When the compote has cooled slightly, add lemon juice to taste. Serve warm or cold.

Sugarless Blueberry Muffins

This recipe is from Mary Ann Guender of the New Jersey Department of Agriculture. With thanks to the North American Blueberry Council.

Makes 1 dozen

***1¾** cups flour*
***2** teaspoons baking powder*
***½** teaspoon baking soda*
***½** teaspoon ground allspice*
***¼** teaspoon cinnamon*
***¼** teaspoon freshly grated nutmeg*
***¼** teaspoon salt*
***1** generous cup blueberries, picked over*
***2** eggs, lightly beaten*
***¼** cup vegetable oil*
***¾** cup orange juice*
Grated zest of 1 orange

1. Preheat the oven to 400° F. Sift the flour, baking powder, baking soda, allspice, cinnamon, nutmeg, and salt into a mixing bowl. Toss the blueberries with about 2 tablespoons of the dry mixture; set aside.

2. In a separate bowl, combine the eggs, oil, orange juice, and orange zest until blended. Make a well in the dry ingredients; pour in the egg mixture. Combine the ingredients gently with a wooden spoon. When only partially combined, add the blueberries. Fold the ingredients together just until moistened but still lumpy; do not overmix.

3. Pour the batter into well-buttered muffin tins, filling them three-quarters full. Bake until risen and lightly golden, 20 to 25 minutes. Cool briefly on a wire rack, remove from tins, then serve warm, with sweet butter.

Lucretia's Blueberry Coffee Cake

From Canter-Berry Farms, a tender sour cream cake packed with juicy berries. Try this for a summer breakfast—eat outdoors, if possible.

Serves 15

2 cups flour
2 teaspoons baking powder
1 teaspoon baking soda
1/4 teaspoon salt
1/2 cup (1 stick) unsalted butter, softened
1/2 cup sugar
2 eggs
1 teaspoon pure vanilla extract
3/4 cup sour cream

TOPPING
3/4 cup light brown sugar
2 tablespoons flour
Pinch of salt
2 tablespoons cold unsalted butter, cut into pieces
2 cups blueberries, picked over
Grated zest of 1 lemon

1. Preheat the oven to 375° F. Butter a 9 x 13-inch baking pan; set aside.

2. Sift onto a sheet of wax paper the flour, baking powder, baking soda, and salt; set aside. In an electric mixer, cream together the butter and sugar at medium speed until light and fluffy. Add the eggs one at a time, beating until well incorporated. Stir in the vanilla. Lower the mixer speed and add the dry ingredients alternately with the sour cream, beginning and ending with the dry mixture. Do not overmix. Scrape the batter into the prepared pan, smoothing it with a spatula.

3. *Topping:* In a small bowl, cut together the brown sugar, flour, salt, and butter until crumbly. Add the blueberries and lemon zest and toss gently. Scatter the mixture over the batter.

4. Bake until the cake pulls away from the sides of the pan and a toothpick inserted in the center of the cake emerges clean, about 30 minutes. Cool on a wire rack, then serve directly from the pan, cut into large rectangles.

Virginia Blackberry Roll

A buttermilk biscuit dough is wrapped around a juicy fruit filling in a loaf pan, then decorated with pastry cutouts and baked until golden. This is an old family recipe from Eileen Proctor Rowe, who tells us:

> *I have also seen this made in a square pan, or in little packets, but these are not official "rolls." My mother always made hers in the "roll" style. She had had them as a child in Goochland County, Virginia. We only had this old-fashioned dessert a few times each summer, so they were special. People who knew we loved blackberries would bring us some, or tell us where the good picking was.*
>
> *Now I am fortunate to have a good supply in a vacant lot next to a shopping mall nearby. My 6-year-old daughter and I go early in the morning or at dusk to pick berries, wearing our bandanas and long sleeves so as to avoid ticks and chiggers.*

Serves 8

BERRIES

- ***1/2 to 2/3 cup sugar (depending on sweetness of berries)***
- ***3 tablespoons quick-cooking tapioca***
- ***Pinch of salt***
- ***4 cups blackberries, picked over to remove stems and unripe fruit***
- ***Juice of 1/2 lemon***

BUTTERMILK BISCUIT DOUGH

- ***3 cups flour***
- ***3 tablespoons sugar***
- ***1 tablespoon baking powder***
- ***1 1/2 teaspoons baking soda***
- ***Pinch of salt***
- ***1/2 cup (1 stick) chilled unsalted butter, cut into pieces***
- ***3/4 cup buttermilk, or more as needed***

GLAZE

- ***1 egg lightly beaten with***
- ***2 teaspoons milk or cream***

Sugar
Vanilla ice cream

1. *Berries:* Stir together the sugar, tapioca, and salt in a mixing bowl. Add the berries and lemon juice and toss to combine. Set aside.

2. *Buttermilk Biscuit Dough:* Place the flour, sugar, baking powder, baking soda, and salt in a food processor and pulse on and off briefly to blend. Add the butter and pulse briefly, just until crumbly. With the machine running, add the buttermilk, just until the dough almost comes together. The dough should be quite soft; if it is still dry, add another tablespoon or two of buttermilk.

3. Transfer the dough to a large sheet of floured wax paper and gently knead once or twice to blend the ingredients. Gently pat or roll the dough into a rectangle about 11 x 14 inches. Neatly trim and reserve the edges of the dough.

4. Generously butter a loaf pan, preferably a Pyrex pan about 4 1/2 x 9 1/2 inches. Very gently invert the sheet of wax paper over the pan, flipping the dough into the pan. The dough should cover the bottom and two long sides of the pan with a slight overhang, and

come just to the top of the short sides. Cut off and set aside any excess dough, leaving an overhang on the long sides; repair any tears in the dough by pressing together gently.

5. Preheat the oven to 400° F., with a rack in the center of the oven, and a sheet of foil underneath to catch any running juices.

6. Pour the berry mixture into the dough-lined pan. Carefully fold one long side of the dough over the fruit. Gently brush a thin layer of the egg and milk glaze over the folded surface of the dough. Gently fold the other long side of dough onto the glazed surface, pressing lightly to seal, and tuck the short ends of the dough onto the surface. Glaze the dough. Cut attractive shapes from the reserved dough (flowers, leaves, and a stem; fruit shapes, diamonds, or other geometric shapes) and lay them on the surface. Glaze the pastry cutouts.

7. Bake until the roll is nearly golden, 50 to 60 minutes; then sprinkle the top with sugar and bake 10 minutes longer. Cool on a rack. Serve warm directly from the pan, cutting the roll into slices and spooning up the berries. Top each serving with vanilla ice cream.

FREEZING WHOLE BERRIES

Raspberries, blueberries, blackberries, and hulled strawberries can be frozen successfully. Here's how:

- ***Place the berries (wash only if necessary) on a baking sheet one layer deep and spaced slightly apart. Place in the freezer.***
- ***When the berries are firm, gently gather them into plastic bags or containers, seal tight, pressing out all air, label and date.***
- ***Store frozen, up to six months.***

Blackberry Dumplin's

An old southern recipe from Merras Brown.

Serves 8

TOPPING

- **½** ***cup (1 stick) unsalted butter, softened***
- **½** ***cup sifted confectioners' sugar***
- **2** ***egg yolks***
- **2½** ***cups sifted flour***
- **2** ***tablespoons ice water***

BLACKBERRIES

- **4** ***cups blackberries, picked over to remove stems and unripe fruit***
- **½** ***cup dark brown sugar***
- **½** ***cup sugar***
- **½** ***teaspoon salt***
- **¼** ***teaspoon freshly grated nutmeg***
- ***Juice of ½ lemon***
- **3½** ***cups water***
- **3** ***tablespoons rum***
- **4** ***tablespoons (½ stick) unsalted butter***

Cream, for serving

1. *Topping:* In a mixing bowl or electric mixer, beat the butter briefly at medium speed, then add the sugar and beat until fluffy. Add the egg yolks one at a time, then lower the mixer speed and add the flour alternately with the water. Gather the dough into a ball, wrap in plastic, and chill at least 30 minutes.

2. *Blackberries:* Place 1 cup of the blackberries in a large kettle with the sugars, salt, nutmeg, lemon juice, and water. Bring to a boil, covered. Cook over medium heat for 20 minutes. Remove from heat and stir in the rum, butter, and remaining 3 cups of blackberries. Set aside.

3. Roll out the chilled dough to a rectangle about 12 inches long and ⅛ inch thick. Cut the dough into strips 2 inches wide; then cut the strips crosswise into 3-inch lengths. Return the berries to the boil, covered; uncover the kettle and boil for 10 minutes. Carefully drop the pieces of the dough onto the berries, using two forks to keep the pieces of dough separated (they will come together slightly; that's fine).

4. When all of the pieces of dough are in, cover the kettle and lower the heat to medium-low. Cook until the dough is set, 12 to 15 minutes. Cool slightly, then serve warm in bowls, passing a pitcher of cream at the table.

Individual Berry Shortcakes with Buttermilk Almond Biscuits

These biscuits are especially light. At one time, all American shortcakes were made with freshly baked biscuits. The spongecake variation was a later development.

For a real treat, try these shortcakes with a combination of strawberries and raspberries.

Serves 6

2 pints (generous) ripe fresh strawberries, picked over, hulled, and sliced
1/2 cup sugar (or to taste, depending on sweetness of berries)

BUTTERMILK ALMOND BISCUITS
2 1/4 cups flour
1/2 cup plus 1 tablespoon sugar
1 1/2 teaspoons baking powder
3/4 teaspoon baking soda
1/4 teaspoon salt
6 tablespoons (3/4 stick) cold unsalted butter, cut into pieces
2/3 to 1 cup buttermilk, as needed
1 egg yolk
1/2 teaspoon pure vanilla extract
1/8 teaspoon almond extract
Milk or cream
1/3 cup sliced almonds

---

1 1/4 cups heavy cream
1 teaspoon vanilla extract

1. Place the sliced berries in a large mixing bowl and toss with the ½ cup sugar. Use the back of a large wooden spoon to crush some of the berries into the sugar. Let stand at room temperature at least 1 hour, stirring occasionally, until the berries have formed a light natural syrup. Chill.

2. *Buttermilk Almond Biscuits:* Preheat the oven to 425° F. Place the flour, ½ cup sugar, baking powder, baking soda, and salt in a food processor and pulse briefly to combine the ingredients. Add the butter and pulse briefly until the mixture is crumbly. Place ⅔ cup buttermilk in a measuring cup; stir in the egg yolk and vanilla and almond extracts. With the processor running, add buttermilk mixture and turn off the machine. Add enough extra buttermilk, blending briefly after each addition, to form a sticky but manageable dough. Transfer the dough to a floured sheet of wax paper; do not overhandle.

3. Sprinkle the dough with flour. With your fingertips, gently pat the dough to an even thickness of about ¾ inch. Use a 3- or 3¼-inch fluted round biscuit cutter to cut out biscuits and transfer them gently to a buttered baking sheet (do not use a black steel sheet). Gather together scraps of dough and cut remaining biscuits. With your fingers or a pastry brush, brush tops of biscuits with a light coating of milk or cream. Scatter the sliced almonds over the tops, then sprinkle with the remaining tablespoon of sugar.

4. Bake the biscuits until lightly golden, 11 to 14 minutes (watch carefully as timing can vary; do not overbake). Transfer biscuits to a wire rack and cool for about 2 minutes. Using a serrated knife and a gentle sawing motion, slice them in half horizontally.

5. Whip the cream with the vanilla (adding a little sugar if you like) until nearly, but not quite stiff. Place the bottoms of the biscuits on serving plates. Spoon berries generously over the biscuits, dividing them evenly and spooning the juices over. Spoon some of the whipped cream over the berries; then replace the biscuit tops. Serve immediately, passing the remaining whipped cream separately.

COOK'S TIP: BRINGING OUT THE FLAVOR OF RIPE STRAWBERRIES

Get the most flavor out of ripe berries with a light natural syrup, whether they're to be served on their own or over ice cream, shortcake, etc. Here's how:

- *Toss hulled fresh strawberries, whole, sliced, or cut up, in a small amount of sugar.*
- *Let them stand at room temperature for 1 hour, tossing them from time to time. The berries will soften slightly, and give off their own natural syrup, with lots of ripe berry flavor.*

Note: This method also works well with raspberries or other soft berries, or with soft fruits such as peaches or nectarines.

Double-Berry Sauce

Try this berry puree studded with whole raspberries over ice cream, melon, or a slice of plain cake.

Makes about 2 generous cups

1 pint ripe strawberries, picked over and hulled
1 pint ripe raspberries, picked over
Superfine sugar, if needed
Few drops of fresh lemon juice
1 to 2 tablespoons crème de cassis or strawberry or raspberry brandy or liqueur (optional)

1. Puree the strawberries and slightly less than half the raspberries in a food processor until smooth. Strain the puree through a fine sieve to eliminate the seeds.

2. Flavor to taste with sugar, if needed, lemon juice, and crème de cassis or fruit brandy. Stir in the reserved whole raspberries and chill. This will keep, refrigerated, three to five days.

Sandy's Warm Three-Berry Surprise

A combination of ripe fresh berries, bathed in a warm sauce of caramel, cream, and vanilla. You can use any combination of available berries.

Serves 4 to 6

1/3 cup sugar
1/4 cup water
1 1/2 cups heavy cream
1/2 vanilla bean, split lengthwise
1/2 pint ripe raspberries, picked over, at room temperature
1/2 pint ripe blueberries, picked over, at room temperature
1/2 pint ripe hulled strawberries or blackberries, picked over, at room temperature

1. Place the sugar and water in a small heavy saucepan over medium heat. Cover and cook, stirring, until the sugar dissolves. Meanwhile, bring the

cream and the vanilla bean to a boil in a separate pan; remove from heat. Remove the vanilla bean. With a small knife, scrape the vanilla seeds from the bean into the cream. Set aside.

2. When the sugar has dissolved, uncover the pan, raise the heat slightly, and bring the syrup to a boil. Boil, without stirring, until the syrup turns a medium amber color.

3. Remove the caramel from the heat. Working carefully, immediately add the hot cream to the caramel, swirling the pan to combine (the mixture will sputter violently). Return the pan to medium heat and boil, uncovered, until the sauce has reached a light napping consistency (it will coat the back of a spoon evenly).

4. Toss the berries into the sauce, stirring gently to coat. Serve immediately.

Quick Raspberry Ice

No ice cream freezer needed for this intensely flavored ice.

1½ pints ripe fresh raspberries, picked over (or two 10- or 12-ounce packages partially thawed frozen raspberries, drained if in syrup)
⅔ cup superfine sugar, or to taste
3 to 4 tablespoons raspberry liqueur or brandy, plus more for serving (optional)

1. Puree the raspberries in a food processor with the sugar and liqueur, adding more sugar or liqueur to taste. Strain to eliminate seeds. Transfer the puree to a shallow pan or freezer tray and place in the freezer compartment of the refrigerator.

2. Freeze until firm around the edges but not quite set in the center, 1 to 1½ hours. Stir the mixture vigorously with a wooden spoon, combining firm and slushy portions. (If the mixture has frozen until solid, cut it into small cubes and process in a food processor until smooth and slushy.) Return the mixture to the pan and freeze again until nearly firm, 1 to 1½ hours longer.

3. The ice is now ready to serve. If you like, drizzle a little more raspberry liqueur over each serving.

Note: If you prepare this ice in advance and it freezes until quite solid, cut it up and process again in a food processor until slushy.

Peach Right-Side-Up Cake, page 215
(Substitute 1 pint blueberries for the peaches.)
M. J.'s Nectarine-Blueberry Cobbler, page 216

...AND SERVE WITH A GALLON OF WHIPPED CREAM.

In 1855, Seth Boyden, an inventive New Jersey man, developed strawberries that grew up to nine inches in diameter! (He had earlier perfected America's first patent leather and its first malleable iron, we learned in John Cunningham's entertaining booklet, "New Jersey's Rich Harvest.") Boyden vowed in 1868 that if he could live another twenty years, he could promise strawberries "as big as pineapples." Since he died eighteen years later, we'll never know. . . .

CHERRIES

Queen Anne cherries, pale yellow flecked with red, and reddish-purple Bing cherries are both sweet and best eaten out of hand, though they are frequently baked in cherry pies.

For a really special cherry pie, we prefer sour Morello cherries, which are smaller, slightly softer, and pale reddish rather than purple. They also have a higher water content than the sweet varieties.

If you cook cherries with any frequency, you might want to invest in a cherry pitter, an inexpensive little hand tool that does the job just right.

BASIC METHOD FOR PRESERVING CHERRIES

This method will enable you to have cherries on hand for all sorts of out-of-season uses: pies, cobblers, sauces for ice cream, etc. Blanched sliced peaches or nectarines, currants, and other fruits can also be preserved this way.

Fresh cherries, pits and stems removed (reserve a few pits)
Sugar Syrup (see box page 202) allowing about ⅔ cup for each pint of fruit
Vanilla beans, split lengthwise, and cut into pieces

1. Sterilize as many canning jars as you need. Place the cherries in the jars. Place a few cherry pits and a piece of vanilla bean in each jar.

2. Prepare the sugar syrup, making sure the sugar is completely dissolved. Bring the syrup to a boil and pour it over the cherries, leaving ⅛-inch headspace. Seal the tops with canning lids and screw bands; process in a boiling water bath for 20 minutes.

Sour Cherry Custard Pie

Adapted from a recipe from Alice Signey in Algona, Washington.

Serves 8

Basic Pastry Dough for a One-Crust Pie (page 241)
- 2 ***eggs***
- 1 ***egg yolk***
- ½ ***cup sugar***
- ¾ ***cup milk***
- ¼ ***cup heavy cream***
- ½ ***teaspoon pure vanilla extract***

Large pinch of freshly grated nutmeg
- 2 ***cups pitted sour cherries, preferably fresh***

1. Preheat the oven to 350° F. Roll out the pastry dough and fit it into a 9- or 9½-inch pie pan, forming a fluted edge if you like. Chill the pie shell while you prepare the filling.

2. In a mixing bowl, whisk together the eggs, egg yolk, sugar, milk, cream, vanilla, and nutmeg until smooth. Place the cherries in the pie shell; pour the custard over. Place the pie on a baking sheet and bake until the custard has set in the center, 35 to 45 minutes. Cool on a wire rack, then serve at cool room temperature.

Cherry Batter Pudding

A puffy pancake, made in minutes—delicious for breakfast. This can also be prepared with apples, plums, blueberries, or prunes soaked in brandy. Be sure to use one of the pan sizes specified.

Serves 6

1 ***cup pitted fresh cherries***
3 ***tablespoons brandy (optional)***
1/2 ***cup flour***
1 ***tablespoon sugar***
Pinch of salt
3 ***eggs***
1/2 ***cup milk***
1/2 ***teaspoon pure vanilla extract***
3 ***tablespoons unsalted butter***
Confectioners' sugar
Sour cream

1. If you are using the brandy, soak the cherries in brandy for 15 minutes or longer.

2. Preheat the oven to 425° F. Sift the flour, sugar, and salt into a mixing bowl. Add the eggs and whisk until smooth. Add the milk and vanilla, whisking until well blended. Stir in the cherries and brandy.

3. Place the butter in a heavy 12-inch straight-sided ovenproof skillet (or a 9 x 13-inch straight-sided metal baking pan). Place the pan in the preheated oven until the butter is sizzling but not brown, about 3 minutes. Pour in the batter, distributing the cherries evenly, and bake until the pudding is puffed and golden brown, about 20 minutes. Sprinkle with confectioners' sugar and serve hot, with a spoonful of sour cream, if you like.

Peach Right-Side-Up Cake, page 215
(Substitute an equal weight of pitted cherries for the peaches.)

BASIC SUGAR SYRUP FOR PRESERVING FRUITS

Many fruits can be preserved in sugar syrup, so you can enjoy their fresh flavors all year round. For each pint of preserved fruit, you'll need about 2/3 cup syrup. Here is a basic light syrup:

Makes about 5 cups

4 cups cold water
2 cups sugar

1. Heat the cold water and sugar (you can make any amount you like, as long as you preserve the ratio of 2 to 1) in a saucepan over medium heat, stirring to dissolve the sugar.

2. Bring to a boil; then remove from heat. For preserving, use when boiling hot.

Note: ***If you like, you can flavor the syrup with a vanilla bean, split lengthwise, lemon or orange zest, brandy liqueurs, spices, etc.***

CURRANTS

In most parts of the country, fresh currants are pretty hard to find. Most often you will encounter "dried currants," which look like tiny raisins, and are actually just that—a dried small grape called the Zante currant. (The name is a linguistic oddity derived from the fruit's French name, *raisins de Corinth,* which was elided and translated as "currant.")

When you do find currants, they're likely to be red ones; though rare, we have seen them in supermarkets in the Midwest. There are also white currants, a pale golden variety that is botanically related to the red, minus the pigment, and sweeter and even more rare. Black currants are the basis of *crème de cassis* (the liqueur that's added to white wine to make the before-dinner drink called a *kir*). For many years, currants (especially black ones) have not been grown in several areas of this country because their roots can serve as a host to a parasitic fungus that causes white-pine blister rust. Black currants and wild gooseberries, it seems, are the preferred hosts for this fungus; though they can survive infestation quite well, neighboring pine trees are destroyed. This blister rust was first introduced here from Europe in about 1900; since then, state laws vary—many outlaw growing black currants entirely, while others require special permits.

However, Doug Miller, who provided us with so much information on berries (page 189), explains that "there's a new variety of black currant being grown here in Oregon, up near Seattle, and all along the Willamette Valley. They have a wonderful flavor, but the only problem is that birds like them, too. You can't keep them away—the birds get right through the holes in the wire netting used to protect the bushes. There have been some red currants around this area, too, but not a lot, until recently."

Currant Sauce for Poultry or Game

Try this with chicken, Cornish hen, squab or pheasant, or even pork chops.

Makes about 1 cup

- ***2** cups Chicken Broth (page 239), or other poultry broth*
- ***2** tablespoons currant jelly, preferably homemade (recipe this page)*
- ***1/3** cup fresh currants, topped and tailed*
- ***Few drops of wine vinegar***
- ***Freshly ground pepper***
- ***2** tablespoons cold unsalted butter, cut into bits*

1. Boil the broth in a heavy saucepan, uncovered, until reduced by about half. (If you wish to serve this sauce with a roast chicken or other bird, you can remove the bird from the roasting pan and add the broth directly to the pan, stirring to scrape up all browned bits. Strain into a saucepan, degrease, and reduce by half.)

2. Stir in the currant jelly until melted. Add the currants and simmer for about 1 minute. Add a few drops of vinegar and some pepper to taste; remove the sauce from the heat.

3. Swirl in the butter, a few pieces at a time, until the sauce is smooth. Serve immediately.

Red Currant Jelly

Makes about 3 half-pints

- ***2** quarts ripe fresh red currants, washed and rinsed*
- ***3 1/3** cups sugar*
- ***Zest of 1 orange, removed in thin strips with a vegetable peeler***
- ***12** black peppercorns*
- ***Pinch of salt, if needed***

1. Place the currants (with their stems), sugar, orange zest, and peppercorns in a large pot. Bring the mixture to a boil, stirring. Lower the heat and simmer, uncovered, for 15 minutes. Skim all possible scum from the surface as the mixture simmers.

2. Remove from the heat and strain the mixture into a bowl, pressing the currants to extract all the juice. Test to see if the mixture has jelled by freezing a spoonful on a saucer (page 178). If the jelly is too loose, return it to the pot and boil, uncovered, until it reaches the setting point.

3. Refrigerate, tightly sealed, for up to three months. If you'd like to can the jelly, pour it while hot into sterilized jars, top with canning lids and screw bands, and process in a boiling water bath for 10 minutes. Keeps for one year.

Plum Cordial, page 220
(For a currant cordial, substitute an equal weight of topped and tailed currants for the plums.)

GRAPES

Grape varieties are, of course, a subject unto themselves. What we find interesting is not only that wine is now being produced in many new areas of the country, but that these wines are now appearing at farmers' markets. Most vendors will be happy to offer you a taste, which—in most cases—will add to the happy market atmosphere. What's also interesting are the new varietal grape juices.

Of the table grape varieties now available, we're partial to the new flame seedless—they're red, with a slightly tart, crisp flavor, and are best just eaten out of hand. But for something completely different, try the recipe on the next page.

DID YOU KNOW....

- ***That Concord grapes are one of the few fruits native to North America? Other familiar ones include cranberries and blueberries.***
- ***That grapes rank fifth in fruit consumption in United States households, after apples, bananas, oranges, and grapefruit?***

Margaret's Special Grape Pie

Ever hear of a grape pie? You'll be surprised at how well it works—juicy and delicious, with a texture that may remind you of a fresh cherry pie, but with a deep flavor all its own. This is from Margaret Zaninovich, who grows grapes in Delano, California. Margaret tells us that she makes this pie with jet-black Ribier grapes, and that it freezes well.

Serves 8

Basic Pastry Dough for a Two-Crust Pie (page 241)
5 cups Ribier, Concord, or seedless red grapes, stemmed (1 pound 10 ounces)
1 tablespoon lemon juice
1 cup sugar, plus more as needed
3 tablespoons cornstarch
½ teaspoon ground cinnamon
¼ teaspoon salt
2 tablespoons unsalted butter, cut into pieces
Milk as needed

Vanilla ice cream, if desired

1. On a lightly floured surface, roll out slightly more than half the pastry to a large circle ⅛ inch thick. Transfer it to a 9-inch pie dish. Roll the remaining pastry to a large circle and transfer it to a foil-lined baking sheet. Chill the pastry.

2. Preheat the oven to 425° F. If using Ribier or Concord grapes (or other grapes with seeds), halve them and remove the seeds. Place the grapes in a food processor in three batches and pulse just until very coarsely chopped. Transfer the grapes to a colander and drain off excess juice. Place drained grapes in a large mixing bowl and stir in the lemon juice.

3. In a small bowl, stir together the sugar, cornstarch, cinnamon, and salt with a fork. Add the mixture to the grapes, tossing to combine. Transfer the grape mixture to the pie dish; dot with butter. Moisten the edge of the crust with cold water, then lay the top crust over loosely. Trim off excess pastry, leaving a ¾-inch overhang; reserve the trimmings. Turn the edges under the pastry, forming a smooth border on the rim of the pie plate. Crimp or flute the border.

4. Using a small knife or a leaf-shape cookie cutter, cut 6 leaf shapes from the pastry scraps. With the dull edge of a knife, lightly imprint leaf veins. Brush the pie lightly with milk; arrange the pastry leaves on the surface, arching them slightly. Cut several steam vents. Sprinkle the pie lightly with sugar and place it on the baking sheet. Bake until golden brown and the juices are bubbly, 35 to 40 minutes. Cool on a wire rack, then serve warm or at room temperature, preferably with vanilla ice cream.

The form of cranberry most people are familiar with is cranberry sauce—and even that's almost always canned. But with their distinctive, tart flavor, cranberries can be used for so much more—jelly, juices and cocktails (page 210), as a glaze for roast poultry (page 210), and more. And when sweetened, cranberries lend delectable flavor to desserts, too (be sure to try the cranberry tart, page 212).

Native to North America, cranberries were first harvested by the Algonquin Indians, who used them not only as food, but as medicine and as a symbol of peace at tribal feasts. Today, Massachusetts is the largest cranberry-producing state, followed by Wisconsin and New Jersey. They are also harvested along the Washington coast and up into Oregon.

Each fall, food writer Mary Goodbody told us, cranberry bogs are harvested by two methods. For the dry harvest method, picking machines are pushed over the bog, scooping up the berries into burlap sacks. Dry-harvested cranberries are sold fresh as whole berries or are used to make whole-berry sauce. For wet-harvested cranberries, the bogs are flooded, machines knock the berries off the vine, and a pump collects them as they float to the surface. The berries are then rinsed of stems and leaves. Wet-harvested cranberries are used for juices and cranberry sauce.

Monique's Cranberry Sauce with Whiskey

From Monique Riechelman, a cooking teacher in New Jersey.

Makes 3 cups

- ***1 cup sugar***
- ***1 cup water***
- ***4 cups fresh cranberries (about 1 pound), picked over***
- ***2 clementines or 1 large orange***
- ***1/4 cup orange marmalade, preferably bitter***
- ***2 tablespoons Scotch or other whiskey***
- ***1/4 teaspoon cinnamon***
- ***Pinch of ground cloves***
- ***1/4 cup chopped walnuts***

1. In a heavy saucepan, stir together the sugar and water over medium-low heat until the sugar has dissolved. Raise the heat and bring the syrup to a boil. Add the cranberries and cook over high heat, uncovered, until most of them pop, 5 to 7 minutes. Remove from heat and let the berries cool for 30 minutes.

2. Use a vegetable peeler or zester to remove the clementine or orange peel. (Remove only the orange-colored zest, not the white pith beneath.) Chop the zest and add it to the cranberries. With a sharp paring knife, remove the white pith from the clementines or orange; discard pith and any seeds. Chop the pulp of the fruit coarsely and add it to the cranberries with the marmalade, whiskey, cinnamon, and cloves, stirring until combined. Chill the mixture. (It will keep, refrigerated, for several weeks.)

3. Just before serving, stir in the walnuts.

WHEN FRESH CRANBERRIES ARE IN SEASON....

Buy a few extra bags and pop them into the freezer. You'll have them year-round—just use as directed in any recipe, right from the freezer.

Hitch Albin's Cranberry Relish

Accented with citrus, ginger, chili pepper, and vanilla, this recipe is from New York's The Four Seasons, where American ingredients have been used inventively for just over a quarter of a century. This relish, excellent with any roast meats, poultry or game, is the creation of the kitchen chef, Christian (Hitch) Albin.

Makes about 1½ quarts

1 large navel orange
1 lime
1 tablespoon grated fresh ginger
2 cinnamon sticks
1 dried hot chili pepper
1 vanilla bean, split lengthwise
2 cups sugar
1 cup raisins
2 pounds fresh cranberries, picked over

1. Cut the orange and the lime, with their skins, into ¼-inch dice, discarding seeds. Set aside at room temperature. Tie the ginger, cinnamon sticks, chili pepper, and vanilla bean in cheesecloth and set aside.

2. Place the sugar in a wide heavy skillet, preferably one with straight sides. Stir constantly over high heat until the sugar turns light amber. The sugar must be cooked carefully to prevent burning; break up lumps as you go. (If there are still lumps of sugar after it begins to color, work over low heat, or off the heat, until the mixture is smooth.)

3. Stir in the diced orange and lime, and the bag of spices, and cook over high heat, stirring constantly, for 5 minutes. Fold in the raisins and cranberries, stirring gently to coat with caramelized sugar. Cook over medium heat, stirring gently, until about half the cranberries pop open, about 10 minutes. Remove pan from the heat and cool. Discard spice bag.

4. Spoon the relish into sterilized jars. Cover tightly and refrigerate for one month before using. This relish keeps, refrigerated, for about 3 months.

Cranberry Jelly
(or glaze for Roast Poultry or Ham)

This tart jelly makes an excellent glaze. Just melt in a small pan and brush on chicken, turkey, Cornish hen, or ham for the final half-hour of roasting time.

Makes about 2 cups

1½ pounds cranberries, picked over
3 cups water
3 cups sugar

1. Place the cranberries and the water in a heavy saucepan and bring to a boil. Stir in the sugar and cook over medium heat, stirring, until the sugar dissolves.

2. Cook, uncovered, over medium heat until the jelly nearly reaches the setting point, about 220° F. (page 178), about 30 minutes. Cool, then refrigerate in a tightly covered jar or plastic container. (If you'd like to can the jelly, spoon it while boiling hot into sterilized jars. Top with canning lids and screw bands; process in a boiling water bath for 10 minutes.)

Cranberry Coolers

The tart flavor of cranberries enlivens several cooling drinks, soft and otherwise. We've made a basic cranberry syrup that can be mixed and diluted in several ways.

Basic Cranberry Syrup

Makes about 3 cups

1½ cups sugar
2 cups water
1 pound cranberries, picked over
Juice of 1 lemon

1. Place the sugar and water in a heavy saucepan and cook over medium heat, stirring, until the sugar has dissolved.

2. Stir in the cranberries and the lemon juice, tossing the lemon halves into the pan. Bring the mixture to a boil and cook gently, uncovered, until most of the berries pop, about 7 minutes. Remove the pan from the heat and let stand for about 30 minutes.

3. Strain the syrup, pressing down on the berries to release all possible juice. Chill.

CRANBERRY COOLER
Place several ice cubes in a 12-ounce tumbler. Add 4 ounces each basic cranberry syrup and soda water or seltzer; garnish with a wedge of lime, or a slice of orange.

CRANBERRY LEMON COOLER
Place several ice cubes in a 12-ounce tumbler or tall glass. Add 4 ounces each cranberry syrup and lemonade and a slice or two of lemon.

CRAN-ORANGE COOLER
Place several ice cubes in a tumbler or tall glass. Add 4 ounces orange juice, 2 ounces cranberry syrup, and a slice of orange.

CRANBERRY KIR
Place 4 ice cubes in an old-fashioned or large wine glass. Add 5 ounces dry white wine and 3 tablespoons cranberry syrup. Garnish with a twist of lemon. (If you prefer, use chilled wine and omit the ice.)

CRANBERRY WINE SPRITZER
Place 4 ice cubes in a tall drink glass. Add 5 ounces dry white wine, 3 tablespoons cranberry syrup, and top with 2 ounces soda water or seltzer. Garnish with a twist of lemon.

Chocolate Cranberry Chunks

Remember the Chunky—as in "What a chunk-a-chocolate"? Here, the rich chocolate chunks are filled with raisins, nuts, and cranberries, which burst with tart flavor as you bite in. This idea comes from Sandy's sister, Sharon Gluck. Cranberries and chocolate are a surprisingly successful flavor combination.

Makes 36 squares

2½ cups cranberries (10 ounces), picked over
½ cup sugar
½ cup heavy cream
1½ pounds (24 ounces) semisweet chocolate, chopped
1½ cups coarsely chopped nuts (almonds, pecans, or hazelnuts)
⅔ cup raisins

1. Line a 9-inch square pan with foil so that all sides are covered. Press foil until smooth. Set aside

2. Place the cranberries and the sugar in a heavy saucepan and stir gently over medium-high heat for 6 minutes. Remove from heat.

3. Place the cream in a heavy saucepan and bring almost to a boil over medium heat. Place the saucepan in a large skillet of simmering water and add the chopped chocolate. Stir over simmering water until the chocolate is melted and smooth. Remove from heat and stir in the cranberries, nuts, and raisins.

4. Pour the chocolate mixture into the foil-lined pan and cool completely on a wire rack. Chill briefly, until firm but not hard. Inverting the pan over a sheet of wax paper, use the foil to remove the block of chocolate from the pan. Gently lift off the foil. Cut the mixture into 1½-inch squares; if you like, place the candies in small paper candy cups. Serve at cool room temperature.

Open-Face Cranberry Tart

You'll be surprised how good cranberries can be, baked in a tart. In fact, the first American cookbook, *American Cookery* by Amelia Simmons (Hartford, 1796), includes a recipe for "Cramberries" that are "stewed, strained and sweetened, put into [puff] paste, and baked gently."

This beautifully glazed tart is based on a recipe from the Hotel Plaza-Athénée in Paris. When Richard was there doing an informal apprenticeship, he was surprised to see the French pastry chefs opening bags of cranberries imported from the United States. They had no idea how cranberries were served here, and were amazed when he told them that we usually eat them with turkey.

Serves 8

Rich Tart Pastry dough (page 240)

ALMOND CREAM FILLING

- **6** ***tablespoons (3/4 stick) unsalted butter, at room temperature***
- **1/3** ***cup sugar***
- **1** ***egg***
- **1** ***egg yolk***
- **1** ***teaspoon Cognac or other brandy***
- **1/2** ***teaspoon pure vanilla extract***
- **3/4** ***cup finely ground almonds***

CRANBERRY TOPPING

- **1 1/2** ***cups sugar***
- **1/4** ***cup cold water***
- **1** ***pound cranberries, picked over***
- **1/4** ***cup raspberry jam, melted and strained, or red currant jelly, melted***

1. Roll out the pastry dough on a lightly floured surface. Fit it loosely into a 9- or 10-inch tart pan with a removable bottom; trim excess dough. Form a high border and flute the edge. Chill the pastry dough for 30 minutes.

2. *Partially Baking the Pastry Shell:* Preheat the oven to 400° F. Line the pastry dough with a sheet of aluminum foil; weight the foil with rice or dried beans. Place the tart pan on a heavy baking sheet and bake until the sides have set, 8 to 10 minutes. Carefully remove the foil and rice and continue to bake the pastry shell until very pale golden, 10 to 12 minutes longer. Prick air bubbles gently with a fork as the pastry bakes. Remove the shell, on its baking sheet, from the oven and lower the oven heat to 375° F.

3. *Almond Cream Filling:* In an electric mixer or food processor, cream the butter with the sugar until light and fluffy. Stir in the egg, egg yolk, Cognac, and vanilla until smooth. Add the ground almonds, mixing gently just until well combined. Spread the mixture in the pastry shell and bake the tart until the almond cream is lightly golden, about 15 minutes. Set aside to cool slightly.

4. *Cranberry Topping:* In a heavy saucepan, heat the sugar and the water over medium heat, stirring to dissolve the sugar. Occasionally brush down any crystals from the sides of the pan with a brush dipped in cold water. Bring the syrup to a boil, boil 2 minutes, and add the cranberries, tossing gently to coat the berries with the syrup. Cover and simmer until the berries are tender but still intact, about 4 minutes. Transfer the cranberries to a bowl and cool slightly.

5. *Assembly:* Raise the oven heat to 400° F. With a slotted spoon, arrange the berries in a single layer on the surface of the tart. Drizzle about 2 tablespoons of the syrup over the berries and bake the tart until the berries are set, about 5 minutes. Remove from the oven, brush the cranberries gently with the jam or jelly, and cool to room temperature. Remove the tart from the rim of the pan before serving.

PEACHES AND NECTARINES

While there are few pleasures to compare with biting into a ripe peach at the height of summer, finding a good one is becoming more difficult all the time. That's because peaches bruise so easily that they are usually shipped before they are ripe—and thus never develop real flavor. While farmers' markets have improved the situation somewhat, peaches are still problematic.

Rarely available in stores, but highly prized by many peach growers as their finest, are white peaches. In fact, because these peaches are so fragile, many farmers save them for their families and friends and for those consumers willing to travel right to farm stands.

The best we can suggest is to seek out a farmer who picks his peaches ripe and transports them carefully. And keep searching.

Nectarines, in fact, are often more satisfying, and can be substituted in any recipe calling for peaches (we made delicious nectarine pies last summer, using a traditional recipe for peach pie). While it's widely believed that a nectarine is a cross between a peach and a plum, it is actually a variety of peach. But whether purchasing peaches or nectarines, choose well-colored fruit, with no brownish blemishes.

Peach Right-Side-Up Cake

We discovered this recipe early one hot summer morning, when we bought a square of a fruit-studded cake from Fred Price and Faye Chan at the Union Square Greenmarket in New York. As we walked away nibbling from their stand, we realized that they had created the perfect cake for summer fruits —tender, moist, and with an incredibly buttery flavor. Fred and Faye's baking business, Fifth Floor Kitchens, calls this recipe Hungarian peach cake; they suggest that you also try it with pitted sour cherries, sliced plums, strawberries, or blueberries. For a picnic, double the recipe and use a 9 x 13-inch pan.

Makes one 8-inch square cake

***2** large ripe peaches*
Lemon juice
***3/4** cup (1 1/2 sticks) unsalted butter, softened*
***3/4** cup sugar*
***3** eggs, separated*
***1/2** teaspoon pure vanilla extract*
Pinch of salt
***1** cup flour*
Confectioners' sugar (optional)

1. Bring a large pot of water to the boil. Preheat the oven to 375° F. Cut a piece of parchment or wax paper to fit the bottom of an 8-inch square baking pan (a 9-inch round pan can be substituted). Fit the paper into the pan; butter and flour the paper and sides of pan. Set aside.

2. Dip the peaches in boiling water for about 15 seconds, then lift out, cool under cold running water, and slip off the skins. Working quickly, stone and slice the peaches thick, tossing them into a mixing bowl with a little lemon juice to prevent discoloration. Set aside.

3. Cream the butter with half the sugar (6 tablespoons) until light and fluffy. Add the egg yolks one at a time, beating until smooth; then add the vanilla.

4. Beat the egg whites with a pinch of salt until they form soft peaks. Gradually add the remaining 6 tablespoons sugar and continue to beat until the whites are stiff and shiny but not dry. Fold about one quarter of the whites into the egg yolk mixture to lighten it. Working gently, alternately fold in the remaining whites and the flour until the mixture is well combined. Pour the batter into the prepared pan. Drain the peach slices and gently arrange them over the batter.

5. Bake the cake until lightly golden and a toothpick inserted near the center emerges clean, 30 to 40 minutes. Cool, in the pan, on a wire rack, for about 10 minutes. Invert the cake gently onto a small rack, peel off the paper, and turn it right-side-up. Cool completely. Sprinkle with confectioners' sugar, if you wish.

M.J.'s Nectarine-Blueberry Cobbler

From M. J. Zirolli, a New Jersey cooking teacher. This cobbler is unusual in that it has a bottom crust, and is topped with a crumbly nut streusel instead of biscuit dough. The bread crumbs keep the buttery crust crisp. M.J. says that this is "something you might want to eat warm from the oven, with a little cream poured over it," and notes that it can be made with a combination of any fresh fruits.

To make half a recipe, serving 6 to 8, halve all the ingredients, and bake it in an 8-inch square pan.

Serves 12 to 15

Basic Pastry Dough for a Two-Crust Pie (page 241)

FRUIT FILLING

- ***3½ to 4 pounds ripe nectarines***
- ***2 cups blueberries, picked over***
- ***Juice of 1 lemon***
- ***⅔ cup sugar***
- ***¼ cup quick-cooking tapioca***
- ***1 teaspoon cinnamon***
- ***¼ teaspoon freshly grated nutmeg***
- ***¼ teaspoon salt***

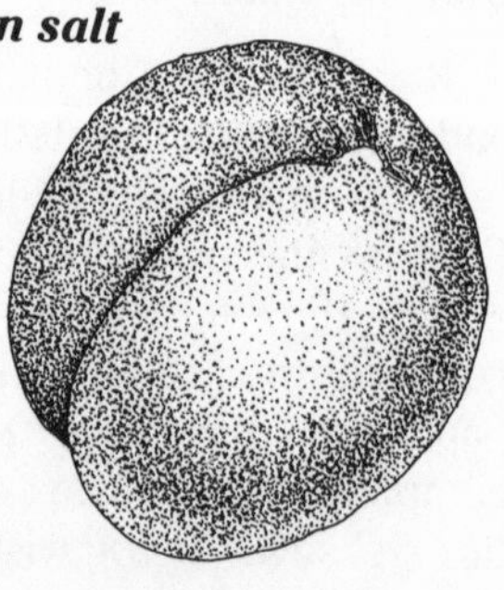

TOPPING

- ***1 cup flour***
- ***¼ cup brown sugar***
- ***Pinch of salt***
- ***11 tablespoons (1 stick plus 3 tablespoons) cold unsalted butter, cut in pieces***
- ***¼ cup chopped almonds***
- ***⅔ cup bread crumbs***
- ***Heavy or light cream (optional)***

1. Bring a large pot of water to a boil. On a lightly floured surface, roll out the pastry in a large rectangular shape about ⅛ inch thick. Fit it into a buttered 9 x 13-inch rectangular baking pan, covering the bottom and sides of the pan with the pastry, with a slight overhang. Fold in the overhanging edges and flute the border. Place the pan in the freezer or refrigerator while you prepare the filling.

2. Preheat the oven to 375° F. Blanch the nectarines for about 15 seconds. With a slotted skimmer or spoon, transfer them to a colander and refresh under cold running water. Slip off the skins with a paring knife. Slice the nectarines about ½ inch thick, letting them fall into a mixing bowl and discarding the stones (you should have about 6 cups sliced peeled nectarines). Toss the nectarines with the blueberries and lemon juice.

3. In a small bowl, stir together the sugar, tapioca, cinnamon, nutmeg, and salt. Toss this mixture with the fruit; set aside.

4. *Topping:* In a food processor or large mixing bowl, cut together the flour, brown sugar, salt, and butter until very coarsely crumbled. Stir in the chopped almonds.

5. *Assembly:* Scatter half the bread crumbs over the pastry-lined baking dish; the crumbs will absorb excess fruit juices. Pour the fruit mixture over evenly. Sprinkle the fruit with the remaining bread crumbs; then scatter the topping mixture on top.

6. Bake until golden brown and bubbly, about 50 minutes. Cool briefly on a wire rack; then serve warm, passing a pitcher of cream, if you like.

Peach Brown Betty

From the Vegetable Growers Association of New Jersey.

Serves 6

7 ***or 8 medium-size ripe peaches***
2 ***tablespoons lemon juice***
1¼ ***cups soft fresh bread crumbs***
4 ***tablespoons (½ stick) unsalted butter, melted***
½ ***cup sugar***
¼ ***teaspoon cinnamon***
¼ ***teaspoon freshly grated nutmeg***
Grated zest of 1 lemon
¼ ***cup orange juice***
¼ ***cup water***

Vanilla ice cream or heavy cream, for serving (optional)

1. Preheat the oven to 400° F. Dip the peaches in a large pot of boiling water for about 15 seconds. Transfer them to a colander and cool under cold running water. Use a paring knife to slip off the skins. Halve the peaches, remove the stones, and slice them thickly into a mixing bowl, tossing the slices with the lemon juice.

2. Toss the bread crumbs with the melted butter; set aside. Toss the sugar with the cinnamon, nutmeg, and lemon zest; set aside.

3. Butter a 1½-quart casserole or soufflé dish. Sprinkle about ¼ cup of the bread crumb mixture into the dish. Top with half the peach slices; sprinkle with half the sugar and spice mixture. Top with the remaining peach slices and sugar mixture. Pour the orange juice and water over; then cover with the remaining crumbs in an even layer. Cover the dish with a sheet of foil.

4. Bake 15 minutes. Uncover and bake until the crumbs are lightly golden, about 30 minutes longer. If you like, run the dish under the broiler briefly to brown the crumbs further. Cool on a wire rack. Serve warm, topping each portion with ice cream or heavy cream.

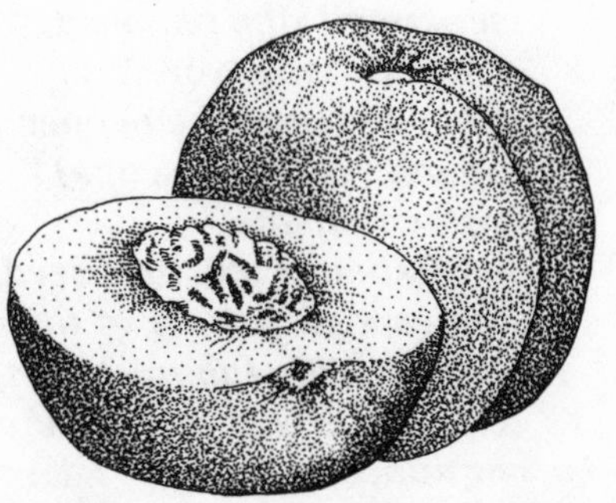

Edna Lewis's Peach Chutney

Edna Lewis, whose *The Taste of Country Cooking* (Knopf) is a beautiful recollection of American country life, is a marvelous cook whose shy, gentle manner conceals a razor-sharp wit. On one of the first summer days we were testing recipes for this book, we found Edna choosing peaches in our local farmers' market. Since we know she bakes a mean peach pie, we assumed that's what they were for. "Oh, no," she smiled, "there's nothing better than just putting them up by themselves, in syrup." (See page 202 for basic sugar syrup for preserving.)

Edna shared her peach chutney recipe with us; it can also be made with mangoes or apples.

Makes about 1 quart

***1** pound ripe peaches, peeled, trimmed, and thickly sliced*
Juice of 1 lime
***1½** cups sugar*
***¾** cups cider vinegar*
***2** ounces peeled fresh ginger, bruised with a mallet or heavy knife (about ⅓ cup)*
***3** tablespoons fresh hot chilies, seeds and ribs removed, finely chopped, or ½ teaspoon cayenne pepper*
***½** pound (about 1¼ cups) golden raisins*
***2** tablespoons mustard seeds*
***1** tablespoon salt, or to taste*
***1** ounce garlic (about 10 small cloves), peeled and crushed or minced*

1. Toss the sliced peaches with the lime juice to prevent discoloration. Set aside.

2. In a noncorrosive saucepan, bring the sugar and vinegar to a boil over medium heat, stirring to dissolve the sugar. Add the peaches and lime juice, ginger, chilies, raisins, mustard seeds, and salt. Bring to a boil, stirring.

3. Boil very gently, uncovered, until the juices are thickened and syrupy, 20 to 30 minutes. Add the garlic, stir for about 3 minutes, and remove from heat. Cool.

4. When cooled to room temperature, remove the bruised ginger, pour the chutney into jars, and store, tightly sealed, in the refrigerator. The chutney will improve with age, and will keep several months, refrigerated.

Note: If you wish to can the chutney, return it to a boil, pack in sterilized canning jars, leaving ¼-inch head-space, top with canning lids and screw bands, and seal. Process for 15 minutes in a boiling water bath.

Individual Peach Shortcakes, page 196
(Substitute 5 ripe peaches, peeled and sliced, for the strawberries.)

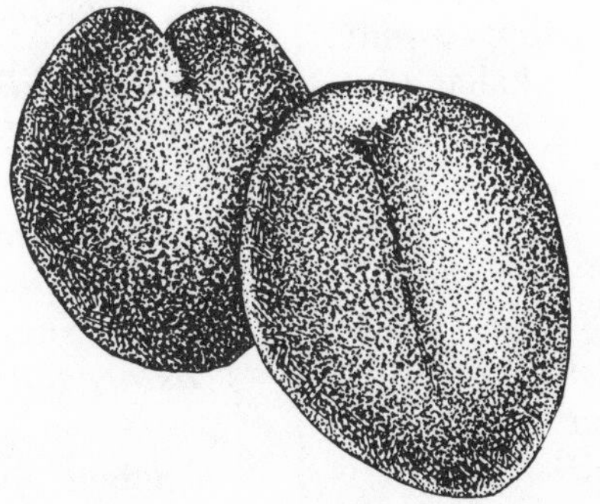

PLUMS

The different varieties of plums can be used fairly interchangeably in cooking, though the small, blue-black Italian plums (a.k.a. prune plums) are firmer and drier than most others. And because they don't give off too much liquid these prune plums are particularly good in cakes and other baked goods.

Mrs. Calvin Dugger of Yakima, Washington, who grows Italian prune plum trees, tells us that "we prop the limbs prior to picking time, so as to allow the light to penetrate the inner portion of the tree, allowing the fruit to color evenly. In the event the trees are not propped, the best and heaviest limbs break off, which reduces the future volume per tree, causing early removal due to reduced bearing surface per acre.

"It requires approximately seven years to grow a tree to a bearing stage. The trees are vigorous for about twenty years with the best of care. The maximum volume per tree is attained in about twelve years."

Some of the plum varieties you might find at your local market include red plums, blue plums, Santa Rosa, and Greengage (reine claude). While they make fine eating out of hand, and excellent cakes and tarts, plums can be used for much more: cooked and pureed as a fruit soup, added to poultry stuffings, or simmered in wine, then sieved and used to sauce roast chicken or duck. And plums make an excellent homemade cordial (page 220).

Plum Compote

This deeply flavored, sweet-tart compote can be served as is, or stirred into plain or vanilla yogurt. It's also excellent over a slice of plain cake or vanilla ice cream (or both), topped with crushed *amaretti* (crunchy Italian macaroons).

Serves 4

1½ pounds (about 9) ripe plums
½ cup sugar
½ cup red currant jelly (page 204, or use a good commercial brand)
1 stick cinnamon
1 strip orange zest

1. Cut the plums in half and remove stones. Put the plums in a heavy saucepan with the sugar, currant jelly, cinnamon stick, and orange zest. Bring to a boil over moderate heat, stirring to dissolve the sugar. Lower the heat to a simmer and cook, uncovered, until the plums are just tender, about 12 minutes.

2. Remove the cooked plums with a slotted spoon, draining all juices back into the pan, and set them aside. Raise the heat and boil the syrup down until it is quite thick. Remove the cinnamon stick and orange zest; pour the syrup over the plums. Serve warm, at room temperature, or chilled.

Plum Cordial

A home-infused version of the plum cordial called slivovitz. Try as an after-dinner nip.

Makes about 1 quart

1 quart vodka
2 pounds ripe plums, halved, stoned (reserve 2 stones), and thickly sliced
2 vanilla beans, split lengthwise
Basic Sugar Syrup (page 202), as needed

1. Combine the vodka and plums in two large jars with tight-fitting lids, dividing vodka and plums equally. Gently crush the two plum pits with a hammer. Tie each pit in cheesecloth; place a cheesecloth bag and a vanilla bean in each jar.

2. Cover tight and let stand in a cool, dark place for one month, turning the jars over once every day to mix the contents.

3. Strain the cordial through a fine sieve lined with cheesecloth. Store refrigerated, tightly covered.

4. *To Serve:* Serve the cordial chilled, in a small liqueur glass, adding sugar syrup to each drink to taste (we find 1½ ounces cordial plus 1 tablespoon syrup a good combination).

Sweet Apple Muffins, page 187
(Substitute an equal weight of diced pitted plums for the grated apples.)

Peach Right-Side-up Cake, page 215
(Substitute an equal weight of plums for the peaches.)

Pear Crisp, page 227 (Substitute an equal weight of plums for the pears.)

Plum Custard Kuchen

A simple biscuit dough, topped with ripe plums and a creamy custard, adapted from a recipe from the American Restaurant in Kansas City, Missouri.

Serves 8

SPICED BISCUIT DOUGH

1¾ cups sifted flour
½ cup light brown sugar
½ cup granulated sugar
2 teaspoons baking powder
¼ teaspoon cinnamon
Pinch each of allspice, ground ginger, and salt
½ cup (1 stick) unsalted butter, melted and cooled slightly
2 eggs
½ teaspoon pure vanilla extract

PLUMS

¾ pound ripe plums, halved, stoned, and thickly sliced
2 tablespoons sugar
¼ teaspoon cinnamon
Pinch of allspice and ground ginger

CUSTARD

2 eggs, lightly beaten
½ cup (1 stick) unsalted butter, melted and cooled slightly
½ cup sugar
Grated zest of 1 lemon

1. *Dough:* Preheat the oven to 350° F. In the bowl of an electric mixer at low speed, mix together the flour, sugars, baking powder, cinnamon, allspice, ginger, and salt. Add the melted butter, eggs, and vanilla, mixing just until a smooth dough is formed. Scrape the dough into a generously buttered 9-inch springform pan. With lightly floured fingers, pat the bottom evenly, and push the dough about 2 inches up the sides of the pan.

2. *Plums:* Arrange the plum slices, skin side down, in a circular pattern over the dough, pressing them gently against the sides of the pan. In a cup or small bowl, stir together the sugar, cinnamon, allspice, and ginger. Sprinkle the plums with this mixture.

3. Bake until the dough is very lightly golden, about 40 minutes.

4. *Custard:* In a mixing bowl, whisk together the eggs, melted butter, sugar, and lemon zest until well blended. With the cake still on the oven rack, pour the custard mixture over the surface of the cake, taking care not to let the mixture run over the edges of the dough.

5. Bake until the custard has set, 20 to 30 minutes longer. Cool on a wire rack; then remove the sides of the pan and serve warm or at room temperature.

Damson Pie

From Eileen Proctor Rowe of Richmond, Virginia. This is an old southern-style pie, quite sweet, which uses preserves instead of fresh fruit. "My mother, Bernice Ransone Proctor, gave me this recipe," Eileen told us. "Her mother-in-law, who would now be 102, and *her* mother both made it often. Some of the family called it 'caramel pie.' It was always served at our family reunions. As you can see, it is wonderfully simple to make."

Serves 8

Basic Pastry Dough for a One-Crust Pie (page 241)
½ ***cup (1 stick) unsalted butter, softened***
1 ***cup sugar***
4 ***eggs***
1 ***teaspoon pure vanilla extract***
1 ***cup Damson plum preserves***

1. On a lightly floured surface, roll out the pastry dough to a large circle about ⅛ inch thick. Transfer it to a 9- or 9½-inch pie plate and trim excess pastry dough, leaving a ¾-inch border. Fold the border under the pastry and crimp or flute the edge. Chill the pastry shell.

2. *Partially Baking the Pastry Shell:* Preheat the oven to 400° F. Line the pastry dough with a sheet of aluminum foil; weight the foil with rice or dried beans. Place the pie plate on a heavy baking sheet and bake until the sides have set, 6 to 8 minutes. Carefully remove the foil and rice and continue to bake the pie shell until very pale golden but not baked through, about 8 minutes longer. Prick any air bubbles gently with a fork as the pastry bakes. Remove the shell, on its baking sheet, from the oven.

3. Meanwhile, cream together the butter and sugar until light and fluffy. Add the eggs one at a time; then beat in the vanilla and preserves.

4. Pour the filling mixture into the partially baked pie shell and bake for 10 minutes. Lower the oven heat to 325° F. and continue to bake until set in the center, about 45 minutes longer. Cool on a wire rack, then serve at room temperature.

TRY THIS FOR A CHANGE....

Mrs. Calvin Dugger told us that she's fond of a pie made with Italian prune plums—great idea. Follow the recipe for Margaret's Special Grape Pie (page 206), substituting 5 cups stoned and sliced plums, preferably Italian prune plums, for the grapes. The plums do not need to be chopped and drained in step #2.

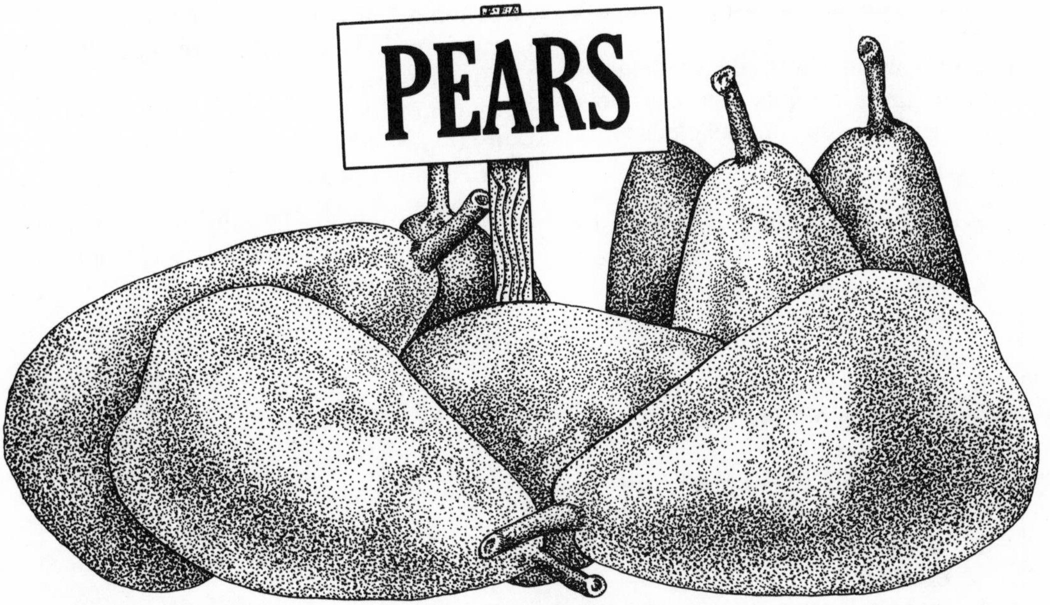

Because Helen Kent of Locust Valley Farm does so much canning, we were under the romantic impression that Helen learned preserving in her mother's farm kitchen. Quite the contrary—she grew up in Brooklyn, worked as a public health nurse in the Milton area of upstate New York and, after she fell in love, moved with her husband Jim to the Kent farm, which had been in the family for over 100 years. "I never did canning as a kid. In fact, I taught my mother canning when she came up here to visit. Then she started in the city, and doing some freezing, too. But it's hard in the city, because your storage space is so limited."

Mrs. Kent grows five varieties of pears: Bartlett, Bosc, Seckel, Anjou, and Clapp. "I use Bartletts for canning," she tells us, "and I recommend them for pies, too. If you're going to bake pears, I recommend Boscs, because they hold their shape. You can cook Bartletts, too, but cook them a little less time, or they'll lose their shape. A lot of people like Anjous for pickling, because there's more crunch."

The intense flavor of ripe pears makes them excellent for cooking. Not only are they good on their own, poached in syrup or wine, but they can be used to make distinctive versions of any of the preparations traditionally made with apples: crisps (page 227), cobblers, butter (page 229) and even such elegant pastry creations as the French *tarte Tatin,* an upside-down tart glazed with caramel.

Pear Biscuits

The pear puree stirred into the dough makes these biscuits nice and moist, and lends a subtle but delicious flavor.

Makes about 1 dozen

1 ripe pear, peeled, cored, and cut up coarsely
½ teaspoon lemon juice
2 cups flour
1 tablespoon sugar
1 tablespoon baking powder
½ teaspoon baking soda
½ teaspoon salt
6 tablespoons (¾ stick) cold unsalted butter, cut into pieces
3 to 6 tablespoons buttermilk, as needed
1 egg, well beaten

1. Preheat the oven to 425° F. In a food processor or blender, puree the pear with the lemon juice until smooth. Set aside.

2. Sift the flour, sugar, baking powder, baking soda, and salt into a mixing bowl. Cut in the butter until coarsely crumbled. Make a well in the center of the mixture and pour in the pear puree, stirred together with 3 tablespoons buttermilk until smooth. Stir the ingredients together quickly, adding just enough buttermilk to form a sticky but manageable dough.

3. Turn the dough out onto a floured surface and pat gently to a thickness of about 1 inch. Use a floured cutter to cut out 2-inch rounds, or cut the dough into squares or triangles. Reroll remaining dough as necessary. Transfer to a well-buttered baking sheet and brush the tops with beaten egg.

4. Bake until the biscuits are golden brown, about 15 minutes. Serve hot, with sweet butter.

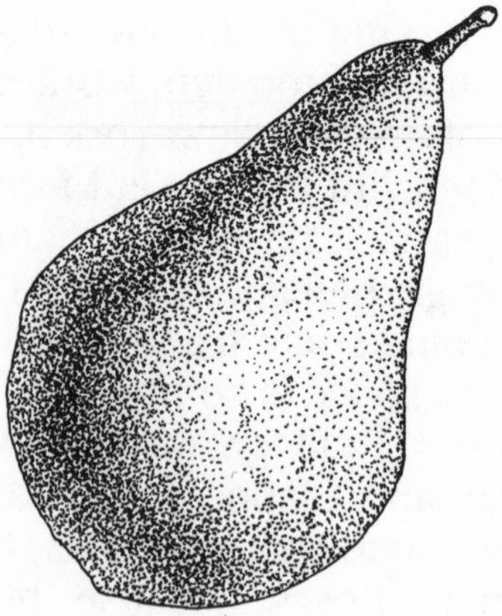

Fresh Pear Cake

From Margaret Stieber, who grew up on a farm near Sheboygan, Wisconsin. Margaret raised eight children on the produce of her large garden, and two of them grew up to cook professionally. Margaret tells us that this moist cake "is good when made the day before needed, keeps well, is nice for picnics, and easy to make. Also, it's nice for morning breakfast with coffee, instead of sweet rolls."

The vanilla frosting is optional; the cake is equally good with just a sprinkling of confectioners' sugar. Try substituting apples for the pears, too.

Serves 12 to 16

2 cups flour
1½ cups sugar
1½ teaspoons baking soda
2 teaspoons cinnamon
½ teaspoon ground ginger
¼ teaspoon freshly grated nutmeg
½ teaspoon salt
4 ripe, medium-size pears (1 pound 8 ounces), peeled, quartered, cored, and diced (4 cups)
½ cup chopped walnuts
½ cup (1 stick) unsalted butter, melted
2 eggs, lightly beaten

VANILLA FROSTING (OPTIONAL)

3 tablespoons soft unsalted butter
1½ cups confectioners' sugar
Pinch of salt
1 teaspoon pure vanilla extract
2 tablespoons milk, plus more as needed

1. Preheat the oven to 325° F. Grease a 9 x 13-inch baking pan; set aside. Sift the flour, sugar, baking soda, cinnamon, ginger, nutmeg, and salt into a large mixing bowl. Add the diced pears, walnuts, butter, and eggs and stir gently to combine the ingredients. Pour into the prepared pan, spreading the batter gently.

2. Bake until the cake springs back when pressed lightly, 1 to 1¼ hours. Cool on a wire rack.

3. *Vanilla Frosting (optional):* Cream the butter; then add the sugar and salt, mixing until smooth. Add the vanilla and enough milk to bring the frosting to a spreadable consistency.

4. When the cake has cooled, either spread with the frosting, or sprinkle with confectioners' sugar. Serve, cut in large squares, directly from the pan.

Pear Yogurt Cake

Adapted from an apple cake recipe from Janet Allison, whose family grows apples in Washington State. One of the best—a moist, buttery, golden cake that keeps well.

Serves 10 to 12

2 cups flour
1½ teaspoons baking powder
1 teaspoon baking soda
¼ teaspoon salt
1 cup (2 sticks) unsalted butter, softened
1½ cups sugar
Grated zest of ½ orange
2 eggs
1 cup plain yogurt
2 tablespoons brandy
2 teaspoons lemon juice
1 tablespoon crystallized ginger, finely chopped (or substitute ½ teaspoon ground ginger)
2 ripe pears (about 10 ounces)
½ cup chopped pecans or other nuts

1. Preheat the oven to 350° F. Butter and flour a 10-inch tube pan; set aside.

2. Sift the flour, baking powder, baking soda, and salt onto a sheet of wax paper; set aside. In an electric mixer, beat the butter briefly at medium speed; then add the sugar and orange zest and cream the mixture until light and fluffy, 5 to 7 minutes.

3. Add the eggs one at a time; then add the yogurt, brandy, lemon juice, and crystallized ginger, mixing until the ingredients are well combined. Lower the mixer speed; add the flour mixture, reserving about 2 tablespoons, and mix at low speed just until the ingredients are nearly combined. Do not overmix.

4. Peel the pears. Quarter, core, and cut into ⅛-inch dice (you should have about 2 cups). Immediately toss the pears with the reserved flour mixture; fold the floured pears and the pecans into the batter just until blended. Scrape the batter into the prepared pan, smoothing the top.

5. Bake until the cake is golden, has shrunk from the sides of the pan, and a toothpick inserted in the center emerges clean, 50 to 60 minutes. Cool briefly on a wire rack; then run a small knife blade around the cake and invert it onto a plate. Invert again onto the wire rack, browned top up. Cool completely before serving.

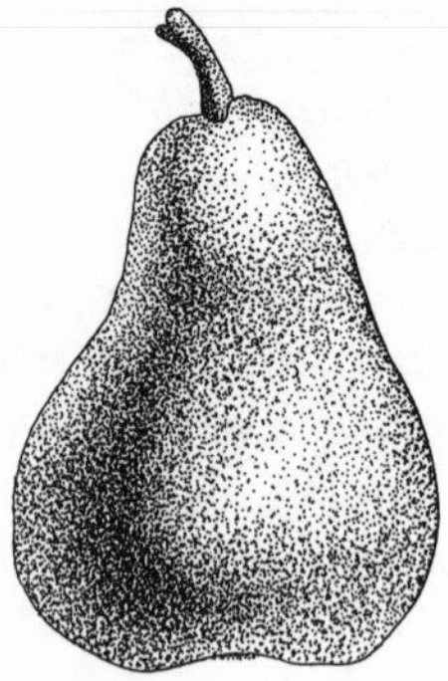

Pear Crisp with Vanilla Custard Sauce

Warm fruit, crisp oat topping, cold sauce—a perfect fall combination.

Serves 8

VANILLA CUSTARD SAUCE

2 cups milk
1/2 vanilla bean, split lengthwise, or 1 1/2 teaspoons pure vanilla extract
5 egg yolks
1/2 cup sugar

PEAR FILLING

9 cups sliced peeled ripe pears (3 1/4 to 3 1/2 pounds; use a firm variety, e.g. Bosc)
Juice of 1/2 lemon
3/4 cup sugar
2 tablespoons flour
1/4 teaspoon salt
Pinch of cinnamon

OAT CRUNCH TOPPING

1/2 cup oatmeal
1/2 cup flour
1/2 cup dark brown sugar
1/2 cup (1 stick) cold unsalted butter, cut into pieces

1. *Vanilla Custard Sauce:* Bring the milk and the vanilla bean nearly to a boil in a heavy saucepan. (If you are using vanilla extract, do not add it yet.) Meanwhile, whisk the yolks and sugar in a mixing bowl until blended. Gradually whisk the scalded milk into the egg yolk mixture; return to the pan. Stir constantly with a wooden spoon over medium heat until thickened enough to coat the back of a spoon evenly, about 7 minutes. Do not boil. Strain into a bowl. With a paring knife, scrape the seeds from the vanilla bean into the strained sauce (stir in the vanilla extract now, if you are using it). Cool thoroughly, stirring occasionally; then chill, covered.

2. *Pear Filling:* Preheat the oven to 375° F. In a mixing bowl, toss the pears with the lemon juice. In a small bowl, stir together the sugar, flour, salt, and cinnamon until blended. Add this mixture to the pears; toss to combine, and transfer the mixture to a well-buttered 8-inch square baking pan (a 9-inch pie plate can be substituted).

3. *Oat Crunch Topping:* In a mixing bowl or food processor, cut together the oatmeal, flour, brown sugar, and butter until crumbled to the size of large peas. Scatter the topping mixture over the pear slices.

4. Bake until the topping is nicely golden, 35 to 40 minutes. Cool briefly on a wire rack; then serve warm, passing the cold custard sauce separately.

Alsatian Pear Tart with Macaroon Crunch Topping

Serves 8

Rich Tart Pastry Dough (page 240)

FILLING

- ***2 firm-ripe pears, peeled, quartered, cored, and sliced 1/4 inch thick***
- ***Pear brandy or lemon juice***
- ***2 eggs***
- ***1 egg yolk***
- ***1/2 cup milk***
- ***1/4 cup heavy or sour cream***
- ***2 tablespoons sugar***
- ***Grated zest of 1/2 lemon***
- ***1/4 teaspoon pure vanilla extract***

MACAROON CRUNCH TOPPING

- ***3/4 cup thinly sliced almonds (about 3 ounces)***
- ***1/4 cup sugar***
- ***3 tablespoons dried currants***
- ***1 egg white, plus more if needed***

1. Roll out the pastry dough on a lightly floured surface. Fit it loosely into a 9- or 10-inch tart pan with a removable bottom; trim excess dough. Form a high border and flute the edge. Chill the pastry dough for 30 minutes.

2. *Partially Baking the Pastry Shell:* Preheat the oven to 400° F. Line the pastry dough with a sheet of aluminum foil; weight the foil with rice or dried beans. Place the tart pan on a heavy baking sheet and bake until the sides have set, about 6 minutes. Carefully remove the foil and rice and continue to bake the pastry shell until very pale golden but not baked through, about 8 minutes longer. Prick any air bubbles gently with a fork as the pastry bakes. Remove the shell, on its baking sheet, from the oven and lower the oven heat to 350° F.

3. *Filling:* Arrange the pear slices in the tart shell in a circular pattern, overlapping slightly. Fill in the center with the remaining slices. Sprinkle the pears with pear brandy or lemon juice. Bake until the pears are nearly tender, 12 to 15 minutes. Do not overcook the pears as they will bake further.

4. In a mixing bowl whisk together the eggs, egg yolk, milk, cream, sugar, lemon zest, and vanilla. Pour the custard mixture carefully over the pears; it should come nearly up to the edges of the pastry. Bake until the custard is barely set in the center, 17 to 20 minutes. Remove from the oven.

5. *Macaroon Crunch Topping:* In a mixing bowl stir together the almonds, sugar, currants, and egg white. The mixture should be very lightly coated with egg white. If too dry, stir in a few drops more egg white. Carefully spoon this mixture onto the surface of the tart in a flat, even layer, smoothing it very gently with a butter knife.

6. Return the tart to the oven and bake until lightly golden, 15 to 20 minutes. Cool on a rack. Remove the tart from the rim of the pan; serve slightly warm or at room temperature.

Spiced Pear Butter

Adapted from a recipe of Jo Ann Aamodt of Aamodt's Farm, Stillwater, Minnesota. Delicious on a muffin or toast.

Makes about 6 half-pints

- ***5 pounds ripe pears (15 to 18 medium), peeled, quartered, and cored (about 12 cups)***
- ***3 cups pear cider or canned pear nectar***
- ***1 cinnamon stick***
- ***2 cups sugar***
- ***1/4 teaspoon ground cloves (optional)***
- ***Juice of 1 large lemon, or more to taste***

1. Place the pears, cider, and cinnamon stick in a large saucepan and bring to a boil, covered, over high heat. Lower the heat and simmer, stirring occasionally, until the pears are tender, 20 to 35 minutes (timing varies depending on type and ripeness of pears).

2. Preheat the oven to 300° F. Set the cinnamon stick aside. Put the pears and their cooking liquid through a food mill with the medium disk into a 9 x 13-inch baking pan. Stir in the sugar, cinnamon stick, and cloves. Bake 2 hours or until the mixture is quite thick when dropped from a spoon. Remove from the oven and stir in the lemon juice, adding enough to bring out the fresh pear flavor.

3. If you wish to can the pear butter, ladle it while hot into hot, sterilized half-pint canning jars, leaving a 1/4-inch headspace. Set the canning lids and screw bands in place and process in a boiling water bath for 10 minutes from the time the water returns to a boil. If not canned, refrigerate the pear butter, in tightly covered containers, up to 1 month.

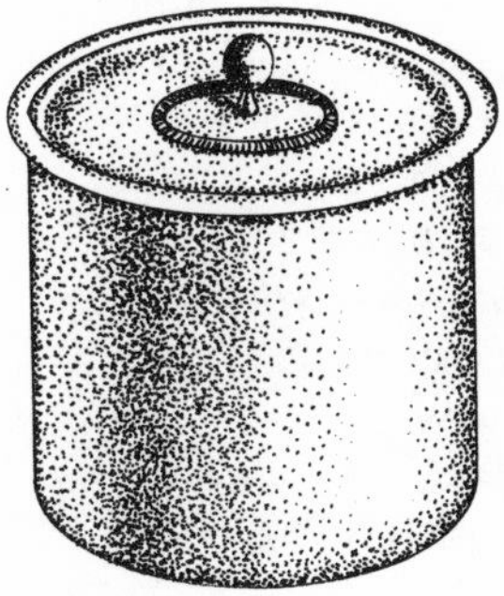

Preserved Spiced Seckel Pears

Lady apples can also be prepared this way.

Makes 2 pints

2½ pounds firm-ripe Seckel pears, peeled, stems left on
2 cups apple cider vinegar
1⅓ cups water
1⅓ cups honey
1 cup sugar
2 cinnamon sticks
12 peppercorns
12 cloves
8 allspice berries
2 small bay leaves

1. Prepare the pears, dropping them into acidulated water (water with a little lemon juice or vinegar stirred in) as they are peeled.

2. In a large saucepan, bring the vinegar, water, honey, sugar, cinnamon sticks, peppercorns, cloves, allspice berries, and bay leaves to a boil. Lower the heat to a simmer and add the pears. Simmer, covered, until the pears are just tender, about 15 minutes. Remove from the heat and let stand until cool.

3. If you'd like to can the pears, transfer them with a slotted spoon to sterilized preserving jars. Return the syrup to a boil and pour it into the jars, dividing the spices as evenly as you can, and leaving ¼-inch headspace. Run a table knife around the edge of the jars to burst any air bubbles. Wipe the jar rims clean, seal the jars with canning lids and screw bands, and process for 15 minutes in a boiling water bath. Cool, label, and store. If you're not canning them, store the pears refrigerated, in a covered container, up to one month.

Dried Fruit Mincemeat Pie, page 168

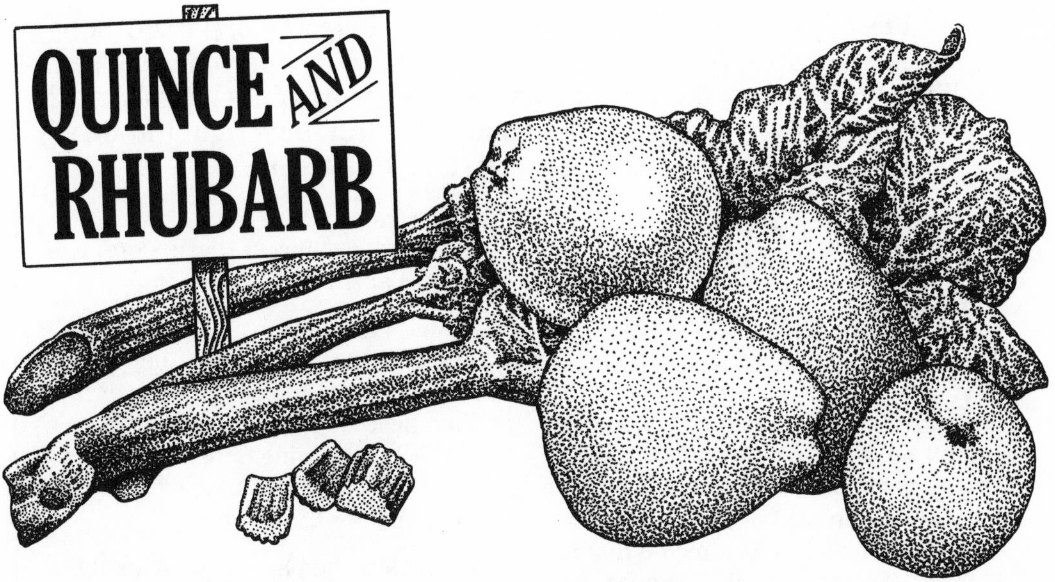

QUINCE

What's a quince? "It's not an apple; it's not a pear [though it's thought to resemble both]. It's a fruit all its own," says Helen Kent of Locust Valley Farm in Milton, New York. "We're one of the few farms that still grow quinces."

Quinces aren't easy to find, and most people have no idea how to cook them. And you *should* cook them. In their raw state, they're sour and hard. "Quinces come from the Mediterranean," Helen explains, "And they're different there. In Greece, they are sometimes eaten raw. We have a few customers that come to the farmers' market and walk away eating them. But they do need to be cooked—gently. They take a while, too. And you have to sweeten them, and then they're delicious. Quinces are used in other places more than they are here. In Germany, they make a soft candy with the pieces of quince that are strained off when making quince jelly. And we've sold lots of quinces to a French chef, who makes a sauce for duck with them.

"My dream," Helen tells us, "is someday to write a booklet called 'What Is a Quince?' You don't see them as they grow—they're covered with fuzz. [In the market, they look a little like lumpy apples.] They're greenish yellow when raw, but when you peel and cook them, they turn a beautiful reddish color, and they take on a flavor something like honey." So many customers, in fact, have asked Mrs. Kent what to do with quinces that she has mimeographed a page of her favorite recipes, which she hands out on market days.

Besides her recipes that we've included here, Helen passed along this helpful tip: "When I bake an apple pie, I put partially cooked, sliced quince over the raw apples. Not too many of them, maybe 12 slices. But it flavors the pie, and it makes the fruit pink right through."

If you haven't tried quinces, you're in for a treat.

Honey-Stewed Quinces

From Chef Ralph Stieber. A good basic method for cooking quinces, with a rosy gold color. Delicious served with heavy cream, or baked in a tart shell (see The Coach House recipe that follows). To preserve the quinces, process in a boiling water bath for 10 minutes as in the Quince Jam recipe, page 235.

Makes 2½ pints

***3** pounds quinces (about 9 medium)*
***½** cup (1 stick) unsalted butter*
***2** tablespoons sugar*
***¾** cup light-flavored honey*
***1½** cups dry white wine*
Juice of ½ lemon
Pinch of salt

1. Peel the quinces. Halve, core, and cut in ¼-inch-thick slices.

2. Melt the butter in a wide heavy skillet. Add the sugar and the quince slices and toss to coat. Cook over medium heat for 5 to 7 minutes, then stir in the honey, wine, lemon juice, and salt. Cover the pan and cook over medium heat for 25 minutes.

3. Uncover the pan and cook until the quinces are just tender, 20 to 25 minutes longer. Cool; then serve warm or chilled.

The Coach House Quince Tart

From Leon Lianides, whose New York City restaurant, The Coach House, has shown for over thirty years—well before it became trendy—how fine American cooking can be. This recipe has been adapted slightly from the original.

Serves 8

THE COACH HOUSE RICH PASTRY DOUGH

2½ cups flour
¼ cup sugar
Pinch of salt
¾ teaspoon cinnamon
1 cup (2 sticks) soft unsalted butter, cut in pieces
Grated zest of 2 lemons
2 egg yolks
3 tablespoons cold water, plus more as needed

3½ cups Honey-Stewed Quinces (see opposite page)
2 tablespoons toasted chopped almonds

Lightly whipped cream, sour cream, or vanilla ice cream

1. *The Coach House Rich Pastry Dough:* In a mixing bowl (or in an electric mixer or food processor), combine the flour, sugar, salt, and cinnamon. Add butter, lemon zest, egg yolk, and 3 tablespoons cold water, mixing until the ingredients are combined. If necessary, add a little more cold water to hold the mixture together. Wrap the dough in plastic wrap and chill at least 1 hour.

2. Remove the dough from the refrigerator. Let stand at room temperature, if necessary, until still cold, but just malleable enough to yield to the rolling pin. Roll out two-thirds of the dough between sheets of wax paper to a circle 12 inches in diameter. Peel off the top sheet of wax paper and fit the dough into a 9- or 10-inch tart pan with a removable bottom. Remove wax paper and form an even edge. Chill dough. Roll out the smaller portion of dough between two sheets of wax paper to a circle 10 inches in diameter; chill.

3. *Partially Baking the Bottom Crust:* Preheat the oven to 375° F. Bake the bottom crust 10 minutes, pricking dough lightly with a fork if it bubbles up. Remove from the oven and cool the pastry slightly.

4. Spoon the quince filling into the pastry shell. Remove the top sheet of wax paper from the pastry circle. Use a fluted pastry wheel or a knife to cut the circle in ¾-inch-wide strips. Lay half the strips over the quinces, pressing them into the edges of the bottom crust. Lay the remaining strips over the tart, placing them at a sharp angle to the others, and pressing them into the edges. Trim off excess dough.

5. Bake the tart on a heavy sheet pan until lightly golden, about 25 minutes. Sprinkle the almonds over the quince filling. Cool to room temperature, then remove the tart from the rim of the pan. Serve with whipped cream, sour cream, or vanilla ice cream.

Helen's Quince Meringue Pie

Another excellent use for quince from Helen Kent. Quince puree flavors the custard filling in this pie.

Serves 8

- ***Basic Pastry Dough for a One-Crust Pie (page 241)***
- ***2 large ripe quinces (about 1 pound)***
- ***2 tablespoons unsalted butter***
- ***½ cup plus ⅓ cup sugar***
- ***1 teaspoon lemon juice***
- ***Pinch of freshly grated nutmeg***
- ***3 eggs, separated***
- ***1 cup milk***
- ***Pinch of salt***

1. Roll out the pastry on a lightly floured board. Fit it into a 9-inch pie pan, flute the edges, and chill the pastry while you prepare the filling.

2. Peel the quinces. Halve them, cut out the cores, and cut each half in 4 pieces. Place the quince pieces in a saucepan with about ½ inch of water. Cover the pan and bring to a boil over medium heat. Cook until tender, 20 to 25 minutes. Put the cooked quinces through a food mill or food processor; you should have about 1 cup coarse puree.

3. Preheat the oven to 425° F. In a mixing bowl, combine the hot quince puree, butter, ½ cup sugar, lemon juice, and nutmeg. Whisk the egg yolks briefly; whisk in the milk. Stir this mixture into the quince mixture and pour into the pastry shell.

4. Bake the pie 10 minutes; then lower the heat to 350° F. Bake until the custard has set, 30 to 35 minutes longer.

5. Shortly before the custard sets, whisk the egg whites and the salt until they form soft peaks. Gradually add the ⅓ cup sugar and beat until stiff and shiny.

6. Remove the pie from the oven and raise the heat to 400° F. Spread the meringue over the pie, swirling the surface. Return to the oven until the meringue is lightly browned, about 5 minutes. Cool on a rack and serve at room temperature.

Quince Jam

A beautiful orange-hued jam, from Helen Kent.

Makes about 7 half-pints

***3** pounds ripe quinces (about 9 medium)*
***4** cups water*
***5½** cups sugar*
Juice of 2 lemons (about ½ cup)

1. Peel the quinces, reserving the skin from 2 of them. Halve the quinces and core, reserving the cores and seeds from 2 of them. Chop the flesh in ⅛-inch pieces in a food processor or meat grinder. Tie the reserved quince peel, cores, and seeds in a piece of cheesecloth.

2. Place the chopped quince, cheesecloth bag, and water in a wide heavy saucepan and bring to a boil. Simmer, covered, until the quince is tender, about 20 minutes.

3. Remove the cheesecloth bag and add the sugar and lemon juice, stirring over moderate heat until the sugar has dissolved. Raise the heat slightly and cook the mixture, uncovered, stirring frequently, until the mixture reaches the setting point (see box, page 178).

4. As soon as the jam has set, turn off the heat and immediately ladle it through a canning funnel into sterilized canning jars, leaving ¼-inch headspace. Top with canning lids and screw bands; process in a boiling water bath for 10 minutes (begin timing from the time the water returns to the boil). Remove from the boiling water and cool. Tighten the screw bands.

RHUBARB

Technically, rhubarb is classified as a vegetable. But since it's cooked and eaten as a fruit, it's here—let's not argue. Whatever it is, rhubarb is underrated. *The New York Times* recently ran an article called "Say, How About a Little Respect for Rhubarb?" ("What is it about rhubarb that makes it so unloved?") It's a shame, because rhubarb can be really tasty.

A WARNING—

Never eat rhubarb leaves—they contain oxalic acid, and are toxic.

Sweet-and-Sour Rhubarb Sauce for Fish or Chicken

This recipe has its origin in Sephardic cooking—a fascinating Jewish cuisine that began in Spain and assimilated the flavors of several Mediterranean countries in which the Jews settled. Sephardic dishes often combine sweet-and-sour flavorings in otherwise savory dishes. This is an unusual, tasty sauce for broiled fish or chicken.

Makes about 1¼ cups

1½ tablespoons olive oil
1 medium onion, finely chopped
2 cups thinly sliced trimmed rhubarb (about 12 ounces)
½ cup peeled and seeded fresh or canned tomatoes, finely chopped
¼ cup honey
1 teaspoon sugar
¼ teaspoon salt
Generous pinch of ground allspice
½ teaspoon lemon juice, or to taste
Freshly ground black pepper

1. Heat the olive oil in a heavy saucepan over low heat. Add the onion and stew gently, stirring occasionally, until softened but not brown, about 7 minutes.

2. Stir in the rhubarb, tomatoes, honey, sugar, salt, and allspice. Simmer the mixture uncovered, stirring occasionally, until it has melted down to a thick puree, about 20 minutes.

3. Add the lemon juice and salt and pepper to taste. Correct all seasonings; the sauce should have a nice balance between sweet and sour. Serve hot, over fish or chicken.

Rhubarb Stewed with Ginger and Vanilla

A good basic way to cook rhubarb, which can be enjoyed on its own, warm or cold, as a sauce for ice cream or cake, or interlayered with whipped cream or a simple custard (page 227) in a fool.

Makes about 3 cups

8 cups sliced trimmed rhubarb (about 3 pounds)
2 cups (packed) light brown sugar
½ cup water
1½ tablespoons finely chopped peeled fresh ginger
1 vanilla bean, split lengthwise

1. Place the rhubarb, brown sugar, water, ginger, and the vanilla bean in a heavy saucepan over medium heat. Bring to a boil, lower the heat, and simmer until the rhubarb has nearly dissolved into a puree, about 35 minutes.

2. Remove the vanilla bean; use a paring knife to scrape the vanilla seeds from the pod into the rhubarb. Serve the rhubarb warm or cold.

Rhubarb Nut Loaf

A moist quick bread, sprinkled with a sugary nut topping, from Marlene Hill of Shelton, Washington. If you like, this bread can be baked in two small loaf pans; decrease the baking time accordingly.

Makes one 9 x 5-inch loaf

1/2 cup vegetable oil
1 1/2 cups light brown sugar
2 3/4 cups flour
1 teaspoon baking soda
1 teaspoon salt
1 egg, lightly beaten
1 cup milk
1 teaspoon pure vanilla extract
1 1/2 cups sliced trimmed rhubarb (about 9 ounces)

TOPPING
1/2 cup sugar
1/8 teaspoon cinnamon
1 tablespoon cold unsalted butter, cut into bits
1/2 cup chopped nuts

1. Preheat the oven to 350° F. Butter and flour a 9 x 5-inch loaf pan; set aside.

2. In an electric mixer, beat the oil with the brown sugar at medium speed until well combined. Meanwhile, sift the flour, baking soda, and salt onto a sheet of wax paper; set aside.

3. Add the egg to the brown sugar mixture; then add the milk and the vanilla. Lower the mixer speed slightly and add the dry ingredients, mixing just until combined. Stir in the rhubarb and transfer the mixture to the prepared baking pan.

4. *Topping:* Combine the sugar, cinnamon, and butter until crumbly; stir in the nuts and scatter the mixture over the batter.

5. Bake the bread until nicely browned and a toothpick inserted in the center emerges just clean, 1 1/4 to 1 1/2 hours. If the bread begins to brown before the inside is done, cover loosely with foil. Cool the bread, in the pan, on a wire rack for about 10 minutes; then turn it out onto the rack and cool completely.

BASIC PREPARATIONS

GOLDEN CHICKEN BROTH

Makes 3 to 4 quarts

5 pounds chicken parts (backs, necks, carcasses, and giblets—no livers)
2 large onions, trimmed but unpeeled, coarsely chopped
2 carrots, peeled, trimmed, and coarsely chopped
2 ribs celery with leaves, trimmed and coarsely chopped
2 garlic cloves, crushed
1 small bunch parsley stems
2 sprigs fresh thyme, or a pinch of dried
1 bay leaf
½ teaspoon coarse (kosher) salt
6 peppercorns

1. Wash the chicken parts well and place in a large stockpot; add cold water to cover by about 2 inches. Bring slowly to a boil, skimming all froth from the surface.

2. Lower the heat and add all remaining ingredients except the peppercorns. Simmer, uncovered, 2 hours; add water as needed to keep solids covered. Skim when necessary. Add the peppercorns for the last 15 minutes.

3. Strain the broth into a large bowl through a colander lined with a double layer of dampened cheesecloth. Gently press solids to extract all liquid; discard solids. Cool broth to room temperature; then refrigerate.

4. When chilled, lift off and discard solidified fat. Pour broth into containers for storage; label and date. This broth keeps three days in the refrigerator, six months frozen.

VEGETABLE BROTH

This can be substituted for meat broth in most recipes.

Makes 2½ quarts

- 3 tablespoons unsalted butter
- 1½ cups sliced onions
- 2 leeks (white portions with some green), bottoms trimmed, halved lengthwise, washed well, sliced
- 3 garlic cloves, smashed and peeled
- 2 large carrots, peeled, trimmed, and sliced
- ½ cup sliced peeled parsnips
- ½ cup sliced celery
- 1 quarter-size slice fresh ginger
- 2 bay leaves
- 2 branches fresh tarragon, or a pinch of dried
- 1 small piece of stick cinnamon
- 3 allspice berries
- 1 teaspoon salt
- 6 peppercorns

1. Heat the butter in a large stockpot. Add the onions, leeks, and garlic, tossing to coat. Sweat over medium-low heat, covered, tossing occasionally, until wilted, about 15 minutes. Stir in the carrots, parsnips, celery, ginger, bay leaves, tarragon, cinnamon, and allspice. Cover and sweat 5 to 7 minutes longer, stirring occasionally.

2. Add enough cold water to cover all ingredients; add the salt. Bring to a boil; then lower the heat and simmer, partially covered, for 1 hour. Add the peppercorns; simmer 15 minutes longer. Strain through a fine-mesh sieve. Cool, then refrigerate. Lift off any fat from the surface.

3. Pour broth into containers for storage; label and date. This broth keeps three days in the refrigerator, six months frozen.

RICH TART PASTRY

Crisper and less flaky than the pie pastry; perfect for open-face tarts. This freezes well, too.

Makes one 9- or 10-inch tart or pie crust.

- 1½ cups flour
- 2 tablespoons sugar
- Pinch of salt
- ½ cup (1 stick) chilled unsalted butter, cut up
- 1 egg yolk
- 2 tablespoons orange juice or cold water, or as needed

1. By Hand: *Sift the flour, sugar, and salt into a large mixing bowl. Cut the butter into the dry ingredients until crumbly, using your fingertips, a pastry blender, or two knives. Do not overmix.*

2. Stir together the egg yolk and juice or water in a small cup. Sprinkle this liquid over the flour mixture, tossing with a fork. Add just enough water so that the dough coheres in a ball; do not make the pastry too wet. Gently flatten the pastry ball into a patty shape. Dust with flour; wrap in plastic wrap, and chill at least 1 hour before rolling out.

3. With a Food Processor: *Place the flour, sugar, and salt in the food processor bowl and mix with several on/off pulses. Add the butter; pulse on and off until the mixture is crumbly; do not overprocess. Stir together the egg yolk and juice or water in a small cup. Add this mixture, pulsing the machine on and off just until the dough begins to clump together (don't let it form a ball); add a few drops of cold water if needed. Transfer the dough to a sheet of plastic wrap and gently press it into a ball. Flatten the ball into a disk, flour lightly, wrap, and chill at least 1 hour before using.*

BASIC PASTRY DOUGH

This pastry freezes well; make several batches and freeze in small portions.

FOR A ONE-CRUST PIE

- *1½ cups flour*
- *1 teaspoon salt*
- *1½ teaspoons sugar*
- *6 tablespoons chilled unsalted butter, cut up*
- *2 tablespoons cold solid vegetable shortening*
- *¼ cup cold water, plus more as needed*

FOR A TWO-CRUST PIE

- *2¼ cups flour*
- *1½ teaspoons salt*
- *1 tablespoon sugar*
- *10 tablespoons chilled unsalted butter, cut up*
- *3 tablespoons cold solid vegetable shortening*
- *6 tablespoons cold water, plus more as needed*

1. By Hand: *Sift the flour, salt, and sugar into a large mixing bowl. Cut the butter and shortening into small pieces, letting them fall into the dry ingredients. Using your fingertips, a pastry blender, or two knives, cut the mixture together until it is crumbly; do not overmix.*

2. Sprinkle the cold water over the flour mixture, tossing with a fork. Add just enough water so that the dough coheres in a ball; do not make the pastry too wet. Gently flatten the pastry ball into a patty shape. Dust with flour; wrap in plastic wrap, and chill at least 1 hour before rolling out.

3. With a Food Processor: *Place the flour, salt, and sugar in the food processor bowl and mix with several on/off pulses. Add the butter and shortening, in large pieces, to the bowl. Pulse on and off until the mixture is crumbly; do not overprocess. Add the water gradually, pulsing the machine, until the dough just begins to clump together, but doesn't yet form a ball; add a little more water if needed to hold the dough together. (Check the texture after a few pulses so you avoid adding too much water.) Transfer the dough to a sheet of plastic wrap and press gently into a ball. Flatten the dough to a disk shape, flour lightly, wrap, and chill at least 1 hour.*

ACKNOWLEDGMENTS

Frankly, we've both seen too many cookbooks that begin with gushing thanks to husbands, wives, and lovers who patiently ate their way through the testing process without complaints. But the many people who came through with generous help on this book should not go without grateful mention.

First, we want to thank all the recipe contributors, for sharing not only their delicious dishes, but also their recollections of life on their farms. They are all credited in the text.

For sharing advice and expertise, we also extend thanks to:

Jean Anderson, who generously pointed us in the direction of real farm food all across the country—a special thank you, Jean

Susan and Robert Lescher

Nach Waxman, an oasis of sanity

Arlene Sarappo

Elizabeth Schneider, whose curiosity is endless, and who is always ready to answer questions

Margaret Wherette of the Pike Place Merchants' Association, Seattle

Linda Burner and Meredith Auerbach of Pacific Kitchens, Inc., Seattle

Barry Benepe, director of New York City's Greenmarket program

John Thorne

Doug Miller of Cascade Conserves, Portland, Oregon

Marilyn Hampstead of Fox Hill Farms, Parma, Michigan

Tom Lunkley of Johnson County Cooperative Extension Service, Iowa City, Iowa

Dr. Stephen Marshall of the Crookham Company, Caldwell, Idaho

Sally Pederson

Mark Titus of Elix Corporation

Ann Bramson at Harper & Row

Hilary Sterne

Claire Reich

The people at Cooperative Extension Services in many states, who went out of their way to put us in touch with farm wives, and who do so much to keep the tradition of good food alive in this country

Professors Fedele Panzarino, Carlo Bussetti, and Joe Tarantino at New York Technical College, Brooklyn, who encouraged us to seek the best always

Mick Violanti and Ralph Stieber, two good men

Matthew and Pamela Starobin, who patiently and generously introduced me to word processing, which, despite a hopeless start, has wound up changing the way I work

Kurt Wallace, talented illustrator, who managed to capture the old-fashioned comfort of farm food in a striking new way

Joel Avirom, whose beautiful design wrapped up the whole package at a key point in our writing process, renewing our energy

Joan Whitman, whose editorial eye is amazing

Rick Kot, who edited this book, nurtured it along right from the earliest stages. Working with Rick, we found the arduous process of writing a cookbook a joy. He is that rare editor whose respect for language is equaled by his love of good cooking. But he also wisely remembers that (to use Sandy's phrase), "it's only food."

INDEX